GETTING
TO PLAN B

GETTING
TO PLAN B

BREAKING THROUGH
TO A BETTER BUSINESS MODEL

———————

JOHN MULLINS
RANDY KOMISAR

HARVARD BUSINESS PRESS
Boston, Massachusetts

Library of Congress Cataloging-in-Publication Data

Mullins, John W. (John Walker)
    Getting to plan B : breaking through to a better business model / John Mullins,
Randy Komisar.
        p. cm.
    ISBN 978-1-4221-2669-1 (hardcover : alk. paper)
    1. Business planning. 2. New business enterprises. 3. Entrepreneurship. I. Komisar,
Randy, 1954- II. Title.
    HD30.28.M842 2009
    658.4'01—dc22

                                                                                2009007185

CONTENTS

Preface   vii

Introduction   1

Chapter 1 Don't Reinvent the Wheel, Make It Better   13
Assembling Analogs, Antilogs, and Leaps of Faith to Get to Plan B

Chapter 2 Guiding Your Flight Progress   37
The Power of Dashboards

Chapter 3 Air, Food, and Water   65
Your Revenue Model

Chapter 4 Avoiding Rocks and Hard Places   89
Your Gross Margin Model

Chapter 5 Trimming the Fat   113
Your Operating Model

Chapter 6 Cash Is King   133
Your Working Capital Model

Chapter 7 It Takes Money to Make Money   157
Your Investment Model

Chapter 8 Can You Balance a One-Legged Stool?   179
Multidimensional Business Models

Chapter 9 Getting Started on Discovering *Your* Plan B   205

Notes   217
Acknowledgments   229
Index   233
About the Authors   251

Why This Book?

In early 2008, venture capital firm Kleiner Perkins Caufield & Byers held a roundtable meeting. The partners, including Randy Komisar, invited CEOs from several early-stage companies they had recently backed. Amid discussions about the common business challenges these entrepreneurs faced, Komisar asked for a show of hands: "Which companies had abandoned their original business plans for a Plan B, or beyond?" Two-thirds of the entrepreneurs raised their hands. In fact, they said, they had restarted their companies nearly three times each! Plan A, the basis on which they had pitched for—and won—Kleiner's venture capital funding, hadn't panned out.

Some seven thousand miles away at London Business School, John Mullins, a professor of entrepreneurship, was analyzing data. Over the previous five years, students attending his Entrepreneurship Summer School had created seventy new businesses, of which sixty-three were still operating and many were thriving. Of those new businesses, more than 60 percent were *not* the ideas that his students had contemplated at the outset of the program. Eight weeks of rigorous scrutiny under the guidance of a mentor led these aspiring entrepreneurs to drop their Plan A for a much more promising Plan B.

These entrepreneurs are among the lucky few. And this book aims to help you join their ranks. It is about taking your good idea and developing it into a business or other organization that has high impact, solves the needs of or even delights your customers, makes you and your investors money, and is sustainable in the long term. More importantly, though, it is a book about experimentation and evolution, about finding a way for your idea to evolve over time into one that's not simply good, but *compelling*!

Entrepreneurship Isn't Easy

Getting to Plan B is also about how to avoid getting stuck in a rut, missing real opportunities, or worse, closing your doors. Don't ever forget that Google and eBay, which have earned billions for their investors, are islands in a sea of start-up failures. There are countless tales of companies that quickly went down in flames. Often, these collapses occurred despite the best minds in the venture capital business plying them with boatloads of cash.

- Webvan, the online grocer, burned more than $1 billion of other people's money before it went down in flames.

- Clickmango.com, the online drug and health Web site started during the dot-com heyday in the United Kingdom, spent £3 million before it, too, crashed.

- At the other end of the new-venture scale, new restaurants, retail shops, and other small businesses come and go like waves on a beach.

In most of these cases, the entrepreneurs tied themselves into their Plan A like a straightjacket. Ultimately, they failed because the economics of their business models didn't work.

The Business Planning Conundrum

Let's consider the business planning culture that pervades all things entrepreneurial today. There are dozens of best-selling books on business planning; Web sites, too—plus software packages, business planning consultants, university courses, and more. Yet amid all this good advice, most business plans fail to deliver.

In our combined fifty-plus years of experience in the entrepreneurial realm (we'll tell you more about that in a few pages), we have read hundreds of business plans—each extolling its Plan A—that never made it past the recycling bin. They were lucky to make it that far.

The problem is that before putting pen to paper, few would-be entrepreneurs consider the lessons to be learned about how other business models might be adapted to work in their own company. Few think in any structured way about whether and how the economics—the business model—are likely to really work. Fewer still test their ideas before pitching investors with spreadsheets promising riches.

Despite these omissions, most business plans explain, in excruciating detail, exactly why Plan A—though it's never called that in the business plan—will work. They present page after page of financials so detailed that they simply *must* be true. But, as most experienced early-stage investors will tell you, "I've made more money on Plan B than I ever made on Plan A." Until now, however, there's been no road map—no systematic process—for discovering a more grounded Plan B. This book provides just that.

Why Not Just Do It? Why Read a Book?

If you "just get out there and do it" you are likely to fail. Why? Today, uncertainty rules. Flux is the only constant. The thesis of this book is simple: the uncertainty that surrounds most innovations and most new ventures can be significantly mitigated by comparing the plan on the table to other businesses already in existence.

Our working assumption is that part or all of Plan A is wrong. By systematically testing a series of hypotheses, the savvy entrepreneur or street-smart executive identifies, through experimentation rather than impassioned persuasion, a better Plan B or, eventually, Plan Z.

Our Goal for *Getting to Plan B*

We have written this book to provide entrepreneurs and executives with a process and a framework to discover the best business model for their venture, whether it's a spanking-new start-up or a new venture hiding in the bowels of a much larger company.

The Process

We will show you how to rigorously and systematically stress-test your Plan A. You'll see how valuable it is to compare your business to other companies—*analogs* and *antilogs*, we call them. And we'll introduce you to *dashboarding*, a methodical way of focusing your precious time and money on removing the critical risks that threaten your best-laid plans. Through the firsthand evidence reflected in your dashboard you will either quickly validate your vision, or course correct before it is too late. All this will make the question that befuddles most entrepreneurs—"Why won't this work?"—easier to answer, to learn from, and to put to work toward your success.

The Framework

You'll also learn a framework for developing a strong business model—something venture capitalists require, but most business plans do not currently deliver. The five elements of the business model—your revenue, gross margin, operating, working capital, and investment models—contain the key to whether your idea and your planned strategy really hold water in economic terms. You will examine how the lifeblood of every business, cash—from customers, suppliers, investors, or all three—can be transformed into a potentially thriving and sustainable venture. The financial framework we explain can yield strategic insights that will lead to customer plaudits and competitive advantage. If you follow the advice in this book, you may even find that you reduce your reliance on investors—and therefore can keep more of the rewards once your business is thriving.

The Birth of This Book

This book itself is the product of Plan B. In late 2006, John spent several weeks in California researching business models, a subject much discussed in entrepreneurial circles but, in John's view, about which there was more glib talk than substance. There he found Randy, who was thinking about similar issues from his venture capitalist's perspective. In recent years, Randy had been working with his portfolio companies on some ideas about how they could more quickly and inexpensively test the core assumptions—the untested *leaps of faith*—on which their initial ideas were based. As Randy saw it, starting and growing a successful entrepreneurial company is a process that can be learned, and he had learned some things he was eager to share.

To make a long story much shorter, Randy's ideas about the *process* of getting to better business models and what John had learned about the *content* thereof—the five business model elements that comprise the framework articulated in this book—seemed to both of us like a win-win combination.

This book is the product of our experiences, and the knowledge we have brought together since 2006. In it, we'll show you how so many of the entrepreneurs sitting in Randy's meeting, and those graduating from John's Entrepreneurship Summer School, succeeded. They viewed their original business plans as mere starting points—a stake in the ground—on a journey of discovery. They succeeded because they studied their potential competitors' and other firms' business models for ideas on how to shape their own. They succeeded because they were wise enough to challenge the assumptions they made about, for instance, their hoped-for customers, or the layout of their stores, or the best distribution channels. They succeeded because they understood that no matter how smart their team, or how innovative their product, their business wouldn't stand a chance unless it was grounded in a strong business model. And in doing all of this, they reduced their companies' exposure to failure. They ultimately won.

Why John Mullins? Why Randy Komisar?

We have been working at the heart of entrepreneurial practice since the 1980s. John Mullins is an associate professor and holds the David and Elaine Potter Foundation Term Chair in Entrepreneurship at London Business School, where he has provided mentorship and advice to more than one hundred active start-up ventures and served on numerous boards. A former entrepreneur and an award-winning teacher, John brings to his teaching and research twenty years of executive experience in high-growth retailing firms, including two ventures he founded and one he took public.

Since becoming a professor in 1992, John has published three books and more than forty articles in a variety of outlets, including *Harvard Business Review*, *Journal of Business Venturing*, and *MIT Sloan Management Review*. His research has won national and international awards. And his trade book, *The New Business Road Test: What Entrepreneurs and Executives Should Do Before Writing a Business Plan*, is the definitive work on the assessment and shaping of market opportunities. Complementing this book, it takes a wider look at assessing new venture opportunities from market, industry, and management team perspectives.

Companies and venture capitalists call on John's expertise regularly. He has consulted with and done executive education on four continents for a variety of organizations, large and small. He regularly provides advice and training for venture capital professionals in Europe, Africa and Asia.

In addition to his day job as a partner at Kleiner Perkins, among the world's most prominent and respected venture capital firms, Randy Komisar has earned rave reviews since 2001 as a consulting professor of entrepreneurship at Stanford University, a hotbed of entrepreneurial ideas and talent. Students have flocked to Randy's lectures to hear about his experiences, which have helped to shape some of the world's most exciting—indeed, daring—technology companies.

In the 1980s, when he was still a practicing lawyer, Randy represented many of the "garage shop entrepreneurs" who defined the personal computing and software industry. He later joined Apple Computer as Senior Counsel for R&D, Operations and Engineering, which is responsible for licensing and technology acquisitions. In 1987 Randy left Apple to cofound Claris Corporation, a PC software applications company that was later sold to Apple.

Since then, he has served as CFO to GO Corporation; CEO of LucasArts Entertainment for George Lucas, breaking new ground in digital gaming and entertainment; and CEO of Crystal Dynamics, a pioneer in the second generation of console games. In 1996 he created a new role as "Virtual CEO," teaming up with a portfolio of entrepreneurs to help them build successful businesses from their vision. His work includes companies such as WebTV, TiVo, GlobalGiving, and Cooliris. His experience covers software, the Web, communications, entertainment, consumer electronics, social ventures, and green technologies to name just a few. In 2005, he became a partner at Kleiner Perkins Caufield & Byers, where he continues to support great entrepreneurs who are changing the world.

Randy is the author of the best-selling book *The Monk and the Riddle: The Art of Creating a Life While Making a Living*—about the heart and soul of entrepreneurship. In 2008 *The Monk and the Riddle* was selected as one of the top one hundred business books of all time. His *Harvard Business Review* article, "Goodbye Career, Hello Success," is a touchstone for the entrepreneurial lifestyle. He speaks about entrepreneurship and creativity frequently on television, radio, and online, in the United States and abroad.

Some Inspiration for Your Journey
from Plan A to Plan B

You will be inspired in this book by the stories of more than twenty companies and their leaders—from little-known start-ups to some of the biggest in the world—that have successfully transitioned from Plan A to Plan B or Plan Z. Along the way, some of them have created business models so disruptive that the competitive landscape in their industry has been altered forever. The "Aha's" are certain to make you think differently about your business. As a result, your Plan A will evolve into a much more promising and productive Plan B. And your Plan B will be stacked with real evidence to support its merit, not just blind faith.

We hope you enjoy reading this book. More than that, though, we hope that by doing so you'll be spared the ignominy of starting a business that quickly bites the dust. Instead, we hope you will join us in what we find to be an energetic and exciting global entrepreneurial community, if you are not already among us. And we hope you'll become another important contributor to making our world a better place through your vision, your experimental and open mind-set, and your entrepreneurial passion. Happy reading, and enjoy your journey to your as-yet-unknown Plan B!

—John Mullins and Randy Komisar,
  February 2009

Introduction

I T WAS THE SUMMER OF 1998, and Max Levchin wasn't quite sure what he was going to do with his life. After finishing his undergraduate education amid the soybean fields of Champaign-Urbana at the University of Illinois, Levchin moved to Silicon Valley to start yet another company, having already started three during his studies.[1]

"I was living in Palo Alto, squatting on the floor of a friend," recalled Levchin. "I had two different ideas that I was considering."[2] After pitching his ideas to a hedge fund manager he had met at a lecture at Stanford University, the two decided to pursue Levchin's idea for security software for such handheld devices as the hot-selling PalmPilot. "I wanted to start a company that would take this scarce skill of implementing crypto on handheld devices and then packaging it into libraries and products. The assumption was that enterprises are going to all go to handheld devices really soon as the primary means of communication. Enterprise requires security; security requires these scarce skills; I have the skills; start a company." Voilà—Levchin's "Plan A" was born! "Any minute now, there'll be millions of people begging for security on their handheld devices," thought Levchin.[3]

The Sad Statistics of Plan A

Every aspiring entrepreneur has a Plan A. And virtually all of these individuals believe, like Levchin, that Plan A will work. They can probably even imagine how they'll look on the cover of *Fortune*, or the comments they'll give when asked, "How did you create the world's best business?"

Unfortunately, they are usually wrong. But what separates the men from the boys, so to speak, is what they do when their first plan fails. The entrepreneurs and other visionaries featured in this book tend to lick their wounds, get back on their feet, and morph their newly found insights into great businesses. Small retail shops selling bags of freshly ground coffee are not what made Starbucks a household word. And an effective free search tool is not what made the word *Google* a verb nor made billions for Google's investors. Both of these now-global brands owe their success not to their Plan A, but to Plan B.

Your Entrepreneurial Dreams

It is a widely accepted fact that successful entrepreneurs and their fast-growing companies deliver the vast majority of economic development—in both the developing and developed worlds. In the United States, for instance, firms that were less than five years old generated all of the net job growth between 1980 and 2001. Those are good results to aspire to. Older firms actually lost jobs![4] But if so many Plan As fail, why on earth are nearly one in ten American adults—and one in fifteen Brits and millions more in almost every country around the world—actively involved in starting or running a new venture, most of which are based on Plan A?[5]

There are many reasons why so many aspiring entrepreneurs are pursuing entrepreneurial dreams today. There's the opportunity to be your own master. No more punching the clock in your look-alike cubicle in a dead-end job. There's the opportunity for the thrill and excitement—the just plain *fun*— of creating and growing an entrepreneurial venture (we know, because we've both been there, multiple times). Some are pulled into entrepreneurship by what they think is a great idea. Others are pushed into it for financial reasons.

Still others hope to use their business' success to contribute to making the world a better place, in some small or not-so-small way. The Body Shop's Anita Roddick, for example, wanted to make the world of cosmetics "greener" and more socially responsible. Google's Sergey Brin and Larry Page wanted to better organize the world's information, no simple task. Great reasons for starting a new venture.

Alas, despite the best of intentions, experience shows that the vast majority of these entrepreneurial dreams will fail to bear the fruit their enthusiastic and passionate proponents intend. And that's a shame. If more people harboring the dreams of Roddick and the Google founders, for instance, were to have a more informed crack at it, society would be stronger for it. A crucial question, then, is why most entrepreneurial dreams—the founders' Plan A—won't work.

Why Plan A—Yes, Yours—Probably Won't Work

Let's step back for a moment and take a candid look at the success and failure of new ventures, whether new products in established companies, small lifestyle businesses, or ambitious new ventures bent on raising a boatload of venture capital to shoot for the moon.

The research on new product success and failure indicates that it takes fifty-eight new product ideas to deliver a single successful new product.[6] Difficult odds! Thus it's often the case that the solution an entrepreneur is pursuing isn't quite what the customer—or user, policy maker, whatever—will embrace. Figuring out what the customer wants and will buy sounds easy. It's not. Figuring out what customers will buy is a process—one that lies at the heart of this book—not a guess. And a handful of focus groups or surveys isn't likely to uncover the answer.

Another common culprit is cash. When a new venture dies an early death, the reason often given for its demise is, "We ran out of cash." But running out of cash isn't a cause, really. It's a symptom. It's a symptom or signal that the company's business model didn't work. Why don't most new companies and their business models work? Perhaps the combination of what it costs to invent, finance, produce, and deliver your dream simply isn't sustainable at a price the customer is willing to pay or at a valuation at which the required investment can be attracted. Perhaps your customers were too few in number or too expensive to attract. Developing viable business models means getting all the economic elements to work together just right. Otherwise—poof!—you're out of business in a heartbeat.

So let's return to Max Levchin. When we left Max, he was feeling pretty uncomfortable camping on his friend's floor, but rather confident that his millions were just around the corner. We reckon you can see the writing on the wall. Let's watch what he does.

Max Levchin's Plan B . . .

You guessed it: Max Levchin's Plan A was not to be. Demand for security on handheld devices never materialized. He remained a vagabond. But he was cooking another idea.

Max pursued a Plan B that centered on cryptography software. "It's really cool, it's mathematically complex, it's very secure," said Levchin.[7] But once again, no one really needed it. Plans C, D, and E didn't work out any better. Levchin's Plan F, still based on his cryptography expertise, was a system for securely transferring cash from one PalmPilot to another. As part of that effort, Levchin's team built a Web-based demo version that did everything on a Web site that the PalmPilot version could do. By early 2000, people were using the Web version for actual transactions, and the growth of the Web demo was more impressive than for the handheld version. "Inexplicable," recalled Levchin. "The handheld one was cool and the Web site was . . . unsexy . . . a demo. Then all these people from a site called eBay were contacting us and saying, 'can I put your logo in my auction?' We told them 'No. Don't do it.' Eventually, we realized that these guys were begging to be our users. We had the moment of epiphany. For the next twelve months, we just iterated like crazy on the Web site version."[8] Levchin finally had a tool that filled a void, allowing ravenous eBay traders to safely transfer cash from buyer to seller.

Plan G—a little outfit called PayPal—was born. And did it strike gold. PayPal is the now dominant system of paying securely for online purchases. Eventually, eBay, whose internally run payment system was floundering, bought PayPal for $1.5 billion.[9] Max Levchin's Plan G was a winner at last!

Creating a Business Model That Works

Breaking through to get from Plan A to Plan B or Plan G is about discovering or developing a business model that really works. This won't happen by duplicating the models already in existence. Draw on them, yes. Play "me-too"?—generally no. If those are working, who needs yours?

But what do we really mean by *business model*? It's a phrase that, since its advent during the dot-com boom and bust, has come to mean everything and anything and nothing at all. By *business model*, we mean the pattern of economic activity—cash flowing into and out of your business for various purposes and the timing thereof—that dictates whether or not you run out of cash and whether or not you deliver attractive returns to your investors. In short, your business model is the economic underpinning of your business, in all of its facets.

What we are advocating is not the same as contingency planning, however. We suggest you put only one plan on the table, starting with Plan A, and devote all of your scarce resources and energy to rigorously stress-testing that plan, as quickly and inexpensively as you can, at its most critical points of vulnerability. At each such point, you'll want to know whether it is still viable. If the emerging evidence says to move on to Plan B—and sooner or later it probably will—move on, and resume the process once again!

Street-Testing Your Plan A: The *Process*

As we will see, creating a business model that can turn your idea into the next PayPal or Google—or turn your long-established company into a juggernaut that disrupts your entire industry—means mixing and matching analogs and antilogs and identifying and addressing leaps of faith.

Let's recap the essentials of the Max Levchin example. Working experimentally, he examined a series of hunches or hypotheses about, among other things, what products his crypto skills might produce, what he might be able to sell, and whether customers would buy what he offered. Levchin was testing ideas and learning to see if they held water. Was he simply lucky? Perhaps. But he was also disciplined, smart, and—after some badgering from eBay users—open-minded about where his process might lead.

Such an experimental process, our research and our experience have found, can lead to the discovery of a new and more attractive customer offering and a potentially attractive Plan B. And the best news is this: you can follow this process systematically, with some helpful structure to keep the seeming chaos in check. Let's explore the four key building blocks of this iterative process:

- Analogs

- Antilogs

- Leaps of faith

- Dashboards

Don't Reinvent the Wheel: Analogs

Perhaps the most fundamental building block in the process we advocate is the recognition by the entrepreneur that others have probably done things at least somewhat like what you are thinking of doing now. There's no point in reinventing the wheel when key elements of it already exist. How can you do this?

To begin with, you'll need an idea that you want to pursue. The best ideas are those that resolve somebody's pain, some customer problem you've identified for which your solution might work. Alternatively, some good ideas take something in customers' lives that's pretty boring and come up with something so superior that it provides what we call customer delight. A fancy latte at the Starbucks on the corner, compared with a 1950s-style cup o' Joe, is an example.

Next, consider the *analogs* to your idea, successful predecessor companies that are worth mimicking in some way. There are many analogs out there, portions of which can be borrowed or adapted to help you understand the economics and various other facets of your proposed business and its business model.

Be Different: Antilogs

Next, consider what we call *antilogs*: predecessor companies compared to which you explicitly choose to do things *differently*, perhaps because some of what they did has been unsuccessful.

Information drawn about analogs and antilogs can be inexpensive and easy to find, because it's sometimes found in what marketing researchers call secondary data—data that's already been created or gathered and is lying around on the Internet, in libraries, in other companies' performance reports, and so on. It is just waiting for you to access it. You stand to learn a lot from it because it has actually happened. Often, primary market data—like responses to surveys and focus groups—reflects what people *say* they will do. But what people *say* is not always what they *do*, so such research can be misleading. Just because they *say* they will buy your new spaghetti sauce based on your grandmother's old-world recipe does not mean that they will actually *buy* it once they have tasted it!

Ask the Right Questions: Leaps of Faith

Having identified both analogs and antilogs, you can quickly reach conclusions about some things that are, with at least a modicum of certainty, known about your venture. But it is not what you know that will likely scupper your Plan A, of course. It's what you don't know.

So the next step in the process is to identify the questions raised by your analogs and antilogs or other questions for which there are neither analogs nor antilogs that provide reliable answers. The questions you cannot answer from historical precedent lead to your *leaps of faith*—beliefs you hold about the answers to your questions despite having no real evidence that these beliefs are actually true. "Any minute now, there'll be millions of people begging for security on their handheld devices," believed Max Levchin.

To address your leaps of faith, you'll have to leap! That is to say, you must experiment. That may mean opening a smaller shop than you aspire to operate, just to see how customers respond. It may mean trying different prices for your newly developed gadget to see which price makes sales pop.

By identifying your leaps of faith early and devising ways to test hypotheses that will prove or refute them, you are in a position to learn whether or not your Plan A will work before you waste too much of your time, and your and your investors' money.

Guide and Track Your Journey: Dashboards

The final step in the process is to adopt a structured, disciplined, and systematic way to guide your set of experiments, track the results as they arise, and provide insight and answers to the questions that underlie your leaps of faith. You need metrics that will yield tangible, measurable evidence capable of telling you whether your leaps of faith are proven or refuted, and whether you are on the path to a strong business model, or a flop (in which case you, like Max Levchin, may decide to move on to Plan B). How is this best done? A *dashboard* is the answer.

A dashboard is a tool that drives an evidence-based process to plan, guide, and track the results of what you learn from your hypothesis testing.

In part, it highlights key indicators of your progress, much as the dashboard in your car tracks key information about your holiday trip to Grandma's house. But dashboards as we use them are much more than the dashboard in the family car. A dashboard in our sense is also a trip planner to help you determine the best route. It provides a detailed map of the hypothesis-testing journey you will take, as well as determining any necessary alterations as you travel.

Your dashboard serves four key roles.

1. It forces you to think strategically about the most crucial issues presently on the table that can—quickly and inexpensively— answer the all-important question, "Why won't this work?"

2. It forces you to think rigorously about how you can examine your leaps of faith by testing hypotheses whose results can be measured quantitatively, wherever possible. Numbers are more persuasive than naïve hopes or dreams.

3. If one or more of your leaps of faith are refuted by the evidence you collect, the results displayed on your dashboard are visible and dramatic indicators of the need to alter your Plan A and move toward Plan B.

4. A dashboard is a powerful tool for convincing others—whether members of your management team, investors or others, even yourself—of the need to move from Plan A to Plan B. If your tenacity or perseverance is questioned, you can show the evidence to support the move toward Plan B. You are not being erratic or flighty. You are systematically testing hypotheses to prove or refute your leaps of faith, and you are listening to what the data tell you.

The process we've just described—finding suitable analogs and antilogs, identifying leaps of faith time and again, and building a dashboard with metrics to guide your journey and keep track of the results of your hypothesis tests—is a straightforward one, really. It inevitably iterates, as will your leaps of faith and the hypotheses you develop to test them. Thus the process never ends, at least not until your final Plan B—in Levchin's case, it was Plan G— is a screaming success. And even then stay alert—things change.

Street-Test Your Plan A: A Framework
to Organize the *Content*

At the heart of every Plan A or Plan B that works lies a set of economic fundamentals that, taken together, make the business viable. There is more cash coming in than there is going out. Or, if this isn't the case just yet, you have enough cash in the kitty to last until cash flow turns positive or until you can raise more capital based on the milestones you have met. If your business model works, you are unlikely to run out of cash unless the economic environment around you starts to crumble.

Every business model, whether viable or not, comprises five key elements. These elements, taken together, determine the economic viability of any business that you might pursue. They determine whether you're likely to run out of cash, or not. They are the *content* of your business model, the building blocks that underlie the financial statements that will eventually measure your company's results. Each of the five elements in our business model framework answers one or more key questions, each focused on cash—cash coming in, or cash going out:

- *Your revenue model:*[10] Who will buy? How often? How soon? At what cost? How much money will you receive each time a customer buys? And how often will they send you another check? This set of questions will not result in one, tidy number. It will produce many elements that should be supported by an analog or, if not, become a leap of faith and properly considered.

- *Your gross margin model:*[11] How much of your revenue will be left after you had paid the direct costs of what you have sold?

- *Your operating model:*[12] Other than the cost of the goods or services you have sold, what else must you spend money on to support the sale?

- *Your working capital model:*[13] How early can you encourage your customers to pay? Do you have to tie up money in lots of inventory waiting for customers to buy? Can you pay your suppliers later, after the customer has paid?

- *Your investment model:*[14] How much cash must you spend up front before enough customers give you enough business to cover your operating costs?

Put Process and Content Together:
The Business Model Grid

Many companies achieve greatness though innovations in—and relentless focus on—just one or two of the five business model elements. For some such companies, their new business models create a Plan B for their industry that can disrupt the entire competitive landscape. Think Southwest or Ryanair in airlines. Skype in telephony. Google in advertising. Zara in fashion. We will dig into the stories of these and other companies in the chapters that follow. But first, we need to bring both process and content together into a single unified whole (see figure I-1)

The column headings in figure I-1 list the *process* issues you'll need to address as you break through to a better business model. These include identifying your analogs, antilogs, and leaps of faith, and developing your dashboard.

The rows list the five elements of every business model. It is these five elements that must ultimately create value for customers, shareholders, and others. Thus, the five business model elements constitute the five themes

FIGURE I-1

The business model grid

Your current idea and the customer pain that it resolves or the consumer delight it offers

Business model element	Relevant analogs and the numbers they give you	Relevant antilogs	Leaps of faith around which you will build your current dashboard	Hypotheses that will prove or refute your leaps of faith
Revenue model				
Gross margin model				
Operating model				
Working capital model				
Investment model				

about which your analogs, antilogs, leaps of faith, and dashboards must inform you as you navigate your way from Plan A to Plan B.

Your task in traveling the road to Plan B and in breaking through to a better business model than you probably have now is to underpin each of the elements of your business model with evidence, in most cases quantitative evidence. The process elements outlined earlier will help you do just that. If all goes well, they will deliver the numbers you need—whether from analogs and antilogs or from hypothesis testing—to answer the questions posed above (and others we flesh out in the chapters that follow) for each row. We'll say more in chapter 9 about how to use the business model grid and your own tailored set of dashboards to successfully travel the road from Plan A to a better Plan B.

What's Next?

We don't want to read about your failed venture in the broadsheets. We want to know that the business model you go on to develop produces an interesting product or service, attracts satisfied customers, pays its employees regularly, keeps the heat switched on, and still has the financial breathing room for some innovation and growth. Thus, in the pages that follow, we offer you a first line of defense against the considerable odds stacked up against your Plan A. By the time you reach the final pages, you will have a process in hand, as well as a deeper understanding of the content you need to consider as you establish a viable business model. Like this pursuit of a surefire business model, we have organized the rest of this book in two sections: process and content.

To start, in chapters 1 and 2, we dig deeper into the *process* of getting from Plan A to Plan B. Chapter 1 examines the case histories of three ventures that have traveled the road from an initial Plan A that didn't work to a vibrant and viable Plan B. We uncover some of the analogs, antilogs, and leaps of faith that got them there. In chapter 2, we examine the dashboarding process, and take a look at the varied forms that good dashboards can take.

In chapters 3 through 8, we address the *content* of the business models that path-breaking entrepreneurial companies—as well as longer-established innovators such as Dow Jones and Toyota—have created to go either from their initially unworkable or industry-standard Plan A to a more viable or more disruptive Plan B. In chapters 3 through 7, we focus on each of the five business model elements one at a time—the revenue model in chapter 3, the gross margin model in chapter 4, the operating model in chapter 5, the working capital model in chapter 6, and the investment model in chapter 7. Chapter 8 deals with companies whose innovative business models are based on not just one of the five business model elements, but multiple elements that work together in intriguing ways.

Along the way, we'll dissect the case histories of twenty companies and the often inspiring characters—entrepreneurs and executives—who led them. Some of them, like PayPal, made successful transitions from a Plan A that was not working or would not work to a Plan B that ultimately worked. Others created a disruptive Plan B that played havoc with the existing industry structure, sometimes creating entirely new industry segments that made life exceedingly difficult for traditional players.

Included are the case studies of particularly inspiring companies with nonprofit (rather than for-profit) mission-driven business models. Their tales will be of particular interest to readers who want to do more than just make money for their shareholders. It is our fervent belief that the best of today's companies do much more than deliver an ever-growing financial bottom line. They make the world a better place. They create jobs where jobs are hard to come by. They accomplish what others in the public or private sector have been unable to accomplish. And they create a more livable planet to pass on to our children and grandchildren. In short, they are not just for-profit. They are for-benefit, too.

Finally, to close the book, we address a concern we coauthors share: all is not well in today's culture of business planning. It is an indisputable fact that, despite the overwhelming interest in all things entrepreneurial, most business plans simply don't deliver. Few plans raise money, and the vast majority of plans never even get read. So, in chapter 9, we explore how the process we articulate in this book, focused on a suitable, perhaps revolutionary, combination of the five business model elements, should make the time and money spent on writing and pitching business plans more productive.

We'd like to see your venture turn out to be one of the standouts, one that promises—with evidence and, ultimately, performance, to back up your promises—the kind of economic and social returns that entrepreneurs in raw start-ups, in lifestyle businesses, in nonprofits, or in large for-profit organizations are so capable of delivering worldwide. Let's get on with our journey!

CHAPTER 1

Don't Reinvent the Wheel, Make It Better

Assembling Analogs, Antilogs, and Leaps of Faith to Get to Plan B

GETTING TO PLAN B is about taking your good idea and developing it into a business or other organization that has high impact, makes you and your investors money, solves the needs of your constituents—sometimes customers, sometimes beneficiaries or others—and is sustainable in the long-term. More importantly, though, it is a book about experimentation and growth, about finding a way for your idea to evolve over time into one that's not simply good, but *compelling*.

This book is also about not getting stuck in a rut or missing real opportunities. Mediocre success—finding a passable business but missing the real potential—is equally problematic. Arguably, it's worse than missing the target completely, because it will tie down your considerable talent in a venture with no real future. You and other entrepreneurs and innovators like you are the lifeblood of today's economy. And to waste your talent on something mediocre would be a real shame.

We'd rather that you make a difference, make the world a better place in whatever way is important to you. If that way is also important to your customers and to other supporters, have confidence—they'll sign on. How then, might you ask, do you go from the germ of an idea to one that's truly compelling with a business model to match? How do you ensure that your epitaph doesn't read, "His business was OK, nothing special. It just kind of limped along"?

Goal for Chapter 1: Don't Start from Scratch

Let's take a step back and think about theater—the world of Shakespeare and Molière, of Rogers and Hammerstein, of Andrew Lloyd Webber. French playwright Georges Polti, drawing on the work of eighteenth-century Italian dramatist Carlo Gozzi, surmised that only thirty-six basic literary plots existed.[1] Thirty-six in total! Polti and Gozzi argued that you could take every play ever written and fit it into one of these thirty-six plot lines. Leonard Bernstein's *West Side Story* is Shakespeare's *Romeo and Juliet*, set in New York's Harlem in the 1950s. *The Magnificent Seven* is just another twist on *The Seven Samurai*. Thus, each time a playwright or screenwriter develops a new script she is really just building on something that has come before.

So, is business like theater? Can you grow your good idea into a successful business as playwrights do, by studying, leveraging, borrowing—even stealing—and learning from that which has been done before?

This chapter is about learning from the experiences of others, using both successful and failed endeavors to inform your decisions, and then develop and test hypotheses and mold your business. The beauty of this method is that by using other people's experiences to shape your decision making, you have the benefit of their mistakes, their blood, sweat, and tears. They have already waded into the water to test for jellyfish while you've been watching from the shore with a gin and tonic in hand.

Each of the companies whose stories comprise this chapter learned from their predecessors' successful and not-so-successful ventures. To learn about product concepts, business models, customer behavior, markets, and operational issues, they used *analogs*—successful predecessors worth mimicking in some way. They also learned from *antilogs*—predecessors (whether successful or not) in light of which one explicitly decides to do things differently. In both cases, they were looking for indications that, based on the experiences of others, their idea would be successful or not. And, for both analogs and antilogs, they took care to frame their comparisons in the context of the current market environment.

Thus, whatever you do, *don't* start from scratch. There are far too many examples that will spotlight the critical unknowns and risks you need to resolve. These examples will answer many of your questions, and they will also identify some crucial beliefs you may hold—what finance types often call *assumptions*—that lack any evidence to either prove or refute them. We call these beliefs your *leaps of faith*, beliefs about which neither analogs nor antilogs can provide satisfactory evidence. By identifying the critical leaps of faith early, you can then methodically focus your limited time and money where it will make the biggest difference, on proving or refuting the hypotheses that grow out of them.

Taken together, the process of uncovering analogs and antilogs, identifying your leaps of faith, and testing your hypotheses can provide the evidence you need to either continue with your Plan A or modify it into what might be a breakthrough to a better Plan B. (Chapter 2 focuses on how best to guide your journey as you undertake such tests.) We examine this process with three examples:

- We explore the transition that Apple made from an innovative but struggling PC hardware and software marketer to a consumer electronics and music distribution powerhouse. Apple shows how relevant analogs and antilogs can be found both inside and outside your own industry.

- We travel to India to examine the rapid growth of Pantaloon, India's largest retailer, and the experimental, trial-and-error process it followed. We'll see that leaps of faith don't always pan out. Failed experiments are good (if inconvenient) news, not necessarily bad.

- Finally, we witness in Africa a story that's unfolding as we write. The African Leadership Academy (ALA) seeks to provide a new kind of educational experience that can create the next generation of African leaders. The ALA's founders have relied heavily on analogs and antilogs to draw lessons from each into their plan. And we see how the ALA quickly made huge strides forward by finding an ingenious way to test its most critical leaps of faith quickly and inexpensively.

Each story offers unique lessons about getting to Plan B. But they also share a few common themes. First, analogs and antilogs can play a variety of roles in helping to get you from Plan A to Plan B, all very useful. Second, analogs and antilogs can only take you so far. Real innovators don't blindly copy the analogs, they mix and match them and turn them upside down or give them their own unique twist. And it's the new twists on old models that sometimes set the world on its ear. Third, the process of getting from Plan A to Plan B is a *systematic* one, we believe—one you can easily learn and apply to your business old or new. So let's get on with the learning!

Case 1: Apple Branches Out from Personal Computers

If you ask anyone born after about 1990 what Apple is famous for, the answer will likely be "the iPod." And with half of Apple's 2006 revenue generated through sales of its iPod and music-related business, this young person wouldn't be all wrong.[2]

But those born before 1990 remember that Apple was once a computer company. Apple built the world's first PC with a keyboard. Apple developed sleek computers that were innovative in design and intuitive to use. By consistently offering the world a different and better computing experience, Apple grew a population of vocal evangelists: people who lived and breathed for Apple products and who were willing to stand in line to get a glimpse at the newest Apple creations.

The iPod catapulted Apple from its computer origins into the world of consumer electronics. The wildly successful portable music device and its associated music store did not magically appear out of Apple's DNA, however. Apple's music portfolio can be traced to a few key analogs and antilogs.

In 2000, Apple was looking for its next big product. The company had struggled for years in the hotly competitive personal computer industry and was in need of some dramatic reinvigoration—something as revolutionary as the Apple II had been to the computer world in 1977. So, rather than sticking to the company's bread and butter, Apple's legendary leader, Steve Jobs, decided it was time to take a stab at the new digital music phenomenon. Music and consumer electronics were not industries where Apple had any obvious advantage. They would have to innovate.

In 2000, the music industry was seeing a flurry of activity and change. Napster, the new peer-to-peer music-sharing site, was wreaking havoc on record companies' bottom lines. In what can only be called a massive theft operation, Napster's users were—illegally, as the courts later decided—downloading millions of pirated songs to their computers. It was no surprise that the music labels grew increasingly hostile to digital music, opting to sue Napster for copyright infringement.

By late 2000, there was a seemingly voracious appetite for digital music. It appeared that everyone under the age of twenty-five was downloading tunes. Piracy of copyrighted music abounded. But without court action, there seemed to be no way to get people to start buying music, versus stealing it. And there were no well-designed products on which to play digital music, in Jobs's view. The scene was set for Apple to pounce.

Apple's Analogs and Antilogs

Jumping into a totally new industry requires more than just guts. It also requires some savvy about what works and what doesn't work. Fortunately for Apple, there were some analogs to light the way, starting with Sony's Walkman. This revolutionary product, introduced in 1979, was the first truly portable, personal music player. Sony CEO Akio Morita said, "Although I originally thought it would be considered rude for one person to be listening to his music in isolation, buyers began to see their little portable stereo sets as very personal . . . We found that everybody seemed to want his or her own."[3] Sure enough, within twenty-five years after it entered the market, Sony had sold more than 330 million Walkmans.[4] The Walkman analog proved that people all over the world enjoyed listening to music on their own and were willing to pay for a device to do so. Most importantly, it proved that personal listening on the go was a socially acceptable activity.

Further, some 26 million Napster users worldwide, sitting around in their jeans and t-shirts sharing their music files, made it clear that individual songs were just as much, if not more, appealing to music consumers than complete albums.[5] Napster proved to the world—and to Apple—that downloading music from the Internet was more attractive than going to the local record store. It also proved that people would go through the trouble of downloading digital music if it were free. Whether they would pay, however, was another question.

It was a question for which the record companies themselves offered some clues. Even before Napster opened the floodgates, the music industry had experimented with selling downloadable digital music online. Various record labels launched Web sites from which music could be downloaded (for a fee, of course). The first, MusicNet and Pressplay, were subscription-based models; users paid a monthly fee to access the songs. With MusicNet, users could download songs to one computer, but as soon as the subscription ended or a bill wasn't paid, those songs disappeared. And MusicNet didn't allow users to download their songs to portable devices, so users had the option of listening to their music on their computer or not at all. Pressplay did allow users to burn a small subset of their songs to CDs for use on the go, but users of these two services didn't really own the music they purchased. And each of the record company sites provided only songs from the musicians that they represented. As a result, neither site contained an exhaustive music library, so users would have to shop from site to site to find the songs and artists they wanted. Consumer response was tepid at best.

From these two pay-for-music antilog sites, it became clear to Jobs and his team that users wanted all of their music in one place. And if users were in fact going to pay for music, they didn't want to rent it, they wanted to own it and be able to play it on their portable devices—not just on their computers. Moreover, people wanted songs, not albums.

Apple could learn from another antilog. In 1998, Diamond Media Systems launched the Rio, the first mass-marketed MP3 player. But its clunky user interface made it difficult for users to find or organize songs. There was only enough storage to play about sixty minutes of music. And transferring music from a computer onto the Rio was painfully slow. "The products stank," recalled Greg Joswiak, Apple's vice president of product marketing.[6] The Rio's struggle in the marketplace confirmed for Jobs that there was no market for anemic or complicated portable digital music players. If it wanted to enter the MP3 player game, Apple would need to solve the storage and user-interface problems that Rio presented.

Apple's Leaps of Faith

Jobs and the Apple team faced some tantalizing questions that led to their leaps of faith. Was there a different business model that would work? Jobs believed there was. Would there be consumer acceptance of a site that offered a huge selection of music for a small fee? It was a leap of faith that music lovers would actually *pay* for their tunes. What if Apple offered both hardware *and* software—an MP3 player and the tunes to play on it—in such a way that the record companies would dance to Apple's tune? Would they play? Jobs was confident they would.

Step one for Apple was taken in early 2001. The iTunes Jukebox, launched in January of 2001, allowed Apple computer users to store, manage, and group their music from any source (otherwise known as creating "playlists") on their Macintosh computers. Around the time of the launch, Jobs also decided it was time for Apple to have its own portable music device, so Apple users could take their newly organized playlists with them. He gave his development team eight months to deliver and launch the new device.

The device—or *iPod* as it was coined—launched in October 2001 just in time for the holiday season. The iPod was a chartbuster from day one, contributing revenue of $143 million to Apple in its first year on the market.[7] Apple had officially entered the consumer electronics industry. But to complete the picture, Jobs needed a way to sell music as well. Let's use Gillette as an analog: Apple was already selling razors (the iPod), but Jobs wanted to sell the razor blades (music), too.

At about the same time, Napster closed its site in accordance with a court injunction. But the Napster analog had shown that an online music store with a large inventory of free music could be successful. Jobs knew the Recording Industry Association of America (RIAA) wanted to take down anyone who dared to enable copyright infringement. So, a pirated-music Web site like Napster wasn't going to work. But customers needed an easy— and legal—way to get digital music. Apple's solution was brilliant.

Jobs personally called individual artists, including the Eagles' vocalist and drummer Don Henley, to persuade them to make their music available on the service.[8] Apple was the first to negotiate and reach agreement with five record companies, allowing Apple to sell hundreds of thousands of songs from artists spanning all five major labels. In a revolutionary move, Apple worked out a deal to sell (not rent) each song for 99 cents. Once they shelled out the cash, Apple's customers could keep their songs indefinitely, share them on as many as three Macintosh computers, burn them to an unlimited number of CDs, and transfer them to any number of iPod portable music players.

The online iTunes Store was born in April 2003. On its first day, Apple sold a million downloads. By the end of July, it had sold 7.5 million tracks.[9]

Apple's iTunes would be named *Time* magazine's Coolest Invention of 2003. The iTunes proposition was straightforward. No subscription was necessary, and there was no variability in the song price: every track cost 99 cents. It was simple, clean, and easy for a user to buy, download, organize, and own music. Musician Seal described the iTunes store, saying, "You can't stop piracy, so you have to work with technology, and you have to get into the rhythm of it. That's what Apple has done here."[10] Best of all, the record labels were happy! One executive said, "Until Apple, it wasn't cool to buy digital music. This was about getting to that pivotal group of people—the people who buy the cool sneakers and wear the right clothes—and showing them that legally downloading music could be cooler than stealing it."[11]

Turning the Razor and Razor Blades Model Upside Down

Of course no one was really going to fill an iPod with thousands of songs at 99 cents each. Sure enough, by 2007, only about 3 percent of music on iPods was downloaded or copied from the iTunes music store.[12] The rest was downloaded from other places and was therefore unprotected and playable on any device. But Apple didn't care. The iTunes music store completed the user experience, and as long as a critical mass of people bought at least some of their music from the iTunes site, Apple could keep itself out of trouble with the RIAA. It didn't really matter to Apple financially if people bought only a small percentage of their music from iTunes, because the 99 cent price tag was barely enough to cover Apple's costs and the record companies' licensing fees. Shrewdly, Apple had turned the traditional "razor and razor blades model" on its head: Apple could make its money selling razors—the growing assortment of iPods—even if customers continued to steal most of the blades!

Lessons from Apple

Steve Jobs moved his well-established business in an entirely new direction—with new profit horizons—and took a bold leap of faith: that people would pay a premium for a snazzy portable music device and purchase at least some of what they had stolen before. Analogs and antilogs suggested—rightly, as things turned out—that his gambit would work. As Jobs unabashedly described his company's strategy, "Picasso had a saying: he said good artists copy, great artists steal. And we have always been shameless about stealing great ideas."[13]

The result of Apple's journey to its digital music Plan B? Apple transformed itself from an innovative but struggling PC maker to what is looking increasingly like a consumer electronics powerhouse, accomplished originally with just a single product line, the iPod, which Jobs has called the "twenty-first-century Walkman," and later with the iPhone.[14] In 2006, the company pocketed $9.6 billion from its music business (iPod, iTunes, and other music accessories).[15] By 2008, Apple had sold 6 billion songs to 75 million customers since its launch six years earlier.[16] How did Apple do it? Jobs and his team enabled the device to play and store large amounts of digital music. They found a way to legalize downloaded music that was sufficient to keep the RIAA off their backs. And they packaged all of it as only Apple can—in a sophisticated, cool, fresh, and usable design. In short, they placed a big bet on their leap of faith, though Jobs' confidence was backed by analogs and antilogs that suggested his gambit would work.

We now look at another company's journey in a different industry in a different part of the world. In the sweeping economic phenomenon that is today's India, we meet a pants merchant who has drawn on the stories of Macy's, Marks & Spencer, Walmart, and others while fine-tuning what has become India's largest retailer.

The Case 2: More Than Pants for Pantaloon

Halfway across the globe, in the world's second-most-populated country, another business mastermind had already begun to make his mark. Kishore Biyani, son of a Mumbai textile merchant, had grown up watching India's population multiply from 600 million people in 1975 to almost double that at the turn of the twenty-first century.[17] He saw that things were changing in India, and changing rapidly. Not only was India's population growing, but its demographics had shifted dramatically.[18] There was suddenly a significant and fast-growing number of young, educated, working-age people. Finding well-paid jobs meant moving to the cities. With incomes that would have seemed low to those in industrialized nations, these households could afford consumer goods like ready-made apparel, plus durables like air conditioners, washing machines, even hired help.

Biyani founded Pantaloon in 1987 (under its first name Manz Wear Pvt. Ltd.). At first Pantaloon was a menswear maker, manufacturing readymade pants sold mostly in independent mom-and-pop retailers and kiranas.[19] In 1997, seeing the growing size and potential of the Indian consumer market and the lack of business savvy of many of the retailers who were his customers, Biyani decided to turn Pantaloon into a retail operation. He felt the world of manufacturing didn't offer enough of an opportunity, didn't provide him with a "big enough canvas."[20] Retail, on the other hand, would provide him with unlimited opportunity. But what did a pants merchant know about retailing?

Analogs in Retailing: Pantaloon Learns from Walmart

The first thing Biyani did was to start reading about leading retailers, looking for lessons—analogs and antilogs—that he could apply in India, noting, "I read every book on Sam Walton, Macy's, Marks & Spencer. And management gurus like Tom Peters, whose book *Re-Imagine!* impressed me." But almost in the same breath he declared that he didn't make a practice of visiting these stores. He reasoned, "By going to a Walmart or a Macy's, you could get overwhelmed into thinking that was the best model and stop learning."[21] Instead, Biyani combined his exposure to foreign retailers with his practical understanding of Indian attitudes and buying behavior.

"When a consumer thinks about Walmart," recalled Biyani, "the first thing that usually comes to mind is the store's huge selection of discount goods spanning hundreds of categories from sporting goods to apparel to food to hair supplies. When a fellow retailer thinks about Walmart, he thinks about the company's maniacal focus on its supplier relationships and merchandising."[22] Traditionally, Walmart purchased a large percentage of its products directly from its manufacturers. In so doing, the company eliminated the cost of doing business with wholesalers and was able to influence and more tightly manage relationships with its manufacturers. By removing the cost of a middleman, Walmart was able to pass along savings to customers. The company was also famous for its merchandising ability, focusing much of its energy on product selection and pricing. It institutionalized the concept of category management, using shopper analysis, customer research, and merchandising plans to determine what should sit on the retailer's shelves. In the end, the Walmart customer always found the right products at the right price.

For Biyani, Walmart served as the perfect analog for both supplier relations and merchandising. Both his hypermarkets, called Big Bazaar, and his grocery stores, Food Bazaar, were modeled in many ways after Walmart. Like Walmart, but uncommon in India, Biyani went straight to his manufacturers rather than relying on wholesalers. Between 50 and 60 percent of Big Bazaar's products were bought directly from manufacturers.[23] Like Walmart, avoiding the middleman allowed Biyani to pass savings along to his customers. Discounts in the Big Bazaar ranged from 5 to 60 percent. And just like Walmart, Biyani was focused on merchandising. He practiced the concept of category management both in his Big Bazaar and Food Bazaar stores, as well as in his growing chain of apparel stores, Pantaloon. He explained, "We have over 150 product categories and each is looked after by a manager who is responsible for its growth and profit."[24] According to Damodar Mall, president of Pantaloon's food business, "By undertaking these activities, the category leader along with the retailer undertakes marketing and promotional activities for the particular category."[25]

Pantaloon Borrows from Marks & Spencer and Zara

Biyani wasn't done gathering his analogs. Marks & Spencer, the U.K.-based food and general merchandise retailer, had sold private labels—goods made exclusively for its stores—almost since its inception in 1893.[26] Its in-house labels provided higher margins than did other brands. To gain the benefits of higher-margin goods, Biyani followed suit, offering private branded products both for his Big Bazaar and Food Bazaar retail stores. The Pantaloon apparel stores carried both branded apparel and vertically integrated private label items for the entire family, including casual, ethnic, formal, sports, and winter wear. The private label items were generally less expensive than the name brands, but delivered high margins. As Biyani explained, "Someone who is unable to afford the premium brand will opt for our brands, which are not exorbitantly priced."[27]

The Spanish apparel retailer Zara provided Biyani with yet another analog, this one for inventory management. Zara's lesson (explained further in chapter 8) was that customers were fickle and that fashion preferences changed with the wind. To ensure that Zara never had an abundance of unwanted inventory, the company utilized an inventive product-design and production process called fast fashion. Most Western retailers took half a year to design a line of clothing, get it produced in a low-wage country, and bring it to market. Zara's fashions moved from drawing board to store in as little as fifteen days.

The benefits were considerable. The faster you could bring a design to market, the better the chance customers' preferences would be the same as when the product was designed. This minimized the risk of launching a product that was already passé, forcing the retailer to mark down its obsolete inventory. And under this system, there was far less money tied up in inventory, freeing up cash for other uses—like opening more stores. "The aim . . . is to respond to the demand of the market rather than try to forecast it months in advance," said Biyani. "This will be the key differentiator between the winners and losers because it reduces working capital requirements and improves return on capital."[28]

Pantaloon's Leap of Faith: Getting the Shopping Experience Right

Biyani knew, however, that all these Western analogs would apply largely to the back end of his retail operation. How his stores should be organized and his merchandise presented was an entirely different matter.

He thought about Walmart, whose stores were orderly, with long, straight aisles and systematically shelved products. Walmart stores were often located in busy suburban areas with plenty of parking. The purpose of Walmart's design and location was to make the shopping experience as convenient as possible for time-constrained American customers. Time and convenience were simply not the driving concerns of Biyani's target market, however. Was the typical clean and orderly Walmart store layout an analog, too? Or was it an antilog that would be rejected by Indian consumers, who were used to spending hours each day haggling in Indian markets?

Biyani's leap of faith—that Walmart's orderly layout would appeal to his customers in India—would be resolved when he launched his first Big Bazaars. Alas, he found that, "The customers never stopped. They kept on walking."[29] And Biyani needed them to stop to pick up goods to buy!

Pantaloon Opts for Some Disorder in Its Plan B

For inspiration, Biyani looked no further than the traditional Indian bazaar. Bazaars, common throughout the country, provided Indians a place to buy just about everything. They were hardly an organized or sophisticated shopping experience. Quarters were cramped, with one vendor bumping up against the next. Customers had to pick through both dirty and clean items to find what they wanted. And, of course, there was no such thing as fixed prices. Bargaining and haggling were the modus operandi for the Indian bazaar, and this was the experience Indian shoppers were used to.

So, Biyani created a totally chaotic front-of-house shopping experience to mimic the Indian bazaar, while keeping his back-of-house efficiencies, unseen by the customer, in place. Letting the buyers choose the vegetables they wanted gave them "a sense of victory," Biyani said. To keep the noise level up, employees announced deals on bullhorns. "The shouting, the untidiness, the chaos is part of the design," Biyani explained.[30]

Biyani was learning that Western analogs could only take his ideas so far. Companies like Walmart, Marks & Spencer, and Zara taught him how to operate his retail stores efficiently and cost-effectively. But none of these chains were targeting this new and still highly diverse market, comprising more than two thousand ethnic groups and four major languages, plus a dozen more languages spoken less widely. It was Biyani's opportunity to put their lessons to use. At a certain point, Biyani had to address some crucial questions, of which orderliness versus chaos was only the first.

He had to experiment where best to locate his stores, how to merchandise his products, and how to design the layout of the stores. He did so systematically and iterated rapidly, continually improving his results. Not everything worked at the outset, but the back-end fundamentals were sound thanks to tips taken from his Western analogs. Biyani's attitude helped his business, too: he was nothing if not adaptable.

Is Pantaloon's Plan B Working?

By 2008, eleven years after Biyani's retailing company was founded, Pantaloon was India's largest retailer, with some one thousand stores—including Pantaloon apparel stores, Food Bazaars, Big Bazaars, and more. And the National Retail Federation in the United States named Pantaloon the International Retailer of the Year for 2007.[31] But the best news was this. Organized retailers only accounted for a mere 3 percent of India's $350 billion in retail sales. There was still plenty of room to grow![32]

Lessons from Pantaloon

All is not lost when your leaps of faith don't all work out. Instead, Biyani's experimental mind-set paid Pantaloon huge dividends, as he tested hypothesis after hypothesis about what his analogs could not convincingly tell him. As is often the case in emerging economies, many of the analogs and antilogs turned out to be U.S. and European companies. Biyani shrewdly realized that while some of the best-in-class paradigms applied to his emerging market, others did not. For those situations where there was no applicable model, or where the analogs seemed not to fit, he had to take a leap of faith and try something totally new. Who knows? If Biyani had not introduced some noise and Indian chaos into his stores, his customers might still be walking rather than buying!

In our next case, you'll meet two inspiring entrepreneurs who put analogs, antilogs, and leaps of faith together to pursue their dream: to provide a world-class education for some of Africa's brightest young students. As we'll see, this methodology is equally helpful to for-benefit ventures as it is to for-profit businesses.

Case 3: The African Leadership Academy Develops Tomorrow's Leaders for Africa

It was the summer of 2004, and Fred Swaniker, a native of Ghana whose family ran a primary school in Botswana, and Chris Bradford, a former brand manager with Procter & Gamble, had just completed their MBAs at Stanford's Graduate School of Business. While living in Nigeria, Swaniker had come to realize the urgent need for effective and ethical leaders in Africa. "I was struck by the disproportionate impact that just a few individuals [like Nelson Mandela and Desmond Tutu] could have and started to envision a way to develop a critical mass of the kind of leaders that could transform African society."[33] Bradford had done a short stint teaching economics and physical science to African boarding school students in the United Kingdom and, on a study tour to South Africa, had also seen firsthand the limited opportunities available to most African youth.

The intrepid pair thought a leadership academy was needed. But before they attempted it, they would need to address five key beliefs that Swaniker and Bradford thought lay at the heart of the African continent's numerous challenges:

- The root cause of many of Africa's problems is an undersupply of leadership across all sectors.

- Individual leaders can catalyze the actions of large groups of people and unleash massive positive change in society.

- It is necessary to invest in Africa's leaders when they are young and dreaming and give them the confidence they need to bring their ideas to the world.

- A pan-African approach is required to catalyze growth and development.

- Africa needs entrepreneurial leaders across all sectors who will throw off the constraints of existing institutions to change the paradigm and create value.

Together, Swaniker and Bradford set out to build an innovative institution that would bring together top students from countries across Africa and inspire and equip them to be ethical, entrepreneurial leaders committed to creating a bright future for the continent. Their Plan A was based on analogs: to build a boarding school that would emulate the elite American and European boarding schools like Phillips Academy Andover, Eton College, and Philips Exeter Academy, which attracted diverse groups of top students and prepared them well for top universities.

These schools nurtured capability and confidence as well as lifelong connections between their often-powerful alumni—all goals of the ALA. Swaniker had met many wealthy African parents who were paying $50,000 per year to send their kids to prep schools in Europe, an indication that a portion of the top African students they were targeting for the ALA could afford to pay substantial tuition.

Analogs and Antilogs Define the ALA's Parameters

As Swaniker and Bradford talked about their concept with a wide range of people globally, they were pointed to another somewhat different analog that neither of them had heard of: Raffles Junior College (RJC). Raffles, a prestigious school in Singapore, offered a two-year course for graduating high school students. On average, 95 percent of RJC graduates attended university, many on scholarships. In recognition of its sterling academic accolades, Raffles had been described by the *Wall Street Journal* as the Southeast Asian "Gateway to the Ivy League." Even more impressive was the fact that numerous Raffles alumni had gone on to assume very significant positions of power in the country, including two former presidents. It seemed to Swaniker and Bradford that Raffles had achieved in Singapore much of what they were setting out to do in Africa. They visited the campus and quickly learned as much as they could about the school and its programs.

The duo then looked to United World Colleges (UWC). At the time, UWC ran eleven two-year, pre-university residential schools worldwide (as of 2008, they counted twelve), offering the International Baccalaureate Diploma curriculum. Their mission was to make education a force to unite people, nations, and cultures for peace and a sustainable future. UWC brought together students from all over the world selected on personal merit—irrespective of race, religion, politics, or the ability to pay—with the explicit aim of fostering peace and international understanding. High academic standards, a strong emphasis on community service, and a wide range of cultural and outdoor activities were all part of a UWC education.

Raffles demonstrated success in building a world-class institution producing extraordinary leaders for a single country. UWC suggested that it was possible to recruit students from many countries and put them through a two-year program that resulted in significant leaps in international understanding.

Swaniker and Bradford also looked to their Stanford MBA experience. Several weeks into his first quarter at Stanford, Swaniker was one of seven students sitting at breakfast with Carlos Ghosn, the CEO of Nissan and Renault. "I realized that if an ordinary person could lead such a successful global organization, so could I." Meeting top executives regularly in courses and extracurricular events at the school helped demystify the process of leadership for Swaniker. "It gave me the gall to think big," he says. If he and Bradford were going to build a new generation of leaders for Africa, the opportunity to meet and interact with high-level business and government leaders would be a critical component of what the ALA had to offer to its students.

Swaniker and Bradford were also mindful of some antilogs. Many of the historically white elite African boarding schools had changed their messaging to a focus on building a new generation of African leaders, but the curriculum and recruiting practices had not been revamped to deliver on that promise. They provided a reasonably good educational experience but did not excel at cultivating leadership capability, in Swaniker's view.

Finally, there were also several short-term African leadership development programs, mostly targeting established leaders and engaging them in community service. While these provided good networking opportunities and some positive outcomes in terms of community focus, they were not really expanding the pool of African leaders or significantly increasing entrepreneurial leadership capacity.

The ALA's Leaps of Faith

Swaniker and Bradford felt building a school was clearly doable. But they had five key questions for which their analogs and antilogs had provided insights, perhaps, but no clear answers:

- Could they successfully recruit the best students from multiple African countries?

- Could they establish sufficient credibility to attract top-notch faculty and administrative staff from across Africa?

- Could they raise the philanthropic capital necessary to launch the school?

- Could they attract high-profile business and government leaders to teach and mentor the students?

- Could they have a self-sustaining financial model for the school's ongoing operations? In other words, was there a business model that would work?

Intuitively, as is almost always the case for committed, passionate entrepreneurs, they felt that the answers to all five questions were yes. In their hearts, though, they knew they had scant evidence to support any of these beliefs. All were huge leaps of faith.

Short of building and launching the school they ultimately envisioned, Swaniker and Bradford needed an expedient way to examine their most critical leaps of faith with some hypothesis testing. They hit on the idea of developing a one-month summer youth program in Cape Town, South Africa, to serve as a small-scale trial for the ALA. They recruited Stanford classmate Ronalee Bayani, the former head of a summer program that prepared minority high school students to enroll at the University of California.

The Summer Academy launched in 2005 in Cape Town. The program featured a robust African studies curriculum, twelve teachers from around the world, and seventy students from thirteen countries. "The impact of the program was tremendous," said Bradford. "Our students gained confidence and recognized their power to positively affect the world, and they became passionate about their community and continent." Through the Summer Academy, Swaniker and Bradford gained credibility and experience while validating some key leaps of faith. What did they learn? There were three points of very good news:

- They had no problem recruiting students from multiple geographies.

- They attracted excellent teachers for the program.

- There was the potential for a financial model mixing traditional philanthropy with fees.

Furthermore, they were extremely pleased with the positive relationships that quickly developed between students from different countries and different socioeconomic backgrounds. Perhaps most importantly, the hands-on leadership curriculum seemed to have a big impact on the students.

Difficult Decisions for the ALA

It was time for Swaniker and Bradford to finalize their plans for the real ALA. Would it be the Plan A already established in elite African education, building a boarding school along the lines of the similarly elite European and American schools, as they had originally contemplated? Or would it be a Plan B along the lines of the RJC model? It was beginning to appear that Plan B was better-aligned with what they were trying to accomplish in Africa.

An early decision to locate the school in Cape Town was also reversed. The Summer Academy taught them that it was difficult to recruit the government and business leaders who were central to the ALA experience because a special trip was required. Bradford explained, "Johannesburg is the business and government hub with a much larger pan-African population of prospective mentors and role models and consequently is a more suitable location. We made the difficult decision to walk away from a scenic part of the country to a less idyllic but more practical location."

So were they ready to forge ahead? The summer experiment had proved some key leaps of faith: it seemed that great students and faculty would sign on. They had also nailed down decisions about the program's format and location. They were feeling confident, thanks to the successful Summer Academy experience that they could show to philanthropic investors. They were ready to dive into deeper water, securing an initial campus and recruiting a dean.

Is the ALA's Plan B Working?

Dive they did, and by autumn 2008 several milestones had already been met. A beautiful campus in Johannesburg had been leased. And more than fourteen-hundred students from thirty-four countries applied to the first class, including the top performers on the national exams in Rwanda, Senegal, and Cameroon. In September 2008, the ALA admitted ninety-seven students from twenty-nine countries.[34] Christopher Khaemba, a Kenyan known for his ability to inspire and develop students from a wide variety of socioeconomic backgrounds, signed on as the inaugural dean. A new generation of African leaders was beginning to come together!

Lessons from the African Leadership Academy

We've seen how drawing lessons from various analogs helps to shape your own unique model. For the ALA, the business and governmental involvement that Raffles Junior College was able to obtain in its Singapore location, as well as the multicountry student body that United World Colleges attracted, served as good indications of what the ALA might achieve. Your dreams are crucially important, but blind copying of analogs in me-too fashion is not what we're prescribing. Instead, choose a little of this and a pinch of that until you've got a recipe that serves up what your customers want and what your business model can support. Crucially, this recipe must respond directly to the market and the industry circumstances you encounter.

From the ALA, we've also seen that ingenious means can sometimes be found to test key leaps of faith—live, in the marketplace—in ways that cost far less than going full speed ahead with your ambitious Plan A. These tests, if they pan out, not only build your own confidence in the path you are following, but they provide tangible evidence to financial backers and others—top students and faculty, in the ALA's case—that you are onto something worth being a part of.

Lessons Learned About Analogs, Antilogs, and Leaps of Faith

We hope that at least some of these key messages have hit home for you:

- Analogs and antilogs have varied roles in developing your new business or transforming your existing one.

- Mixing and matching—not simple copying—is the best way forward.

- Oh, it's a process—and a systematic one, at that!

Let's examine each of these themes in some detail to be certain that these messages sink in.

The Varied Roles of Analogs, Antilogs, and Leaps of Faith

Analogs, antilogs, and the testing of hypotheses to prove or refute your most crucial leaps of faith can inform all kinds of decisions, including operational and marketing plans, without breaking your piggy bank. And they can provide insights into issues much broader than whether your customer will buy.

There's another role, too, that's probably even more important, because walking before you decide to run is a very good idea. Testing your leaps of faith early and often helps safeguard your company against risk. Thus, doing so deserves focused managerial attention until the questions you pose and the untested beliefs you hold are convincingly resolved, either proved or refuted.

Mixing and Matching, Not Simple Copying

Mixing and matching snippets of one analog here, an antilog there, provides a creative melting pot out of which can stew new strategies and business models that can enable your company to stand out in your industry. Each of the companies in this chapter drew lessons from companies that had gone before them, and each of them applied those lessons in new and creative ways. New twists on old models, as we saw from Apple, rather than blind copying, is what you are after. That is what many successful entrepreneurs do. Had Apple tried to replicate the razor and razor blades model faithfully, with low-priced iPods and high-priced tunes, we doubt they would have been nearly as successful.

Starting an Innovative Business Is a Systematic Process

The process of uncovering and critically examining analogs and antilogs, and identifying leaps of faith to be examined, is a systematic one, and one you can learn. By exposing the strengths and limitations of your initial strategy, the process often leads to changes in Plan A. These changes can be a series of subtle adjustments, as seen with Pantaloon and the African Leadership Academy, or far more dramatic ones, as with Apple's assault on the consumer electronics and music industries.

Though it doesn't always feel that way at the moment, change is good news, not bad. Refining your plan will make your business more successful. Blind adherence to your original plan is a path to disaster.

In the end, it's often the gaps in the analogs and antilogs, the leaps of faith—and the testing thereof—that are crucial, that make the difference between failure, mediocrity, or slam-bang success. As we'll see in later chapters, some of the most noteworthy successes in business history have arisen when a new kind of business model—mixing lessons from an analog here, an antilog there, and some insightful leaps of faith that turn out favorably—is concocted.

Sometimes, these new recipes create a Plan B not just for the company, as was the case for Apple, but for the industry. Will Apple's digital onslaught on consumer electronics and the music industry turn out that way for the legacy players? What about for artists? And will the iPhone do the same for the cell phone makers like Nokia and Samsung? Time will tell, but we suspect that Steve Jobs and his musical and consumer electronics adventures have only just begun to hum.

Q&A with John and Randy

We've jumped into the deep end in this chapter. There are probably at least a few questions that you cannot yet let go of:

- Aside from this book, where else should I look to find analogs and antilogs?

- How do I know which analogs are "right" or most useful (and which antilogs are "wrong")?

- When is an analog or antilog good enough, and when do I need to test what it tells me as yet another leap of faith?

Where Might You Find Analogs and Antilogs of Your Own?

As the Apple story suggests, the most useful and revolutionary analogs and antilogs may be those from industries other than your own. That's in part because your lead-footed or narrow-minded competitors aren't as likely to notice, examine, or understand them. The razor and razor blades analog can probably be applied in many more industries than it is today. Steve Jobs proved that it can be turned on its head with surprising success. Can you do it in your business? Would it help you break through to a better business model?

So where should you start looking? With reams of data, annual reports, books, and articles on the world's publicly traded companies, there is certainly no shortage of analogs and antilogs. You can start in the pages of the business sections of your local, national, and international newspapers and magazines.

Even better, strong social networks, which are among the most useful assets of most successful entrepreneurs, are a great place to look. Why? Because building a network can help you not only find relevant analogs and antilogs for your business model, but also provide you with trusted insight into how those analogs and antilogs really work. Insights shared among friends can provide the clarity and depth that newspaper articles or financial statements lack. And perhaps most important, a strong social network might help to lift you from an emotional rut if a leap of faith doesn't pan out as you had hoped!

Which Analogs Are "Right" or "Wrong?"

At the end of the day, there are neither "right" nor "wrong" analogs—or antilogs—until they are proved in the marketplace. Thus, in most cases, the customer—as well as the cash flow—is the final arbiter of whether you have chosen them well and followed their advice appropriately for your situation. It's a hard, cold world out there, and you won't always be right. But being "wrong"—whether about an analog, an antilog, or a leap of faith you test—is OK, as we've noted above, as you can then move forward more knowledgeably to Plan B. So, don't worry too much about what's right and what's wrong. Get on with the process and let your learning begin.

When Is an Analog or Antilog Good Enough to Move Forward?

If you are in the throes of starting a new venture, whether a raw start-up or a new venture within your established company, you simply cannot test everything with an experiment. There are not enough hours in the day or—most likely—money in the till. Using your best judgment, if an analog or antilog looks like a close enough parallel to your situation, if you and your investors gain comfort from what it tells you, and if you're happy to assume an element of risk, then you'll have to simply trust some of your analogs and antilogs. That will free you up to focus your attention on other more critical issues—your leaps of faith—where the advice you get from analogs and antilogs isn't so clear.

What's Next?

Leaps of faith are pivotal to the innovation process. They emerge from a thorough understanding of what has come before—analogs and antilogs—and they should be the focus of the scarce time and resources necessary to arrive at the ultimate plan, whether it remains Plan A or evolves into Plan B. The process is systematic and continual, with new questions and hypotheses at each and every critical juncture. But the process is neither dumb luck nor black art. On the contrary, embarking on the journey from Plan A to Plan B requires methodical, experimental thinking and requires a different kind of tool, one we call the dashboard. Building dashboards and using them to guide your journey toward a fruitful and viable Plan B is the topic of chapter 2.

CHAPTER 2

———

Guiding Your Flight Progress

The Power of Dashboards

AT THE RIPE AGE OF ELEVEN, Johnny Tart experienced his first summer heat wave. Temperatures maxed out at a sticky 104°F. As he sat lazily at his front window one Friday afternoon, he noticed how miserable the commuters looked walking home from the train station. His Chicago suburb was a sleepy one. There was nowhere to stop for a cold drink. Johnny leapt from his perch as an idea took shape in his mind. He would quench the thirst of the local commuters! He would set up a lemonade stand.

Johnny was not the first person in his neighborhood to sell lemonade. The previous summer, his neighbor Jennifer had set up a stand at the end of her driveway, but Johnny had the sense that he could do a better job. For starters, she ran her stand in the early afternoon, long before the commuter rush. She didn't open for business every day, as he planned to. And if he was honest, her lemonade, made from a sugary packet, didn't taste very nice. Jennifer's lemonade stand was more antilog than analog. Johnny assumed that his homemade lemonade, offered every afternoon to commuters, would combine for a great little business. But he had two lingering, unanswered questions—Will commuters stop and buy?, and How much will they pay?—which led to two leaps of faith:

- LOF 1: Commuters, eager to get home, will take a few minutes to stop in front of my house to buy a refreshing drink.

- LOF 2: People will happily pay a premium for a glass of my ice-cold homemade lemonade.

Without realizing it, Johnny was starting a process that we prescribe to data-starved entrepreneurs: dashboarding. Johnny had just accomplished the first task of dashboarding, asking the right questions about his venture. He also had two hunches (hypotheses) about the answers to these questions:

- H1: At least ten people per day will stop and buy my lemonade, if they are not in a rush.

- H2: With a bottle of Coke priced around $1 at the convenience store on the other side of the tracks, they will gladly pay $1.50 per cup.

He believed these hunches, but he had no evidence that they were true.

Let's take a break from Johnny's learning for a moment, because this is where many entrepreneurs make the mistake of stopping. They take their assumptions (Johnny's hypotheses) as fact. Some reckless entrepreneurs embrace this naïveté, having heard that "entrepreneurship is all about tenacity, so I'm going to barrel down this highway at one hundred miles per hour, because my Plan A is wonderful!" Their ventures are the wrecked cars you spot on the side of the road.

If either of Johnny's hypotheses were untrue—if few people stopped to buy his lemonade, and if shoppers thought his lemonade was extortionate at $1.50 a glass—and he failed to respond swiftly, he would probably go out of business. When you leave stones unturned, you run the same risk. We prefer that you reach your destination.

Dashboards Defined

Let's revisit our analog and antilog process. At some point, we exhausted our ability to learn from other companies. Their examples would have given us "good enough" answers to some of our questions, and we could move on. But when analogs and antilogs reach the limit of what they can tell us, we are left with leaps of faith, each driven by a burning question that we cannot answer without some real-world data. So, as we saw in chapter 1, we draw from our leaps of faith a few hypotheses that state what we hope and believe to be true, and we then test them in some way, as quickly and cheaply as possible, and we measure the results. This process—systematically recording our leaps of faith, the hypotheses that grow out of them, and the results of our hypothesis tests—is what we call dashboarding. Scientists do this in their sleep. They begin with a small set of critical leaps of faith, generate hypotheses with which to address them, and determine metrics to measure the results.

A dashboard—the systematic record you keep to guide and track this process—is a flexible tool for addressing your leaps of faith. It forces you to keep track of the questions you have about your venture, while keeping your assumptions (often guesses, really) in mind. It focuses your attention on the critical issues and more efficiently deploys your precious time and resources to removing the critical risks. And it provides a way to respond to the real-life data you generate.

Moving into the dashboarding stage in developing your business model means moving from *spectator*—observing others as you gathered analogs and antilogs, as Johnny did by recalling his neighbor's limited success—to *doer*.

Johnny Dashboards His Way to Plan B

As we know, Johnny had hunches as to how his questions would be answered in practice. So he put into place some metrics to gauge his success (or not!):

- Number of customers and glasses per day that he sells

- The price at which customers most readily buy

On Monday, Johnny placed his family's old card table at the end of his driveway and formally entered the lemonade business. He jotted down some interesting results:

- He only sold two glasses of lemonade at $1.50 per glass.

- Several people stopped to chat without buying, and one grandfatherly gentleman told him that $1.50 was too pricey; the lemonade stand he'd had in his youth had only charged five cents per glass.

Alas, Johnny's hunches were wrong. He needed to make some changes if he wanted to make money. Armed with the data from Monday's experiment, he made two improvements. First, he posted signs at the end of the street to advertise "Fresh Lemonade." Second, he lowered his price to 50 cents for a small glass and $1 for a large. Unfortunately, on Tuesday it rained, but on Wednesday, business picked up, with six glasses sold—and $5.50 in revenue. By dashboarding, Johnny spared himself from the hard lessons of failure and saved his customers from a thirsty walk home!

If Johnny was as systematic as we hope you will be as you dashboard your way to a better Plan B, he would have kept careful records so that he could make midcourse corrections if necessary. His record might have looked something like the one shown in figure 2-1.

Johnny's is a simple but prototypical dashboard that illustrates the key building blocks of the dashboarding process that we hope you will follow:

- Your leaps of faith

- The hypotheses you will test

- The metrics you will use to measure your results

- The results of your hypothesis tests over one or more periods

- The insights you draw for decision-making, based on the results you've obtained

FIGURE 2-1

A prototype dashboard for Johnny

Hypotheses	Metrics	Actual Monday	Actual Tuesday	Actual Wednesday	Insights obtained, course corrections needed
Leap of faith 1: Commuters will stop and buy a refreshing drink					
H1: At least 10 customers per day	Customer count	2 customers	No one stopped in the rain	6 customers	High pricing deters sales, they look, don't buy; no point in setting up if it rains; seems like demand is somewhat less than Johnny thought.
Leap of faith 2: People will pay a premium price					
H2: $1.50 per glass will be acceptable	Total sales, price paid	$3.00 total sales, $1.50 per glass	—	$5.50 in sales (1@ 50 cents, 5@ $1)	$1.50 too high, $1 looks about right.

A dashboard is much more than routine paperwork to complete. It is a tool to help you to frame and respond to the lingering questions your venture faces. As you'll see in our examples in this chapter, dashboards must reflect the nature of your business, the management team, and your questions. In other words, one company's dashboard will look different from another's. And the dashboard you build before your venture takes off will be quite a different beast from the one you create two years into the business!

Why Should You Dashboard?

In business, we love to measure things. In an era where established companies suffer from data *overload*, it is rightly considered good business practice to keep a close eye on a much smaller set of metrics to focus everyone's attention on how the business is operating. After all, if it gets measured, it will get done, as the saying goes. Managers like to know how their sales teams are performing. A CEO appreciates quick snapshots of everything from employee turnover to sales results to bank balances.

In a growing number of companies large and small, these metrics are captured and reported each day, week, or month, using a dashboard that's not all that different in concept from the one Johnny would have prepared. Like the dashboard in your car or in a Boeing 777, these companies' dashboards keep track of the most critical indicators of how they are proceeding on their journey. The good news is that, in most established companies, crunching the numbers might take time, but at least the numbers exist to crunch!

Entrepreneurs, on the other hand, tend to suffer from the flipside: data *underload*. Most nascent ventures lack sufficient experience or enough solid information to launch their businesses outright. Based on only a wild guess, doing so would be as ill advised as flying in bad weather with no instrumentation. Pantaloon's Kishore Biyani (from chapter 1) wasn't sure that his Indian customers would respond well to his orderly store. After a small test, he saw that they never stopped walking the aisles to shop! He quickly refashioned his stores to mimic the chaos and racket found in traditional Indian markets, and sales shot up.

Entrepreneurs such as Biyani have a healthy respect for the fact that their business is toast if their assumptions are incorrect. And in case you missed this little point, initial assumptions—whether about a raw start-up or a new venture in a larger organization—are usually wrong. Testing and measuring is excellent business practice in the start-up world. It's a process that you cannot afford to ignore.

Goal for Chapter 2: Learn to Iterate with Dashboards

A key theme of this book is that, most often, it is necessary to constantly iterate to find a path that will work—for your would-be customers, for you, and for your prospective investors. If all goes well as you iterate, identifying still more leaps of faith and testing hypotheses to address them, you'll eventually find your way to a Plan B or C or Z that will deliver you the kind of success you seek.

Doing this does not mean flying by the seat of your pants—nor without instrumentation. Both flexibility and methodical iteration are the keys to finding entrepreneurial nirvana. Dashboards will record the results of the tests of your hypotheses as they occur. But mere record-keeping isn't why dashboards are so important. More crucially, they will signal the midcourse corrections necessary to reach a viable Plan B. And they have some other tricks, too, as we'll see.

In this chapter, we examine two inspiring case histories. The first is a nonprofit where the analog-antilog-leaps of faith-dashboarding process is every bit as applicable as it is in the for-profit world. The other story is one of those rare cases where Plan A initially worked, though continued dashboarding ultimately revealed the need for a Plan B.

- In the GlobalGiving story, we see how analogs, antilogs, and leaps of faith lead directly to dashboards to interpret what is learned from real-world evidence, and how that learning—whether about initial plans or unanticipated market shifts—brings into crystal-clear focus the need for changing from Plan A to Plan B.

- Aggregate Knowledge's first dashboards confirmed that its Plan A was, remarkably, on track. But the founder kept dashboarding, uncovering some interesting challenges and opportunities for his business.

There are also three common themes that permeate these two stories. The first is their founders' laserlike focus on the biggest risks on the table at each point in time. Second, we see how their dashboards changed over time, and how the founders used them to evolve their businesses. Third, there was a clear emphasis on quantitative measures, even though some hypotheses were more qualitative in nature. At the end of the day, though qualitative issues are important, getting the numbers nailed down is the only way to know whether you've got a business model that will work.

Case 1: GlobalGiving: Inspired by an Antilog

It was late 1998, and Dennis Whittle had just spent a year developing new processes that would help The World Bank, where he was a senior executive, fight poverty.[1] He had a $5 million budget and the services of a top consulting firm. He, his colleague Mari Kuraishi, and their team of development professionals were running a program that had funneled billions of dollars to the Russian Federation for economic development.

Their efforts were deemed innovative and successful. Yet the *results* were disappointing and unsettling: Whittle and Kuraishi were not confident that the large amounts of money they were injecting into the country had had the impact they were seeking or that it had reached the people on the ground who needed the most help.

Theirs was a familiar problem: funds targeted at urgent human needs didn't always end up where they were intended to go. All too often, the funds wound up in the personal Swiss bank accounts of government officials. In Whittle's view, a radical new approach was needed. He asked Kuraishi to join him and help shake things up.

Kuraishi quickly pulled together strategy staffers and personal friends from other parts of the bank for an all-day brainstorming session. They divided a whiteboard into two sections. The left side was labeled "Existing World Bank Processes" and the right, "What Is the Opposite?" On the left, they wrote things like "top-down loans; $100 million; and two-year processing time; two hundred pages of documentation," and on the right, "bottoms-up grants; $100,000 loans or grants; two-day processing time; two pages of documentation."

The outcome of this antilog-driven process was nothing like what constituted business as usual at The World Bank. Tagged The World Bank Development Marketplace, the resulting program would prove to be an important analog for GlobalGiving.

The First Development Marketplace Sparks an Idea
for Whittle and Kuraishi

In February 2000, seven hundred people crowded around 270 cramped booths in the usually pristine atrium of The World Bank. Each was intent on pitching an idea for alleviating poverty in the first-ever Development Marketplace. These finalists were selected from 1,130 applications from more than one hundred organizations based in more than eighty countries. The proposals were limited to four pages, and a fifteen-minute presentation.

At the end of this two-day carnival of ideas, James Wolfensohn, the president of The World Bank, stood on the stage and made awards totaling $5 million to forty-four teams. The event was an overwhelming success. As Whittle explained, "The Development Marketplace not only surfaced exceptionally innovative ideas and projects, but it enabled funding decisions to get made in two days, lightning speed by World Bank standards. This was a radical and eye-opening innovation."

When the awards ended, a South African woman approached Whittle and Kuraishi. In a strong voice, she said, "I did not win." Whittle replied, "Well I am sorry, but this is a competition, and not everyone can win." She retorted, "I am telling you that my idea is a good one, and just because The World Bank did not finance it does not mean that there are not others out there who will finance it."

Whittle was haunted by the truth of the woman's words. Several months later, he and Kuraishi walked away from successful careers in the development establishment. They were committed to building a true marketplace for development project funding where there could be more winners than losers. It would prove to be a challenging journey.

Whittle and Kuraishi Assemble Their Analogs

Whittle and Kuraishi felt strongly that the discipline and rigor of a for-profit business would be critical to the success of their new venture. That would mean raising capital, something neither of them had done. They were encouraged, however, by an analog—eBay—which by matching buyers and sellers for all kinds of goods had grown to more than 20 million users, a dazzling success in the dot-com world. Was an Internet marketplace the right vehicle for their noble venture?

The pair wondered if there were other organizations from which they could learn. Heifer International had been very successful with a charity model, using traditional marketing techniques like direct mail to raise upward of $100 million a year for projects promoting economic self-reliance for individuals in developing countries. But the marketing cost was significant, reducing the funding that actually reached projects. And there was no direct connection between donors and projects. Heifer would be both an analog—demonstrating the possibility of engaging large numbers of donors—and an antilog, for the costly manner in which it raised its money.

GlobalGiving Builds a Dashboard and Takes Crucial Leaps of Faith

With very little effort, Whittle and Kuraishi identified more than one thousand compelling projects in developing countries that could make a significant impact with a small to moderate infusion of funding. It seemed logical that if projects like these could be made visible to a large community of potential funders, money would flow. But their business was far from proven, and it felt too early to establish a foundation to channel charitable contributions to their favorite projects. So the pair established a partnership with the nonprofit Calvert Foundation. The Calvert Foundation had the necessary apparatus for accepting tax deductible donations under the U.S. tax system, an important incentive for U.S. donors.

But the crucial issue, a real leap of faith, was whether Whittle and Kuraishi could harness the Internet to generate direct philanthropic contributions to global development projects in an economically sustainable manner. In particular, there were three key questions:

1. Will attractive, high quality, legitimate projects participate over the Internet?

2. Will sufficient numbers of donors contribute directly over the Internet?

3. How can we fund and structure the marketplace to achieve financial sustainability? In other words, is there a business model that would work?

Though the analogs and antilogs were informative, there was only one way to answer these questions: launch a pilot site and test some hypotheses.

The pair's network in California's Silicon Valley helped to hook them up with a development team in India to create a barebones Web site. In 2002, their new venture, Development Space, came to life with twenty-five projects. Their initial dashboard is shown in figure 2-2.[2]

Though their dashboard does not look just like Johnny's prototype, the same elements—leaps of faith, hypotheses, metrics, results, and insights—are there. Unlike Johnny's, some of Whittle and Kuraishi's hypotheses—the quality of the business plans submitted, for example—are qualitative in nature. Dashboards can be used to gain insights into qualitative issues, too. Like Johnny's, though, a clear focus on the most critical issues that would determine the survival of the business is apparent.

The Data Speak

Happily, there was an immediate and positive response to the Development Space concept. Donations began to trickle in. The news media gave the venture positive coverage as well. But the challenges outweighed the good news. Development Space's results showed that customers needed an assurance as to the quality—indeed, the legitimacy—of the projects listed on their Web site. Based on the eBay analogy, Whittle and Kuraishi envisioned the same kind of user rating system that was so powerful for eBay. Why couldn't donors rely on the ratings of other donors to gain comfort about project quality?

Two things made this clearly unworkable. First, the Patriot Act, introduced after September 11, 2001, required significant vetting of charitable contributions to ensure that they were not going to organizations with terrorist ties. Second, before making a charitable contribution, donors wanted assurance from a credible third party that the project was sound. As Whittle explained, "People were comfortable buying things on the basis of the opinions of other consumers, but they wanted reliable expertise involved in helping them find legitimate projects to fund with their philanthropic dollars." The model would have to be adapted to identify projects through credible sponsor organizations who could conduct due diligence on the ground.

Another problematic hypothesis involved donors. Again, based on the eBay experience, the hypothesis was that if the marketplace existed, donors would come. But the marketplace for "used stuff" that eBay brought to the Web already existed in the form of classified ads and garage sales. The same wasn't true of the marketplace for global development.

FIGURE 2-2

Development Space start-up dashboard

Leap of faith question	Hypothesis	Metrics	Finding	Insight/response
1. Will attractive, high-quality, legitimate projects participate in the marketplace?	Projects will self-identify with minimal guidance. Business plans will be a good proxy for project quality. Due diligence can be conducted after projects apply.	• Number of projects submitted • Size of projects • Type of projects/descriptions • Existence and quality of business plans • Value of business plans to prospective donors • Cost and reliability of due diligence	100 projects submitted; 25 qualified. Size range: $1,000–$250,000. Some too conceptual to appeal to donors (e.g., Argentina fiscal adjustment). Most projects had no business plans or needed extensive technical assistance to create them. Donors didn't care about business plans. Due diligence after the fact was unaffordable and unreliable.	Need to find projects by mining relationships in the field. We need a Plan B! Smaller, community-based projects most attractive to donors. Compelling project descriptions key to marketplace success. Solid relationships with sponsor organizations and a "chain of trust" are needed to ensure project quality and legitimacy, particularly post-Patriot Act. We need a Plan B!
2. Will sufficient number of donors participate in the marketplace?	As with eBay, if the marketplace exists, donors will come.	• Number of donors in first 8 months	<100	Marketing to prospective donors is required. We need a Plan B!
3. How can the marketplace be funded and structured to achieve financial sustainability?	Social and strategic investors will be the best sources of capital.	• $ raised	$3 million investment from HP and World Bank's IFC seemed almost certain, but fell through. $100,000 raised in relatively small increments.	After the dot-com bubble burst, investment capital unavailable. Are philanthropic grants the answer? We need a Plan B!
	A for-profit structure paired with a foundation partner could work.		Having an online marketplace branded "Development Space" and directing donors to a nonprofit partner to make the contribution was a problem in terms of brand identity and credibility.	A structure is needed that would allow for a unified brand. We need a Plan B!

Source: GlobalGiving.

Total spending on foreign aid programs was running close to $100 billion per year, with roughly one-quarter to one-third of the funds coming from private individuals, companies, and foundations. But there were few vehicles other than Heifer International that allowed donors to contribute directly to international development projects. And even Heifer made no clear link between individual donors and specific recipients.

Whittle and Kuraishi's idea was based on a new paradigm. Development Space would connect individual donors with specific projects. As was the case for Heifer, they would have to spend a significant amount of time and money educating and marketing to potential donors. Heifer, the hoped-for antilog, was looking like an analog after all, though a disappointingly expensive one.

Finally, the team found that relying on the Calvert Web site to process donations created a disjointed customer experience. In fact, donors felt as if they didn't know where their cash was going once they were sent to the Calvert Web site.

Development Space Faces a Funding Drought

To make matters worse, the dot-com bubble had burst. Financial investors weren't lining up to put money into an Internet marketplace for global development. And unfortunately, Whittle and Kuraishi needed a small infusion of cash to stay true to the pleas of the South African woman, as well as many other worthy projects. It had been more than two years since her words had kick-started their entrepreneurial journey.

Taken alone, their difficulties might have caused them to give up. But Whittle and Kuraishi were determined to keep going. As Whittle recalled, "Even though the marketplace was not taking off as quickly as we had expected, we could see that the potential was there. We were learning at a rapid pace and needed to adapt our approach based on what we learned." The data, as reflected in the initial dashboard shown in figure 2-2, were speaking loudly and clearly. It was time for Plan B.

Plan B: Development Space Becomes GlobalGiving

Whittle and Kuraishi created a Plan B that was markedly different from their first set of ideas. On the project side, new emphasis was placed on building a sponsor network and relying on sponsors to identify and help position suitable projects for the marketplace. Ashoka, a highly credible organization that identifies and builds networks among promising social entrepreneurs in the developing world, signed up as the first project sponsor. With Ashoka came a chain of relationships, as well as trust, giving projects credibility.

But the venture was desperate for new donors. This was the area where the initial hypotheses were furthest from the reality that unfolded. Hewlett-Packard (HP) had been interested in Development Space from the start. As a technology company committed to innovation and social responsibility, HP was looking for ways that technology could accelerate economic development beyond the then popular "bridging the digital divide" concept of giving everyone access to the Internet. Excited by the possibility of using the Internet to transform global development funding, HP invited Development Space to be a part of its employee giving campaign. This was a big "Aha," a way to aggregate donors in a potentially much more efficient fashion, without spending scarce resources on marketing.

The time was ripe for Development Space to establish a foundation of its own, to clear up the confusion created when donors were directed to the Calvert Foundation. At the same time, the company changed its name from Development Space to GlobalGiving, a name that the new foundation took as well. A separate board was set up for the foundation. Appropriate mechanisms were put in place to provide the level of independence needed to ensure legal compliance.

GlobalGiving had evolved a financial model that depended on many components, one of which was philanthropic support of the foundation. About the same time, Whittle and Kuraishi launched a major fundraising campaign, targeting foundations and high net worth individuals. Despite the drought, they attracted enough money to take the next steps.

Finally, the original, barebones technology platform needed work. Whittle and Kuraishi needed better tools for tracking and analyzing traffic and user behavior, and they needed a new-look Web site to improve usability and the overall donor experience.

With all of these changes, it was time for a new dashboard to affirm or refute their new leaps of faith (see figure 2-3). The three initial leaps of faith remained unchanged, as neither the company's ability to attract enough good projects, enough donors, nor build a business model that would work had been proved in the first iteration. Based on the learning from the earlier dashboard, however, the hypotheses were changed to reflect the decisions that embodied GlobalGiving's Plan B.

FIGURE 2-3

GlobalGiving second dashboard

Leap of faith question	Revised hypothesis	Metrics	Finding	Insight/response
1. Will attractive, high-quality, legitimate projects participate in the marketplace?	A network of trusted sponsor organizations will identify attractive, quality projects.	• Number of projects submitted • Size of projects • Type of projects/descriptions	300 qualified projects <$100,000 in size. Community-based projects.	Project sponsors (first was Ashoka) created credibility; floodgate opened. Hypothesis confirmed! Must limit number of projects to maintain balance with donor volumes.
	Project sponsors will validate quality and legitimacy, create a chain of relationships and trust.	• Number of trusted project sponsor organizations • Cost and reliability of due diligence	Ashoka signed on first, four others followed. Projects are donor-ready.	Sponsorship is the way to go. No follow-on due diligence necessary. Hypothesis confirmed!
2. Will sufficient number of donors participate in the marketplace?	Donors can be aggregated through companies/corporate partnerships.	• Number of corporate relationships • Number of donors achieved through relationships • $ in donations	3–4 key corporate partnerships/sponsorships to build credibility and momentum.	Good vehicle for getting started, but expense of doing customization and servicing relationships is too high for this to be a viable long-term strategy. We need a Plan C as a donor strategy!
3. How can the marketplace be funded and structured to achieve financial sustainability?	Corporations and foundations are the best targets.	• $ raised	Less than the $5 million in corporation and foundation money sought.	The sale cycle is long. Time to breakeven will be significantly longer than originally expected. Major time and energy will have to be invested in raising money for an extended period of time. Plan C needed here, too.
	Need to create a foundation to collaborate with for-profit organization under a coherent brand.	• Structure acceptable to funders? • Ability to accept private investment maintained? • Flexibility to reinvest earnings in foundation?	All foundation funders OK with hybrid structure. YES YES	Hybrid structure provides flexibility but governance is complex.

Source: GlobalGiving.

When the new site was launched, things started to pop. With Ashoka as a project sponsor, the floodgates opened, in part due to the credibility that Ashoka lent. Three hundred projects came so fast and furiously that the team temporarily stopped adding projects to avoid an untenable imbalance between the number of projects listed and the volume of contributions coming in. Once HP's employee giving campaign got under way, the almost immediate uptick in the number of donors and dollars provided an all-important psychological boost for the team. Perhaps Heifer's aggressive marketing spending could remain an antilog, after all!

HP also helped promote this idea to other companies. Partnerships with several other companies, including Visa, Advanced Micro Devices, and The North Face soon followed, augmenting the original open marketplace model with customized sites for specific organizations.

Is GlobalGiving's Plan B Working?

As we write, more than five years after Development Space was launched, the company has funded more than a thousand projects, and GlobalGiving has established a strong sponsor network, as well as robust mechanisms to ensure project legitimacy. While these numbers are not on track with early projections, momentum continues to accelerate and the team remains committed and optimistic. Whittle and Kuraishi now laugh about some of their early hypotheses and how much they have learned. Importantly, they continue to learn not only from their own experiences but from new analogs as well.

What lies ahead for GlobalGiving? Building its growing base of donors is the highest priority. The focus here is on providing such a compelling experience that visitors can't wait to tell everyone they know. Whittle and Kuraishi believe this is possible, in part based on the experience of another analog, Kiva, which delivers microloans by donors in the West to individuals in the developing world. There are two elements in the Kiva analog from which GlobalGiving has learned. First, donors giving through Kiva have felt a connection to the people they are helping, and they've spread the word. Kiva's adeptness at telling the stories of the individuals seeking loans—from the baker in Kabul who needed a new oven to the fish seller in Kenya who needed additional supplies—made each loan request a compelling human interest story. For Kiva, effective storytelling has been a key ingredient in getting donors to open their hearts and their wallets.

Second, offering projects at a sufficiently small size lets donors have a direct impact—a key element to opening wallets. GlobalGiving, as it enters its third phase, is determined to leverage as much as it can on Kiva's successful approach.

By 2008 GlobalGiving had successfully facilitated a reported $14 million in donations from 41,500 people to more than 1,300 projects worldwide. In the process it managed to create a viable business model.[3] The philanthropic support it receives is its most important source of cash. But it also derives revenues from small transaction fees and from the corporations whose employees it services. A very innovative way to fuel a venture endeavoring to change the world.

Lessons from GlobalGiving

The GlobalGiving experience demonstrates the power of the analog-antilog-leap of faith-dashboard process in launching a bold social venture that faced many unknowns at the outset and breaks new ground. By remaining focused on their leaps of faith while making major changes to key strategies—all based on the insights revealed through their dashboards—Whittle and Kuraishi have overcome seemingly insurmountable obstacles and moved ever closer to their goal of making their operation a financially sustainable one.

We now turn to another pair of entrepreneurs. They shared an equally bold vision, one focused on an entirely different problem and a different set of customers. And they are the lucky ones—their Plan A met early success! Read on to see how their dashboards took them further still.

Case 2: Aggregate Knowledge Does Online Discovery

In Paul Martino's view, search engines can't solve every Web user's needs, especially when users do not know quite what they're looking for. Martino's discovery engine was developed for just such instances.[4] He reasoned that individuals' affinity to certain topics (what someone likes to read, for example) provided a better indication of their interests than what they *said* they were looking for.

His concept was a "formative" one: what you read online "formed" and informed a clearer view of what kind of person you might like to date—someone who reads similar things, listens to similar music, likes the same sorts of food, and so on. Martino's insight was that technology could suggest areas or items of interest to users based on the behaviors of other like-minded people. Add to this affinity idea the concept of the wisdom of the crowds en masse and voilá, his vision of "online discovery" was born.

AK's Analogs and Antilogs

In 2005, Martino and Chris Law, his good friend and colleague, cofounded Aggregate Knowledge (AK). Their goal was ambitious: to provide users with information about events, media, and commerce that was deemed relevant based on each person's previous decisions. For example, if you searched for the score of the latest Chicago Bulls game, AK's discovery engine might provide you with upcoming Bulls game times and locations and the ability to purchase courtside tickets. Or, if you were looking at buying a red dress online, the AK engine would suggest other items that people who bought the same red dress had ordered. How about a flashy pair of red heels? The top-selling salsa CD?

Unlike existing online recommendation systems, however, Martino's system would employ the wisdom of crowds across the entire Internet, not just the commonalities of a discrete group on a particular site.

The genesis of Martino's idea for AK was simple. He and Law were working at Tribe.net, an online classified service that combined social networks with groups and listings. Tribe could provide information for finding San Francisco's most recommended orthodontist, but it didn't do a good job helping users find dating partners. Martino figured that the key to finding good dating partners online was to connect individuals based on the news and message boards they read, something Tribe didn't do.

Personify Inc., another start-up, was both an analog and an antilog. The company provided analytics software to help companies gain insight from their customers' behavior, and Personify's idea and its team had attracted substantial venture capital.[5] Personify's value proposition was compelling; however, the company's analytics engine was not scaling sufficiently. It could only process and provide suggestions when there was a limited amount of data. But with so little data, its discovery results tended to be inadequate. Thus, in Martino's view, Personify didn't have the technical firepower it needed to succeed. The AK engine would have to be vastly more scalable.

Fortunately, searching for things on the Internet was not a new concept in 2005. So when Martino and Law considered their company's revenue model, they looked to a number of analogs for lessons. Google topped their list. Google's technology and reach proved that it was feasible to search from hundreds of millions of sources of data and provide almost instantaneous results. And the bigger its dataset the more useful Google was to its users. Google had become the paradigm of choice for how users found things on the Web. And fortunately for Google's founders and investors, Google had become a targeting tool for paying advertisers who used keywords to offer relevant marketing messaging to online searchers. "Can we be another Google?" Martino wondered.

There was an antilog, too. Epiphany Inc. helped companies keep track of and support their customers. It was proving that its customers had little tolerance for long and complicated software deployment cycles. The fact that it took Epiphany months to deploy its tool to customers instead of days or weeks was proving to be a drag on sales. Martino's tool would have to have short deployment cycles. Clunky architecture simply wouldn't do. Martino reasoned that if he could provide discovery like Personify, make his solution scalable like Google, and make it easy, fast, and inexpensive for customers to deploy, unlike Epiphany, then Aggregate Knowledge would have a winning solution. Easy to say, but was it possible to do?

AK's Leaps of Faith

Three leaps of faith were crucial, as shown on AK's June 2006 dashboard.[6] In keeping with Martino's deep background in science and technology, this first of his dashboards was focused on just the three pressing issues, using simple, pared-down language (see figure 2-4).

> LOF 1: Would B2B customers use AK's technology on their own sites? Martino believed they would—a leap of faith for which, at the outset, Martino had no evidence.
>
> LOF 2: Would the AK research engine really scale, technically speaking? It would, in Martino's view—a second leap of faith.
>
> LOF 3: What was the best route to market? Who knows?

FIGURE 2-4

Aggregate Knowledge dashboard 1

Hypothesis	Metrics	Results
LOF 1: Would B2B customers use AK's discovery technology as part of their sites?		
3 trials	# of trials in development	2 under way, who to do the third?
LOF 2: How well does AKRE 1.0 work?		
1.0 Feature Set compelling	Deliver essential features that exercise core product value	Engineers on board, getting up to speed
Scaling 1 billion/month	# of data hits	Early data is exceeding expectations
LOF 3: How do we go to market?		
Merchants or publishers	Identify subset of potential merchants and publishers that have a strong interest in product value	Initial market segments identified
Fee or revenue share pricing model	Test various pricing scenarios against actual customers	Early discussions, not as important until after-market selection

Source: Aggregate Knowledge.

If these leaps of faith had been left unexamined, Martino would not have been able to confidently say that his technology was on the optimal path, and he would have been running very high risks of failure. Martino used dashboards regularly and relied on them to navigate this early period of AK's development. And as we'll see, he relied on even more granular dashboards following from each successive wave of leaps of faith as his company evolved. "Keeping the multiple moving parts of a nascent business organized and accounted for is always a challenge for a start-up CEO. I used a dashboard to keep track of every point of development because I wanted to make sure that we were spending our time and our investor's money on the things that would be determinative of our ultimate business model and success. If we had it wrong we wanted to know, and quickly, so we could course correct before we ran out of time."

The second leap of faith had to do with the technology. Could the team build a product, Version 1.0, which would operate at Web scale and in real time? If not, Martino would find his idea in the discovery graveyard with the likes of some other infamous antilogs!

The final leap of faith was AK's go-to-market strategy. Which customers should they start with? Were media sites more likely to want what AK offered, or were commerce sites? Who would be willing to pay? How much? And what was the top-line sales potential of each of the potential market segments?

To test his hypothesis that such a system could, indeed, be built and that users could be attracted, Martino needed a couple of well-known B2B clients with millions of unique monthly visitors and hundreds of thousands of transactions. If the technology faltered under stress he would have to rethink his approach. He convinced two pilot customers—one media company, one e-commerce site—to let AK run trials. It was AK's first real test, and his first leap of faith answered!

The Data Speak

Martino kept close tabs on AK's performance. He measured the number of results served, the number of hits, the number of page views, the speed with which the results were delivered, and other metrics. These were the metrics that would indicate whether the technology would work.

From this limited set of data, it seemed as though the company's technology could scale. Good news, both for AK's technology and its ability to attract customers who would pay. Having easily found pilots from each of his target industries, Martino surmised that both media and commerce would make good target segments. But he had some new concerns.

Aggregate Knowledge's Second Dashboard

Martino had two new leaps of faith: First, it was far from clear how much customers would pay. Second, it was not clear what the true market potential really was. Excerpts taken from AK's second dashboard to address these issues are shown in figure 2-5. This second iteration, in January 2007, applied more of a functional lens and additional quantifiable metrics including the number of prospective customers in the sales pipeline, the number testing AK's product, the number of paying customers, and more.

This new dashboard read like a list of critical tasks for key functional leaders in marketing and sales. Instead of dashboard items being strategic leaps of faith, this was more granular, penetrating into the next layer of issues. The metrics assigned to each of these tasks gave functional leaders clear and measurable objectives to shoot for. For the sales team, how many

FIGURE 2-5

Aggregate Knowledge dashboard 2 (+ 6 months)

Sales			
Hypothesis	**Metrics**	**Results**	**Insight**
Pipeline (Y qualified leads)	# of engaged prospects	>Y	Well on the way. Getting correct retail/media mix in the pipe now.
Trials (Z new)	# of trials under way	>Z	Several this month and a few more next month already signed.
Paying customers (W new)	# of customers under contract	<W	Need to figure out right time period for trials to convert

Source: Aggregate Knowledge.

sales meetings were they having? What was the pace of commitment? How many trials were started? If the answers to Martino and Law's leaps of faith proved correct, then the sales team should be able to generate sales, right? In the front office, were the office processes working well enough to keep the product moving forward and customers satisfied?

As a direct result of what Martino and Law had learned from their antilogs, the marketing group closely watched the product's setup wizard, measuring the number of days it took to deploy the solution with a new customer (not shown in the excerpted portion of the AK dashboard that appears in figure 2-5). And, since discovery was all about the quality of the recommendations, the new dashboard closely tracked the percentage of attribution (also not shown). How often could a B2B customer attribute a sale or mouse click to the recommendation provided by Aggregate Knowledge?

While pleased with the level of detail that this new dashboard gave him for managing the growing business, Martino found it somewhat difficult in another way. It covered the key functional questions, but it didn't provide him with focus on the larger priorities for the company. As a result, Martino and Law had to regularly step back and ask themselves whether they were measuring the right things.

Ramping Up: An Audacious Plan B

By July 2007, AK had grown to forty employees. The company had proved that it could generate a positive gross margin on the paying pilots that were in place. It had proved that the discovery notion resonated with customers across the retail and media spaces—both with users and with the online sites where the AK discovery engine had been deployed. The AK team could work effectively together to upgrade and improve their service. And the technology worked well enough to make their customers more money. A winning proposition, it seemed!

Indeed, Patrick Byrne, CEO of Overstock.com, a pilot customer, said, "Over 20 percent of all products purchased on Overstock during the holiday season were directed through the discovery window that Aggregate Knowledge powers on our site. Our customers love the new choices they are given, and we are thrilled with the results—higher sales conversions, larger shopping cart sizes, and increased customer engagement and satisfaction."[7] Martino, Law, and their team had developed and launched a recommendation engine that helped Overstock more effectively sell its eight hundred thousand SKUs, and had deployed it on Overstock's site in a manner of days, not months. Proven progress, indeed!

With so many proven hypotheses under the company's belt, AK was moving into acceleration mode. No longer did the company simply want to be a discovery tool for individual companies, it aspired to become a discovery platform across multiple online businesses.

It would create a larger network to pool data from and market a new network-based product. It would provide each B2B customer with the benefits of everyone else's experience and a chance for each customer to build new on-site real estate that they could monetize across the network, like online advertising. AK's customers would make money by selling their click-stream assets to one another, with Aggregate Knowledge tending the store.

The key to such a breakthrough was scalability. Martino and Law did not want to settle for good, they wanted to be great. Rather than execute against a plan based solely on the product and value proposition they had already proved, they wanted to see if there was a chance to reach for something much bigger. Growth was their primary concern. Another dashboard, AK's third, was needed to guide this stage of the journey (see figure 2-6).

AK's third dashboard focused on making the business and technology into a scalable network and platform. Functional leaders were assigned larger company priorities—including, for the VP of sales, getting companies with large networks on board—and were responsible for tracking their

FIGURE 2-6

Aggregate Knowledge dashboard 3 (+ 1 year)

Top priorities			
Hypothesis	**Metrics**	**Results**	**(Function head responsibility) insight**
Network product deployed with acceleration	# of installations	On track	(VP Eng) Product plan completed; hiring in place; launch with new small to midsize Discovery Networks; v1 done.
Agreements with X midsize to large discovery networks	# of networks	Trailing	(VP Sales) Trial agreements signed for the basket of Discovery Network tests we need to do.
Competitive assessment completed	Identify strategic partners	On track	(CEO) Determine friends, foes, best/worst partners. This includes the analytics and reporting strategy.

Source: Aggregate Knowledge.

progress toward achieving those priorities. This method allowed leaders to create and manage their own functional dashboards, drilling down to the task level with their own functional teams, while permitting Martino and the executive team to address the critical leaps of faith regarding scale.

Let's focus on the product area again to see how AK's third dashboard tracked its progress at a functional level. As the leader of the product team, Law's priority was to develop and implement a companywide product-management process. This included not just staffing and integrating with the rest of the organization that touched the product, but also driving the product road map and customer feedback process. These major priorities were assigned to leaders in his organization who then managed them as part of the marketing dashboard with specific performance metrics. Take for example the VP of engineering. His dashboard now tracked tasks related to the process flow—including getting the new network product deployed—and integration of the science into the process, in order to test its speed, responsiveness, and flexibility. No longer did Martino need to track every detail. He watched his team's progress on their priorities and let each leadership team manage the nitty gritty. Getting himself out of the proverbial weeds allowed him to make the big, strategic decisions—based on an updated competitive assessment—more quickly because he could focus on the newly emerging leaps of faith concerning the network and new platform opportunities.

Is Aggregate Knowledge's Plan A Still Working?

By the end of AK's third year, Martino noticed something unusual in its dashboards: the sales team was not acquiring as many new customers as expected and competition was putting pressure on its pricing. He decided to spend ninety days on the road speaking directly to customers. What he found was that few customers had the sophistication to realize the value of Aggregate Knowledge's full power, and competitors were offering a smorgasbord of alternatives that could incrementally address the customer's smaller and more immediate needs. Paul needed a Plan B. He looked for new analogs (advertising networks) and antilogs (Web analytics companies) and determined that Aggregate Knowledge's special sauce had the potential to uniquely address a serious customer pain: targeting the best personalized advertising message to each user. This was his new leap of faith. Fortunately, through dashboarding Martino was quickly alerted to the slowing pace of sales and was able to swiftly refocus his resources. Doing what any smart entrepreneur would do, he began to test his hypotheses using yet another dashboard. Stay tuned.

Lessons from Aggregate Knowledge

The AK example shows how useful a dashboard can be, even when it affirms that Plan A is on the right track. It shows how both quantitative and qualitative data provide insights into progress, and it shows the wider use of a dashboard, as we discuss more fully below. It also shows how AK's dashboards evolved over time, from crucial, high-level strategic questions—huge leaps of faith—to more detailed performance measures as the company matured.

For Aggregate Knowledge, the dashboard was much more than a navigational tool. The company used it to set priorities, provide transparency for the employees, and motivate the right behaviors. Every week, Martino published the dashboard to the entire company. Doing so had positive results. First, it provided all employees with a clear understanding of the company's priorities. Second, it sparked communication among the executive team. Martino also tied his executive team's bonuses to their dashboard results, motivating his leaders to work on the things that mattered most to the company. While specific objectives were subject to change, getting answers was rewarded regardless.

Finally, the Aggregate Knowledge story shows how fast a company can progress when its hypotheses are spot-on. With a store of analogs and antilogs to draw on, Martino and his team hit the ground running. Similarly, AK's dashboards saved it when the company ran into trouble with its initially successful Plan A. Without benefit of dashboards, the problem could have gone unnoticed or unheeded for too long, making Plan B unachievable.

Lessons Learned About Dashboarding

We opened this chapter on dashboarding with a simple story about Johnny and a simple prototype dashboard to illustrate the basic ideas. Then we pushed you quickly into the deep end, showing you real dashboards for more complicated real organizations. There are three themes that we hope have come through about which we'd like to say a bit more:

- The laser-like focus that dashboards provide

- The way dashboards evolve over time

- An emphasis on numbers, though not exclusively

Dashboarding for Focus

In the GlobalGiving story, we saw how the company's dashboards brought into crystal clear focus the need for changing from Plan A to Plan B. In contrast, AK's dashboards made it clear that, for an extended period, AK's strategy was largely on track. Whichever the outcome, dashboards help entrepreneurs—and managers in established companies, too—focus their time and energy on the crucial issues that matter most at the current moment in the company's development.

Dashboards Evolve over Time

In both of this chapter's cases, we saw how the dashboards evolved based on the learning they uncovered. Thus, there's no simple formula for what a dashboard should look like in one company or another, at a given point in time. There's art in their development, and science in their use.

Focus on Numbers

This book is about breaking through to better business models, about getting to a Plan B that, as we saw for GlobalGiving, is better than Plan A. Doing so is an inherently quantitative task, as the next several chapters will make abundantly clear. While some elements of most dashboards address qualitative issues, you'll be missing the boat if the vast majority of your hypotheses are not quantitative in nature.

Finally, there's one more insight we hope you have gleaned from the cases in this chapter: to get the most out of dashboarding, there are three things that matter most:

- The quality of the questions you ask to identify your leaps of faith

- What you do with the data

- The speed at which you get on with your next steps

In Johnny's trial run, he proved his hypotheses wrong. The next day, he made adjustments, and his lemonade business was stronger for it.

Drawing on what we discussed in this chapter, it should be clear that quality questions are what drive your leaps of faith. Which questions about your company make you feel uneasy and keep you up at night? What would you like to know that you don't? What assumptions have you made that might be wrong? What information would lead you to a different conclusion than the one you are operating under? Your dashboard must address these big questions—your leaps of faith.

The way in which these questions are asked and tested depends on the culture of the company and the context of the situation. If you are in an early stage, like GlobalGiving and Aggregate Knowledge, many of the questions are fundamental. They are about whether your idea will work technologically and whether it holds any value in the marketplace. As you grow and evolve, your questions become foundations for how you refine your plan for greater success. They help you focus on the right market and market segments, customer preferences therein, the right pricing and payment strategy, the right distribution channel, the right financial model, the right partners, and so on. In all of these cases, as leaps of faith are answered or dismissed as no longer relevant, new ones emerge.

Q&A with John and Randy

At this point, you may be harboring a couple of questions about how to apply dashboarding to your new venture—or even to your old one! Here are two that come to our minds:

- How formal must my dashboard be? Must I have all these parts?

- What are the implications of dashboarding for business planning? It seems as if, in these examples, the key figures normally found in a business plan materialize over time.

How Formal Must Your Dashboard Be?

The cases in this chapter relied on dashboards that differed in their formality. GlobalGiving's dashboards were much like the prototype we set out for Johnny in figure 2-1, the textbook example, in a sense. There were specific leap of faith questions, one or more specific hypotheses for each of them, and clearly specified metrics that indicated how progress was to be measured. In addition, in the final two columns there were places to record the results and—importantly—draw conclusions about just what those results meant and what to do next.

Aggregate Knowledge was perhaps less formal, but no less rigorous in identifying what the key questions were at each stage in the company's development. There's no single right answer about how you must do this in your company, but these two examples indicate the range of how dashboards can be effectively employed.

The dashboards shown here also differ in how the leaps of faith were presented. Some companies treat them as questions to be answered and state them accordingly. Others identify them as assumptions or untested beliefs that have been identified and state them declaratively. Either approach works—do what is comfortable for you.

What About Business Planning?

We'll return to this question in more detail in the final chapter, chapter 9. But at this point, it should be clear that a detailed business plan would have been a disservice to companies like GlobalGiving and Aggregate Knowledge. That's because a detailed plan would have obfuscated the burning questions and lessened the focus on critical priorities. Any revenue projection would have been sheer folly. And without really knowing what shape the business would take, in GlobalGiving's case, any forecast of expenses would have been pie in the sky.

In each of the two cases, dashboarding allowed the teams to identify the leaps of faith that would mean life or death to their companies. As a result, they could focus their scarce time and precious resources on resolving those issues before moving on to tackle the next set of hurdles.

The stories of GlobalGiving and Aggregate Knowledge hint at one more key issue for which dashboards are especially well suited: developing an evidence-based business model whose economics will stack up. We saw how GlobalGiving's conception of the business changed to make its project sourcing much more efficient. We saw how AK's evolving set of dashboards provided real-world, in-the-marketplace evidence of how quickly customers could be acquired and a host of other issues that make the difference between staying in business and running out of cash. This kind of learning translates easily into numbers, and numbers—not words—are the language of every company's business model.

What's Next?

The *process* for developing a viable business model—whether Plan A, Plan B, or Plan Z—is now in place, with analogs, antilogs, leaps of faith, and dashboards laying the foundation.

In the chapters that follow, we turn our attention to the *content* that can make an innovative business model sing and dance. We dive into the five elements of a business model: revenue, gross margin, operating expenses, working capital, and investment. And we check in on Johnny to see how his lemonade stand is faring.

As we shall see, whether in early- or later-stage companies, creating a business model that can turn your idea into the next eBay or Amazon—or turn your long-established company into a juggernaut that disrupts your entire industry—means mixing and matching analogs and antilogs and identifying and addressing leaps of faith, then dashboarding your way to mid-course corrections as you learn.

The content issues are the lifeblood of the business—the arteries through which cash flows—that creates value for customers, shareholders, and others. And—if you apply them well—value for you, too!

CHAPTER 3

Air, Food, and Water

Your Revenue Model

W HEN WE LEFT Johnny Tart in chapter 2, he was sitting confidently behind his lemonade stand, with newly revised prices
and better signage. Johnny's family was a source of real support as he nav-
igated the hiccups of entrepreneurship. His mom had graciously made an
extra trip to the grocery store to buy lemons, sugar, and paper cups. By
Thursday afternoon, with temperatures in the high nineties, commuters
knew where to find him. They were certainly thirsty. And on Friday,
Johnny tallied his sales: $18.75! That's not bad for four short stretches
(remember, it rained on Tuesday!) of daily work!

Revenue Model Defined

In Maslow's well-known hierarchy of needs, air, food, and water sit at the
base of the pyramid—signifying mankind's most primitive, most fundamental, most essential needs.[1] Revenue is to any business—and to most
other organizations, too—as air, food, and water are to mankind. Without
revenue, a business is as lifeless as a plant without water. As management
guru Peter Drucker observed, if you don't have customers sending you
money, at least eventually, you don't have a business, either.[2]

By *revenue*, we mean money given to you by customers in return for
whatever it is that you sell. And by *customer*, we mean the one who pays
for whatever it is that you sell.

In the introduction, we briefly identified the five elements of any company's business model that, taken together, determine whether a business or organization can survive and prosper. Chapter 3 is the first of our five chapters that address these key elements.

In our experience, the most likely reason that your Plan A won't work is that there are not enough customers who will send you money—soon enough, often enough, in large enough amounts—to keep your venture afloat. Thus we begin our examination of the five elements of business models by focusing on your revenue model. In particular, we examine six key questions that underlie every revenue model:

1. Who will buy?

2. What will they buy?

3. What pain are you resolving for your customers, or what delight are you offering?

4. How soon, how often, and how much or many will they buy?

5. At what price will they buy, and on what basis will they pay?

6. With what effort and cost on your part?

Examining these questions isn't a simple form-filling exercise. For each of them, you'll need evidence that shows, to you and to others, where your cash from customers will come from and why. But a word to the wise, if your only source of cash is "investors" rather than customers, it's unlikely that you'll actually *get* any investors.

So to answer these questions—with evidence, not hopes—we suggest following the process outlined in chapters 1 and 2. That requires finding relevant analogs and antilogs; identifying your leaps of faith for your revenue model, based on the questions above that are not adequately answered by analogs or antilogs; then dashboarding to test your hypotheses to either prove or refute your assumptions. Why must you do this? Without building an evidence-based foundation for what you plan to do with your venture, you'll have nothing more than a house of cards, a series of leaps of faith, none of which have been proved. If living in a house of cards is the level of risk you are prepared to take, good luck. But most investors won't give you a minute of their time.

What if you've not been able to identify any analogs to jump-start this process? Being rudderless isn't ideal—we don't recommend it. But if that's the situation you find yourself in, then you'll simply have many more leaps of faith to prove or refute than you otherwise would. The questions above will guide you in identifying your leaps of faith and dashboarding will be the process you'll use to resolve them.

Goal for Chapter 3: Develop a Revenue Model That Paying Customers Will Support

Customers are unlikely to part with their hard-earned cash unless what you offer them resolves some sort of pain—a more fuel-efficient car, a squirrelproof bird feeder, a fireproof mask for firefighters, or whatever—or, in consumer markets, what we call customer delight, an experience that transcends what customers have come to expect in the past. The more pressing, urgent, and severe the pain, or the more delightful the experience, the better your chances of developing a revenue model that works. *Your* task is to find a customer pain that you can resolve—or consumer delight to offer—while making money. *Our* task in this chapter is to help you to do just that: build a healthy, working revenue model in which customers pay.

To address this challenge, we examine the stories of three companies. Each addresses one or more of the revenue model questions listed above.

- For Google, a revenue model was actually far from its founders' immediate priority. In fact, there was essentially no revenue in Google's early days. Google counted users aplenty, but it lacked customers—the ones who pay, remember? The Google story shows how the analog-antilog-leaps of faith process eventually uncovered a pressing customer pain—better-targeted ads for advertisers—that turned Google from the world's best search engine into one of the world's best money-making machines.

- Boulder, Colorado–based Silverglide Surgical Technologies had a planned revenue model from the outset. However, Silverglide's Plan A was not attracting customers. The Silverglide story shows how much you can learn by simply focusing on a narrowly defined target market—not being all things to all people—and then listening to customer feedback. And it shows how one's transition from Plan A to Plan B—by addressing a couple of key leaps of faith through hypothesis testing and dashboarding—can resolve not just one, but several of our revenue model questions.

- Revenue models sometimes get tired and run out of steam, especially when the products on which they are based are easily copied or imitated. The revenue model that served China's interactive gaming leader, Shanda Interactive, began to fail after about four years. Analogs are wonderful to copy, but the copying works both ways. If you can imitate somebody else, so, too, can others imitate you! So, what if this happens and your products no longer excite your customer? The Shanda story shows that offering customers a completely different payment model can reinvigorate a revenue model.

Just as in most start-ups, this trio completed the same painful rite of passage. First, they came to the realization that their first revenue model would not generate enough money to keep them in business. Second, by systematically questioning what was working—and what was not—by applying new analogs and antilogs and by identifying and resolving new leaps of faith, each eventually developed more finely tuned revenue models that worked.

Case 1: Google's Plan A: Who Needs Revenue?

You don't need an exhaustive search to find one of the most impressive Plan A–Plan B stories in recent business history. At its inception, Google's founders wanted nothing to do with advertisers. Tracking the evolution of Google from its Plan A—with no revenue model—to its net income of $4.2 billion in its 2007 fiscal year, uncovers a metamorphosis that every aspiring entrepreneur and every manager who wants to go places in an established organization should study.[3]

With the Internet boom came the advent of the search engine. Search engines were (and continue to be) to the Internet what the Dewey decimal system was to turn-of-the-twentieth-century American libraries. In the mid-1990s, there were plenty of search engines—Magellan, Infoseek, AltaVista,

Yahoo!, Excite, and HotBot, to name just a few—each boasting a slightly different way to find information on the Web. These search engines were good enough for most users. However, Sergey Brin and Larry Page were not fans.

In 1997, Brin and Page were pursuing PhDs at Stanford University. They lived in the heart of Silicon Valley during the hottest period in California economic history since the gold rush. Page and Brin set out to create a better search engine, more of an academic exercise than an entrepreneurial venture. It reflected their passion for organizing and delivering to Web users relevant and useful information on any topic in an easily accessible manner. Theirs was no small undertaking!

For the next year, along with a few Stanford buddies, they developed a new search engine to replace then-popular AltaVista. "We had to solve several problems. One was relevance: How do we determine if a web page relates to what you ask? Next, although many results may be relevant, which are the most relevant and the most useful?" Brin recalled.[4] Their search engine differed because it used a new algorithm called "PageRank," a word play on Larry Page's last name. This algorithm weighted the importance or relevance of search results and displayed the results in their rank order. With PageRank, the "best answers" found their way to the top of the page. Page and his team also added brief summaries for each search result, plus bold fonts for key words and terms, and *voilá*, Google was born. "They didn't set out to build a company," Stanford professor Terry Winograd recalled, "but they did set out to do a better search."[5] In so doing, they solved a pain—finding all kinds of information with far more ease and speed—that customers didn't know they had.

The result was a great search engine, initially available to a limited set of individuals, mostly Stanford graduate students. Through word of mouth and a bit of free publicity, the Google search engine became more widely used. By early 1999, Google was handling about one hundred thousand searches per day. But, as with anything else, there were costs associated with a search engine. As their engine gained popularity, Brin and Page had to continue to build and maintain a hardware infrastructure. Some serious cash was required.

Google's Plan A was a great academic feat. It was award-winning, and was nurtured by some talented individuals. But it wasn't making a penny. There were users galore, but paying customers were another story. No venture—for profit or not-for-profit—can live for long without bringing in cash from somewhere.

Google's Plan B

Fortunately for Brin and Page, two venture capital firms in the San Francisco Bay Area saw a glimmer of brilliance in Google. Each invested $12.5 million. Even though $25 million is a sizeable chunk of change, the Google founders knew this funding wouldn't last forever. And the investors were banking on the hope that Brin and Page would devise a plan to generate, in the short term, at least enough revenue to cover their costs and hopefully—in the long term—much more.

Internet search had long been established as a free good, for which the user was not asked to pay. If not the searcher, who would be Google's paying customer? Answering the question became an urgent priority.

Google's answer, its first attempt at Plan B, was to license its search engine to other Internet businesses. Believing such companies would pay, and pay enough, for superior search, was a crucial leap of faith. Google targeted Internet companies such as Yahoo! and Red Hat, which licensed the Google search engine for their own sites. In 1999, Google would generate only $220,000 in revenue and $6.1 million in losses.[6] While the Google guys had begun to turn the corner by finally making a bit of revenue, they did not have a revenue model that could support the costs of running their growing business. Their leap of faith had not really panned out, and all six of the revenue model points remained very much up in the air.

A Villainous Plan C?

Realizing that their licensing model was only marginally effective, the Google team set out to find a better customer. Who else might pay? What about advertisers, who had a problem that Google's technology could solve: namely, finding a way to serve up targeted ads to online consumers? Perhaps here was a set of customers with acute pain that Google could serve!

This new leap of faith, if it worked out, would be music to investors' ears. However, to Google's founders, it felt like marching to the dark side and dealing with the devil. From the outset, "advertising" had been considered evil by Google (see "Was 'Plan C' Evil?"). Brin and Page had been adamant not to include advertisements in their search. But with a rising cash flow shortfall, they finally acknowledged that advertising was potentially the best way to attract customers' cash to support the growing costs of maintaining the world's fastest-growing search engine. It was another leap of faith that might lead to a more cash-rich Plan C.

Was "Plan C" Evil?

The Google board appointed the company's first CEO, Eric Schmidt, in late 2001. In an interview with *CNN Money* in 2005, Schmidt recounted his first run-in with the "Don't Be Evil" mantra: "I was in a meeting where an engineer said, 'That would be evil.' The whole conversation stopped, but then people challenged his assumptions. We ultimately decided not to do what was proposed, because it was evil." Similar conversations occur regularly in all corners of Google, where "Don't be evil" serves as as an organizing principle about values.[a]

In 2004, Sergey Brin and Larry Page expanded on the topic of being evil in their "Letter from The Founders":

> Don't be evil. We believe strongly that in the long term, we will be better served, as shareholders and in all other ways, by a company that does good things for the world even if we forgo some short-term gains. This is an important aspect of our culture and is broadly shared within the company.
>
> Google users trust our systems to help them with important decisions: medical, financial, and many others. Our search results are the best we know how to produce. They are unbiased and objective, and we do not accept payment for them or for inclusion or more frequent updating. We also display advertising, which we work hard to make relevant, and we label it clearly. This is similar to a newspaper, where the advertisements are clear and the articles are not influenced by the advertisers' payments. We believe it is important for everyone to have access to the best information and research, not only to the information people pay for you to see.[b]

a. "The 70 Percent Solution: Google CEO Eric Schmidt Gives Us His Golden Rules for Managing Innovation," *CNN Money*, November 28, 2005, http://money.cnn.com/2005/11/28/news/newsmakers/schmidt_biz20_1205/.

b. http://investor.google.com/ipo_letter.html.

But Google still needed to determine how to make money from advertisers, so Brin and Page looked to an analog for ideas. Overture Services was providing searches on a paid-listings basis, so inspired by Overture, Google incorporated the concept of paid listings into its search (and later paid Overture to settle a lawsuit in which Overture had charged Google with violating its patents. Using analogs is good, but watch out for patents!). When a user searched for information, relevant ads would show up on the search results page, and advertisers were charged for each ad impression. Later (Plan D) Google would switch to a cost-per-click model.

But unlike Overture, Google's ads appeared in rank order with the most relevant ads appearing at the top of the page. Sticking to their guns, another leap of faith, Google did not allow advertisements on their home page, nor did they allow unsightly, distracting banner ads. They were also careful to make sure that users knew which of their results were sponsored ads versus results that were unsponsored (i.e., purely informational). "There's a clear, large wall between the objective search results and the ads, which have commercial influence," said Brin. "At Google, the search results cannot be bought or paid for."[7]

Google also thought about how to make it quick and easy for advertisers to sign up. It automated the process, which lowered its operating costs. This also made the process more affordable, allowing smaller companies—which make up the bulk of the economy—to get into the Google mix. Once advertisers signed up, their ads appeared almost immediately. By combining the best ingredients from their PageRank algorithm and an analog, Overture, Google finally had iterated its way to a revenue model that popped.

As things turned out, everyone won. Advertisers went gaga over Google's truly targeted, high-traffic medium for their ads. Users benefited from having both the most relevant information and relevant ads displayed prominently, with a transparent source. By the middle of 2000, Google was fielding 15 million searches per day. In 2001, Google had its first profitable year, with $86.4 million in revenue and $7 million in profits. By 2002, revenue had increased to $439.5 million with profits of $99.7 million.[8]

Google Looks for More

In 2002, things looked good for Google. The company's revenue far exceeded its costs. The founders were millionaires. Why not stop there? Is it pure avarice that motivates a company like Google to continue to look for revenue-making opportunities? Not really. Staying ahead of the pack ensures sustainability. The better you are at what you do, the harder it is for others to replicate your product or surpass your performance. The more reach you have in the marketplace, the tougher it is for your competitors to catch up.

So Google reinvented its revenue model yet again. Who else might pay for Google's knack for searching and its deep pool of advertisers? The company took a close look at some of the companies displayed on their own results pages. These company Web sites often offered searches of their own. Might there be a way to incorporate Google's search technology and advertisers on other companies' Web sites?

TripAdvisor, an online travel community that provides information and customer reviews of hotels and tourist attractions worldwide, was among the first to see the potential. Here's how it worked. Say, for example, we were going to take our spouses to the Greek Islands for a weeklong vacation and some joint work on this book (a great idea in hindsight, but we've thought of it too late!). As we searched the TripAdvisor site for "Santorini," dozens of hotels and reviews would appear, alongside a few targeted, sponsored ads. Google served these ads. And if we chose to click the ad for bed-and-breakfast listings in Greece, then Google would collect payment from the sponsoring advertiser. TripAdvisor and Google would split the payment.

How effective was this new partnership-based revenue model? In 2003, Google grew to $1.5 billion in sales, more than triple the prior year's revenue, with a modest increase in profits to $105.6 million. By 2004, according to Google chronicler David Vise, "Most of the growth and half of sales were coming from a growing network of websites that displayed ads Google provided."[9] Further innovations on the Google model continued, and by 2006, Google surpassed $6 billion in revenue with $1.5 billion in profits.[10]

Lessons from Google

Google's ascendance, achieved in just ten years, is a classic case of not resting on one's laurels, but instead relentlessly searching for even better ways of generating revenue, with whatever new revenue model might apply. The Google story shows how a key analog, Overture, helped Google eventually uncover a pressing customer pain—better-targeted ads for advertisers— that turned Google into something much more than the world's fastest growing search engine.

The Google story also shows us that, if you are really, really fortunate, you can survive for a while without any revenue model at all! Hotmail, MySpace, Facebook, and others would eventually reach similar conclusions. Such a path is a risky one, however, and most who travel it end up in the gutter. When the music stops, if your business does not have a seat at the revenue and cash flow table, the game is over. At some point, revenue from paying customers is essential.

The Google story offers some wider lessons as well. We've seen how its progress was guided every step of the way by a crystal-clear focus on a core purpose: organizing the world's information and making it universally accessible and useful; and core values: don't be evil.[11] Being clear about why your company exists and the values you wish to follow can provide a useful lens through which to examine possible alternatives to your current and future revenue models.

Finally, we note that Google produces many of its breakthroughs by actively embracing innovation throughout its organization, not just at the top or in an out-of-the-way new product development organization. Google engineers are expected to spend 20 percent of their time working on projects of their liking. Many of today's Google offerings stem from this program—Google News, Google.org, which is helping the U.S. Centers for Disease Control and Prevention to monitor outbreaks of the flu, Froogle, and Gmail, to name a few. Finding new ways, new revenue models, for your company to encourage users or customers—advertisers, in Google's case—to send you money is a task that most companies don't delegate widely enough. How many companies have the courage to ask their employees to spend 20 percent of their time working on some innovation that's not really their job? Does yours?

Unlike Google, our next company expected revenue from day one. But would customers send money? Initially, the answer was not encouraging.

Case 2: Silverglide Surgical Technologies: Customers Love You, but Are Not Spending Much Money

Silverglide Surgical Technologies is a story of an entrepreneur, Jonathan Thorne, who did not want venture capital funding and the restrictions that come with it. He wasn't based in Silicon Valley. And in the late 1990s, he wasn't focused on the Internet craze. Thorne's is an instructive story of a typical entrepreneur's journey toward a revenue model that works, and about listening to and acting upon early customer feedback. And his is a story that shows how the various components of a revenue model— bulleted at the outset of this chapter—can come together when your revenue model works.

Like many entrepreneurs, Thorne had tired of working for others. Ready to take his skills and experience out on his own, he founded Silver-glide Surgical Technologies based on a patented product he had developed (and had since licensed) while working for his former employer. In this initial leap of faith, Thorne believed that his surgical probe would be particularly attractive to plastic surgeons. His device was reusable. And unlike most electrosurgical instruments, it would not stick to human tissue. As he put it, "Sticking tissue can cause complications that mar the final appearance of the surgical procedure."[12] The probe, with its proprietary nonstick technology, effectively cauterized bleeding at the point of incision, a crucial step in nearly every surgical procedure. And it did so without sticking, a significant source of frustration for plastic surgeons.

In early 1998, with $80,000 worth of backing from family and friends, Thorne, the engineer, and his partner, Kevin Morningstar, an expert in regulatory compliance for medical products, launched the company. By December, Silverglide had won approval from the Food and Drug Administration (FDA). In early 1999 Thorne and Morningstar started making sales calls and presenting at surgical trade shows. They made some headway with a few plastic surgeons who raved about Silverglide's nonstick probe. However, they counted just $5,775 in revenue by July of that year. And Silverglide had burned through $54,000 of its initial capital. Plan A was not working.

Thorne's Quest for a Revenue Model That Would Work

Jon Thorne had simply assumed that if he built a better mousetrap, the mice would come. But the mice were not even sniffing the cheese! Why? There were several possible explanations for Silverglide's modest progress. One was that it had targeted the wrong customer. Another was that a reusable product line provided too little motivation—too few repeat sales—to interest surgical product distributors. Perhaps the surgical probe was to blame: a surgical instrument that few surgeons would use. Thorne and Morningside had been frugal with their cash—they rarely paid themselves that year—so runaway expenses were not the culprit.

Thorne realized that his revenue model was the problem. Revenue of $5,775 might as well have been zero. And hemorrhaging (no pun intended) their friends' and families' investment was not the business model he or they had in mind.

Thorne took a careful look at his target customers, plastic surgeons. To make a sale, Silverglide had to "convince the surgeon that the probe doesn't stick, and that a probe itself is a useful surgical tool."[13] But Thorne realized that the probe was not a tool that most of them had used before. He didn't have a good grasp of who was going to buy his product. What's more, few distributors wanted to flog his limited and reusable product line (only probes, in only five sizes). Thorne was forced to admit that there wasn't a pressing customer pain that his new tool actually resolved.

Time for Plan B, but Which Way to Turn?

Thorne and Morningstar were convinced that nonstick instruments still made sense. A few early customers of the Silverglide probe had told them that forceps were tools for which sticking was also a problem. And forceps, unlike probes, were used in nearly every electrosurgical procedure. Said one surgeon, "If you can make nonstick forceps, I'll buy them."[14] But developing forceps—a leap of faith—would take all of Thorne's and Morningstar's time, as well as their remaining money. And raising more cash based on the meager results to date probably would not be easy.

There were other questions as well. As Thorne noted, "Plastic surgeons use forceps, as most other surgeons do. But there's another target market that could be attractive: neurosurgery. Sticking tissue is a problem in the brain (a few brain cells here and there really matter!) or near the spine, where they do most of their work. Electrosurgical forceps are one of the neurosurgeon's primary instruments."[15] The Silverglide team wondered whether focusing on neurosurgeons would be a more fruitful route. Neurosurgeons did most of their operations in hospitals. In a given day, a busy hospital might see more than a dozen surgeries. And, since forceps were such a fundamental device for neurosurgeons, an average hospital would have to stock a large supply. Thorne and Morningstar were uncertain of which way to go. Probes or forceps? Plastic surgeons or neurosurgeons?

Which strategy would start the revenue flowing? Or were they already on the right path and just being too impatient? After all, Rome wasn't built in a day!

Though Silverglide's founders had numerous analogs and antilogs from a variety of medical instrument makers serving a variety of markets with which to assess their options, at the end of the day their decision would be not one but two huge leaps of faith. There was no way to know whether one surgeon's statement that he would buy forceps was enough to go on. Thorne knew that what customers say is not always what they will do. He did not even know for sure whether he and Morningstar could apply their growing understanding of nonstick technology to surgical forceps in a way that would work. But he knew that Plan B and its revenue model would *have* to work.

Fortunately for Silverglide and for Thorne's investors, Thorne's Plan B—and then his Plan C—found traction. One step at a time, Thorne moved from probes to forceps, from plastic surgeons to neurosurgeons, and on to a wider range of other nonstick surgical instruments for use by an increasing range of surgical specialties. By 2002, with revenues north of $700,000, at sharply higher pricing, Silverglide's cash flow turned positive. Thorne and Morningstar were out of the woods.

It took about four years for Silverglide to develop a healthy revenue model. But once Silverglide got there, surgeons had clear reasons to buy Silverglide's nonstick forceps. Frustration with sticking forceps proved to be a *real* customer pain. Better yet, the pain was sufficient to earn premium pricing. And with the range of sizes that were required, the money generated from each sale was attractive. Suddenly distributors, too, had reason to energetically sell the Silverglide line. Not long thereafter, other companies saw value in what Silverglide's technology offered. In 2006, Thorne and Morningstar sold the company to Stryker, a diversified medical technology company, for a price that could reach fifteen times revenue, assuming its future projections panned out.

Lessons from Silverglide

From Silverglide we've seen the power of focusing on winning a significant share of a very narrowly defined target market, an objective that, most often, is far easier to accomplish than winning a small share of a very large market, at least at the outset. Why? Focusing helps you better understand your customer, thereby helping you learn what a better Plan B revenue model might look like. What sort of needs does your customer really have? What benefits must you deliver to convince them to buy? Focusing also limits the resources you need, whether people or capital, thereby enabling you, the founder, to do fewer things better and to keep more of your company once you get things figured out. It's far easier to change from Plan A to Plan B if you've not already burned millions of dollars of your investors' money. (If that's what you've done, by the way, your investors may well embrace a change from Plan A to Plan B, but they may decide that you'll no longer be on board for the journey!)

The Silverglide story also shows that there's more than one way to build a multimillion dollar company. Rather than raising venture capital and shooting for the moon, Thorne proceeded carefully and experimentally, hoarding cash until he had a Plan C that worked. This strategy has its risks—a competitor may pass you by, for example, leaving you in the dust—and is not for everyone, but it's often worth considering. The entrepreneur as risk manager rather than risk-taker is much more common than the folklore reveals.

The Silverglide story is a typical one, especially for technology-driven companies. Most of the time, whether in B2B or in consumer markets, the initial application of the technology, the initial product or services, or the initial target market does not turn out to be where the real money is eventually made. We've seen it with PayPal in the introduction, with Pantaloon in chapter 1, with Aggregate Knowledge in chapter 2, and yet again with Silverglide. Iterating your way from Plan A to Plan B to find revenue you can count on is beginning to look like a road well traveled. But once you find willing customers, do they necessarily stay with you? Let's turn to the story of Shanda Interactive, whose revenue model worked for a time, but then lost its fizz.

Case 3: Shanda Interactive Plays Games in China

The Shanda story shows us that in consumer markets, breaking through to a better business model is not always about resolving customer pain. Sometimes providing consumer delight—an experience so captivating that customers can't get enough of it—is an equally attractive path.

Along with his wife and younger brother, Chen Tianqiao founded Shanda Interactive Entertainment in China in December 1999. Shanda's Plan A was Home Valley, an online virtual community that allowed users to enter and explore virtual fantasy worlds.[16] Unfortunately, Home Valley didn't prove to be the colossal success Chen had envisioned. Users just weren't interested. He soon abandoned ship, but remained committed to finding another way to tap into online communities.

Finding Analogs to Uncover a Product That Will Sell

As Chen looked for analogs to learn from, he saw that the online gaming industry showed promise. In September 2001, Chen jumped into the deep end. His humble goal was to emulate the likes of Bill Gates, doing for gaming and entertainment what Gates had done for software. He started by importing three massively multiplayer online role-playing games (MMORPGs, for short) from South Korea. MMORPGs are online environments in which a large number of individuals can interact and compete with one another at the same time. If you want to serve a large market like China, with its population of 1.3 billion, why not serve lots of customers all at once? MMORPGs would be Chen's Plan B.

First, Chen made certain that his new games were suitable for the Chinese market. His team modified the South Korean games, making their look and feel appeal to the Chinese audience. Next, Chen pondered his revenue model. Should he ask users to pay each time they logged on to play? Or would a subscription model be better, so that users could access the game as often as they wanted? Chen chose the latter as his leap of faith. He would sell prepaid, pay-to-play cards online through Internet cafés and at convenience stores. His prepaid model meant that users required only Internet access to play Shanda's games. This was particularly important, he reasoned, as many Chinese gamers didn't have high-speed Internet access at home.[17]

Chen's revenue model worked like a charm, proving his leap of faith in the prepaid pay-to-play model. In 2003, Shanda took in $76 million in revenue, not exactly matching Bill Gates just yet, but off to a very good start. In May 2004, with international interest in the Chinese market surging, Chen took Shanda public in an initial public offering on NASDAQ in the United States. He raised $152 million, enough cash to fuel even more rapid growth. By the end of 2004, Shanda's revenue had more than doubled to

$165.2 million, and 1.9 million users accessed its games in the fourth quarter alone.[18] In 2004, at the age of thirty-one, Chen was named the second-wealthiest man in China, worth just over $1 billion.[19] In 2005, Shanda earned revenue of $245.7 million and a market capitalization of $2.6 billion, the largest of any Chinese Internet company. Chen was on top of the world, right? Not so fast.

A Changing Market Requires a Plan C

Actually, Chen was getting worried. Four years after Shanda's entry into the Chinese gaming market, its games were losing their stickiness. Its number of average concurrent players slid precipitously to 233,000 in the third quarter of 2005, down from 381,000 in the previous quarter. The June entry of *World of Warcraft*, a competitors' MMORPG with fresher graphics, was stealing Chen's customers.[20] The young Chinese gaming population was getting restless, wanting more from their gaming experience.[21]

Chen had wealth on his side but knew that the tide was turning. Should he stay the course and hope that he could continue to collect on his still reasonably popular game? Or, should he do something drastic? The key questions on his mind were around pricing: what and why will customers buy, and on what basis will they continue to pay? Another leap of faith was on the table.

Audaciously, perhaps, Chen decided to turn his revenue model on its head. In late 2005, observing that several top titles in Korea—still a relevant analog—had gone to a free-to-play revenue model, Chen made two of Shanda's most popular role-playing games, *Legend of Mir II* and *The World of Legend*, free.[22] His goal was to shift his revenue model from one dependent on gaming subscriptions to one reliant on the sale of virtual weapons and costumes for virtual characters, or avatars. The new revenue model invited new, less diehard players to play the older games, and it also extended the lifecycle of each game.

In effect, Chen was betting the company on a bold new strategy underpinned by a new revenue model. Chen's Plan C, in essence, was to evolve from a pure online gaming company to an interactive entertainment and media company, to be "China's Disney," as Chen put it.[23] The Bill Gates software analog was out. Walt Disney's entertainment analog was in! Chen would develop new characters like Disney's Mickey Mouse and market them widely, in many ways.

To become this new breed of company, Chen believed that it was in Shanda's best long-term interest to both expand its user base and increase its average revenue per user. Shanda's goal was to attract gamers and then, when they were online, to sell them books, movies, music, and other forms of digital entertainment.[24] Zhou Donglei, Shanda's director of business development, said, "Instead of hanging around and waiting for these older games to lose more and more users, we proactively changed the revenue model."[25]

Following his new Disney analog, Shanda also added another dimension to its revenue model. Chen and his team started selling products such as dolls, action figures, and cartoon books in retail stores. "The revenue coming from the game-character product business is four times more than that from the game itself in mature markets such as America and Japan," Chen said.[26] Observing the hot demand for electronic gaming devices in Western markets, Shanda also started selling a new product, a small set-top box (called the EZ Station) that provided access to games and video content to be played on an owner's TV.[27]

As Chen had warned, however, the effects of these changes on Shanda's performance were not pretty. Revenue continued to slide, and in the fourth quarter of 2005, profits turned to losses and Shanda lost $69 million. The company's shares plummeted to a fifty-two-week low of $12.36 by April 2006.[28]

Shanda's weak results didn't last long. "The move to 'free-to-play' was not easy, but it was the right one," Chen said.[29] In February of 2007, Shanda reported better-than-expected 2006 fourth-quarter earnings of $22 million, with the 2006 year as a whole delivering $67.8 million in earnings, up more than threefold over the company's $21.3 million in 2005.[30] Chen remained optimistic about what the new revenue model would bring: "The (new) model was proven to be successful in 2006, and we will enhance it in 2007."[31] Indeed, Shanda's revenue rose nearly 49 percent to $337.8 million. And in 2008, Shanda's population of registered—and, in many cases, captivated—users hit the 20 million mark.[32] In another move towards its goal to become a more complete media company, Shanda has acquired three literature Web sites since 2002. In June 2008, the company combined these to form Shanda Literature Limited, which tallies more than 20 million registered accounts.[33]

Lessons from Shanda Interactive

From Shanda, we've seen the power of analogs to help an aspiring entrepreneur break through from an initial Plan A that flopped to a better Plan B and to a Plan C that struck NASDAQ gold. Along Shanda's journey, we've seen the power of analogs for building and adapting one's revenue model. Not once, but twice, Chen copied the South Koreans to get his business back on track, and then Walt Disney. There is nothing wrong with emulating or recreating an effective model. Mimicry, as the saying goes, is the sincerest form of flattery.

But we've also seen just how difficult it can be to remain competitive in industries where imitation is easy and competition rampant. Changing how customers pay for their products provides one alternative for staying ahead of the pack, though changing the basis on which customers pay is easily imitated, too. Thus, in industries where differentiation is hard to sustain, long-term success often comes down to superior execution. Will Chen and his team be able to regain the former $2.6 billion market cap that Shanda once enjoyed? Time will tell.

Lessons Learned About Revenue Models

At the outset of this chapter, we identified the key questions that need to be asked to develop or redevelop a revenue model:

1. Who will buy?

2. What will they buy?

3. Why will they buy?

4. How soon, how often, and how many will they buy?

5. With what effort and cost on your part?

6. At what price will they buy, and on what basis will they pay?

For all three of the companies highlighted in this chapter, Plan A generated little or no revenue. But their subsequent plans, with more fruitful revenue models, created breakthroughs. As they evolved, each company found better answers to one or more of these revenue model questions. So what have we learned in this chapter about building a revenue model, whether for Plan A or Plan Z, that will work for you? We hope two themes will have hit home:

- The importance of resolving customer pain (the Google and Silver-glide cases) or providing consumer delight (Shanda)

- The need for actual evidence of how customers are likely to respond

Let's elaborate briefly on each of them.

Painkiller or Delight: Choose One or the Other

At the foundation of almost every business-to-business revenue model that bears fruit—and many revenue models in consumer markets, too—is the notion of resolving some customer's problem or pain. As renowned venture capital investor John Doerr points out, "Great business opportunities emerge from solving big, painful problems."[34] Alternatively, in the case of some consumer-focused businesses, rather than resolving pain, the new venture delivers what we call consumer delight, a new level of consumer satisfaction in a previously boring, perhaps uninspiring, hum-drum category. Think Starbucks and its coffee experience. The Walkman—and later the iPod—for portable music. Or Andrew Lloyd Webber's long-running hit musical, *Phantom of the Opera*, in London's West End.

If your Plan A neither resolves customer pain nor delivers consumer delight, why should the customer divert her precious cash to your company? The good news is that customer pain can be found practically everywhere. Try making a bug list—a list of things you encounter that are not quite right, or not done as well as you think they could be done. Its length will surprise you! Whether you can come up with solutions for which customers will pay is a lengthier task, of course.

Ground Your Revenue Model in Evidence

We've also learned that at every step, evidence is required, to show, with some confidence, that the revenue you foresee will actually materialize. Analogs and antilogs are your best starting point for gathering such evidence, because they—unlike much of what passes for marketing research—are based on actual history of what customers (albeit customers of other companies, most likely, not yours) have done. Talk is cheap; actions are what count.

But, at some point, analogs and antilogs will leave you with one or more crucial leaps of faith. At these junctures, you must build hypotheses and test them, with marketing research if you must, or better yet with real-world, in-the-marketplace experiments, guiding your journey with dashboards and course-correcting as you go. We've already seen how this process works in chapters 1 and 2. In this chapter, we have learned that to develop your revenue model, you'll have to find evidence that responds to some crucial questions. Who will buy? How much will they pay? and so on. (See the checklist at the end of this chapter for a concise reminder of the things for which this evidence is required.)

Q&A with John and Randy

Having come this far on your revenue model there are three questions that probably remain:

- How will you know which customers to target?

- Where should you look for the right analogs and antilogs for your revenue model? How, specifically, should you gauge a company's revenue performance?

- How will you know whether your analogs are likely to hold true?

How Can You Know Which Customers to Target?

It's a matter of insight into their customer pain. Sometimes, customers will tell you what hurts, as one of Silverglide's surgeons eventually did ("If you can make non-stick forceps, I'll buy them"). As we have seen, focusing clearly on a narrowly defined target market can aid in this learning. If the customers respond, great. If not, try another target. Unless you are very insightful—or lucky—iteration and experimentation will probably be necessary.

Where Should You Start to Find Analogs or Antilogs That Will Provide Useful Insights for You?

From all three of the companies profiled in this chapter, we've learned that analogs and antilogs are out there, just waiting to be identified. And in your case, waiting for you to apply them—for free!—to your current plan.

It's easy, as entrepreneurs or executives sitting alone in the CEO's hot seat, to forget that others have probably already faced the challenges and dilemmas on your plate. Many have, indeed, many times over. So, get out of your cloistered garden and get to know them—in your industry and elsewhere. Start with the printed word in news articles, financial, and annual reports. Then get closer through your networks. These people have been there before and their lessons are instructive. And they are your best source for detailed insights about the revenue model questions—how revenue is really generated, from whom, and at what cost. Most financial statements don't reveal the detail you need because they are not required to disclose such information.

How Will You Know Whether Your Analogs Will Pan Out?

Identifying the leaps of faith that you will take, testing the hypotheses you generate, and using dashboards to guide the process and signal the need for the almost inevitable midcourse corrections, is a powerful way forward. It's an iterative world, and there are few right answers that can be known with any certainty up front. So equip yourself with an experimental mind-set and go discover your answers. If your initial hypothesis does not pan out—Google's first licensing deals were inadequate, Silverglide's probe sold poorly, and Shanda's Home Valley was a flop—chalk it up to learning and move on to Plan B.

There is one more takeaway from the three examples in this chapter. Though the world abounds with innovation, few products are truly new. Google's revenue model was copied from Overture. Silverglide's initial product was licensed from Jonathan Thorne's former employer and his eventual winner, surgical forceps that didn't stick, were just better forceps, no more, no less. Shanda's first games were licensed from South Korean gamers. You don't have to reinvent the wheel to create a successful new venture.

Whether you are innovating or imitating, all is not lost if your Plan A generates little or no revenue. Analogs, antilogs, and well-chosen leaps of faith, all of which eventually led to well-thought-out revenue models, created the breakthroughs we have observed. They can do so for you, too. If that's your mind-set from the get-go—imitate some old stuff, add your new stuff, thoughtfully, in a disciplined and measurable, experimental way—so much the better.

What's Next?

There is more to a successful business model than revenue, of course. The real work begins once you have identified your customers, the pain you resolve or delight you provide, and how much you can entice customers to pay for your product. It takes money to produce a product. So while Johnny celebrated his initial take-home of $18.75, he has yet to figure out just how much of that cash he can keep for himself.

In chapter 4, we'll take a close look at your gross margin model. In other words, we'll see how other companies have managed to save bundles of money on the cost of their products. Money saved here will help you in chapter 5, when we try to keep the other costs related to your business in check as we examine operating models. In chapter 6, we'll take a look at working capital and cash flow. These two phrases are critical ones to understand, because if cash from your customers doesn't reach your company's coffers in time to pay your suppliers and lenders, it doesn't matter how good your product is, you won't be able to run the operation to produce it. In chapter 7, we'll take a hard look at your investment model, which is to say the money it will take for you to get your idea off the ground and into profitable territory. So, to the rest of the economics we now turn!

John and Randy's Revenue Model Checklist

Every robust revenue model is constructed from a well-established set of building blocks. For each of these building blocks, you'll need a strategy and evidence—hard, cold facts rather than hopes or dreams—either from analogs you know and trust, from marketing research (always tenuous at best), or ultimately and most reliably from testing the hypotheses that arise from your leaps of faith in a dashboard. What are these building blocks?

✓ Who will buy: A clearly defined target market, please!

✓ What will they buy?

✓ Why will they buy? Are you resolving customer pain? Offering consumer delight? Or neither, if you are honest about it?

✓ How soon will they buy once you start trying to sell, and how often will they repeat their purchases?

✓ How much or many will they buy?

✓ What price and on what basis will they be willing to pay? (A subscription? Pay per use? Give away the game to sell the weapons?)

✓ What will it cost you to acquire each customer, to make each new or repeating sale?

Finally, which companies' analogs and antilogs, or what other tangible evidence, underpins your thinking about the questions above?

CHAPTER 4

Avoiding Rocks
and Hard Places

Your Gross Margin Model

WHEN WE LEFT JOHNNY in chapter 3, he was celebrating the revenue from his first week in business: $18.75. He had his mind set on purchasing a video game for $17.50. But as he touted his financial success to his mother over dinner, she interrupted. Of course, she was very proud of Johnny's success. But she said something to the effect of, "Johnny, I don't want to knock you off of your high horse, but you don't really have $18.75 to spend. You owe me money for the lemons, sugar, cups, and for the gas-money I spent driving to the grocery store." His face fell. She continued, "Don't worry, I won't charge you for the time it took me to go back and forth to the store. I'll cut you a deal. You only owe me $6.50." Johnny sulked over his $12.25 profit. There would be no video game.

As we saw in chapter 3, revenue is the lifeblood of a company, as important as air, water, and food are to a human. If we continue with Maslow's analogy, gross margin is one step higher on the needs pyramid than revenue. Gross margin is the safety or security one also needs. Generating adequate gross margin from your revenue ensures that there's money available to pay the rest of your company's costs. And if the revenue and the gross margin it generates are abundant enough, there will be leftover money (after paying all other costs) that can be used to grow the business or pay out for other purposes—like the sailing trip around the Greek Islands that you've dreamt of for years! On the other hand, if your gross margin is insufficient to cover your other costs, you'll find yourself squeezed between rocks and hard places, and profitability will be elusive.

Answers to just a few simple, but crucial, strategic questions underpin every viable gross margin model:

1. How large is the spread—in absolute and percentage terms— between the price you can get for what you sell and what it costs you to procure or produce it? Or, in finer-grained detail:

   – How low can you drive your cost of goods sold (COGS)?

   – How high can you drive your pricing and have your customer still buy?

2. How should you best manage your margin mix across your product line? Some products might merit higher gross margins, some lower.

3. How can your gross margin model give you competitive advantage in ways that others in your industry lack?

As you'll remember from chapter 3, these questions must be addressed with evidence—data from the real world, not your imagination. If they cannot be answered by analogs and antilogs, then they become the source of new leaps of faith and into the dashboarding process they go!

Gross Margin Defined

Gross margin is simple in concept, but sometimes tricky to apply. For those of you who have not picked up an accounting book recently, let's spend a minute reviewing what gross margin, sometimes called *gross profit*, really means.

Gross margin = Revenue − Cost of goods sold (COGS)

COGS includes all the expenses *directly related* to producing or delivering whatever it is that you sell. It is often expressed as a percentage of revenue, ranging from near 0 percent (for the virtual weapons and costumes Shanda Interactive sells to its gamers, as we saw in chapter 3) to figures approaching 100 percent (some manufacturing businesses incur very high COGS, in percentage terms, resulting in razor-thin gross margins).

COGS excludes the various other costs of being in business. For instance, Johnny's card table and sign, as well as his product-development expenses, such as the cost of tasting various recipes—always tough duty for a lemonade merchant!—are operating expenses, which we tackle in chapter 5.

All else being equal, the higher your gross margin percentage, the better. Let's take Johnny's lemonade. His revenue was $18.75. His COGS was $6.50, or 35 percent of revenue. That left him with a gross margin of $12.25, or 65 percent of revenue. The percentage figures are important. Johnny's mom shopped at a fairly inexpensive grocery store. His friend Randy's mom shopped at the organic market. As a result, the COGS at Randy's lemonade stand was higher, leaving him with a gross margin of just 42 percent, at the going price of a dollar per large cup.

But your business probably isn't as simple as Johnny's lemonade stand. Maybe yours is a chain of women's apparel stores. What's your COGS? It's what you pay for your garments, including the freight expense to ship them from factories in China, for example, to your stores. What's your revenue? It's the amount you actually receive from your customers. If you don't have to mark anything down, your gross margin might reach the 60 to 70 percent range. You'll need a healthy gross margin level like this to cover your operating expenses, such as the rent for your stores, the utilities to keep the lights on, the staff you hire, and those important trips to Paris and Milan to stay abreast of next year's hot fashion trends. If your total gross margin at the end of the year covers all these and your other costs, you'll earn a net profit. However, if you place your fashion bets on fuchsia for next year and the market wants tangerine, you'll probably have to mark some garments down in order to sell them, and your gross margin—hence your profits—will suffer in both absolute and percentage terms.

In businesses where you buy and sell simple things, such as Johnny's lemonade stand or most retailing businesses, the calculation of gross margin is relatively straightforward. But in many businesses, the calculation gets tricky. The accounting profession has developed a set of rules and conventions about what, for most kinds of businesses, is—and is not— allowed to be included in COGS when you report your financial performance. If yours is a publicly held company, these rules are important. For our purposes in developing business models, though, we're far more concerned about *understanding* your cash flows—where money will come from and where it will go—than about *reporting* your results. So let's set the arcane accounting rules aside and consider some examples to illustrate how we'd like you to think about your gross margin and its flip side, your cost of goods sold.

Suppose you have in mind a new business model for a new airline. What's your COGS? By our definition above, it's the cost of producing or delivering what you sell, say, a business-class seat from London to San Francisco. To say this includes just the free meal and the hot nuts and drinks, though, would be incomplete, as it takes other costs—pilots, flight crew, and jet fuel—to get you there. So these costs, too, are part of your COGS. Calculating gross margin is getting tricky, isn't it? What about the plane? Should you somehow allocate part of the cost of leasing or buying the airplane itself? It's getting trickier! A long flight, like the one from London to San Francisco, uses a lot more plane time than a short hop from New York to Boston. So, for the purpose of planning your business model, one might argue that you should also include in your COGS a prorated portion of owning and operating the plane, too. Now we're on a slippery slope that really never ends. So, where should you draw the line between what's included in COGS and what is not?

For business model purposes, our suggestion is this. Simply draw a line that, in your particular business, most meaningfully separates the cost of *what your customer actually buys* from all the other costs, your operating expenses, of being in business, like buying or leasing some airplanes and airport gates. So COGS is the cost of the garment for the fashion boutique, the cost of flying you from LHR to SFO (however widely or narrowly you figure it), or the cost to Microsoft of duplicating a software CD and putting it in a fancy box. In some businesses, like many service businesses, COGS as a percentage of sales will be very low, and most of your expenses will be operating expenses. If you are in the haircutting business, the stylist's time is about all the COGS you'll have. Your gross margin percentage will be high. The same is true in the software industry. The cost of the CD and the pretty box that contains it is negligible compared with the cost of developing the software in the first place. Ditto for movies, whether made in Hollywood or Bollywood.

As you work toward building a viable business model, it is critical to find a way to make the combination of the five business model elements work together so that, at the end of the day, there will be cash left over after paying all your expenses. With a revenue model in hand, the next key step in doing so is determining, in percentage terms, the gross margin that you can expect from each bit of revenue that your revenue model brings in. Thus, there is an intimate connection between your revenue and gross margin models. If your overall business model "works," and your gross margin covers all your other expenses, you will find yourself in the enviable position of deciding what you'd like to do with the extra cash.

Goal for Chapter 4: Give Yourself Some Breathing Room

In this chapter, we'll try our best to give your company some financial breathing room. We'll help you devise a gross margin model—whether for Plan A or Plan Z—that puts those of others in your industry to shame. A tall order? Absolutely. But do it and prosper!

To address this challenge, we examine the stories of three well-known, but inspiring companies, one of which is more than seventy-five years old.

- First, we explore the eBay story, an uncommon case of hitting the nail on the head with its Plan A, which turned out to be a disruptive Plan B in the auction industry and in the retailing of used goods of all kinds. The online auction site demonstrates gross margin nirvana, with gross margin approaching 100 percent of revenue, while cost of goods sold is near zero. For more and more companies in today's digital world, such a possibility is no longer a dream.

- Next, we take a look at a company whose current gross margin model, though arrived at iteratively, has over time disrupted the world's automotive industry and very nearly put Detroit out of business. Toyota's relentless drive for efficiency and quality is legendary. The Japanese company found ways to manufacture better automobiles for less money, while pricing their automobiles at levels that deliver higher gross margins than their competitors. But the best and most ingenious part of Toyota's gross margin model is its ability to apply competitive pressure across one part of its product mix by taking wider gross margins elsewhere.

- We close the chapter with the story of entrepreneur Yvon Chouinard and Patagonia. Patagonia's vigorous environmental advocacy was funded, in its iteration to Plan B, by an ambitious gross margin model. By catering to environmentally conscious customers who could afford and appreciate top-quality outdoor clothing and gear, Patagonia provides lessons about gross margin and more: that an entrepreneur's values don't have to take a back seat to the company's bottom line. And it demonstrates just how hairy things can get if you don't keep a close tab on costs from the start.

All three of these companies developed killer gross margin models. They did so by finding ways to fatten their gross margins, either by keeping cost of goods sold in check or by giving sufficient value to their customers that kept the spread between COGS and price at a very healthy level. Or both.

Their stories also make clear how the notion of Plan B can be employed in two quite distinct ways. The first, as we've seen in earlier chapters, is the kind of Plan B that follows or grows out of a sometimes not-fully-successful Plan A in an iterative manner. The second, including the first two cases we examine in this chapter, is the kind of Plan B that disrupts or revolutionizes how business is done in its industry. These kinds of Plan B (whether arrived at iteratively or ingeniously conceived from day one), in effect, rewrite the business model rulebook in their industries, creating in some sense a new and disruptive "industry Plan B." Companies that create disruptive business models like these often wreak havoc on their legacy competitors who still do business the old way.

Case 1: eBay, Gross Margin Nirvana

What if you could create a company with no costs of goods sold at all? Recall our equation:

$$\text{Gross margin} = \text{Revenue} - \text{Cost of goods sold}$$

If there were no COGS, every $1 in revenue would generate $1 in gross margin. This is a very nice daydream, unattainable for most companies. Unlike most of our other case studies, which evolved their business models over time, eBay launched a revolutionary business model that came close to gross margin nirvana from day one.

What prompted Pierre Omidyar to start AuctionWeb (the eBay name came later) was not what most people think. He was not trying to find a way for his fiancée to get rid of unwanted trinkets in her basement. He was not even trying to strike it rich. As nerdy as it might sound, he wanted to create a "perfect market." In this market, buyers and sellers could interact freely. Buyers would have access to perfect information. Sellers would have equal opportunity to sell their goods. He thought the Internet would enable just such a market.

So, in 1995, over a fabled Labor Day weekend, Omidyar developed a little auction Web site. The site, AuctionWeb.com, allowed users to list, view, and place bids on items free of charge. As he described it, "Instead of posting a classified ad saying I have this object for sale, give me a hundred dollars, you post it and say here's a minimum price. If there's more than one person interested, let them fight it out . . . The seller would by definition get the market price for the item, whatever that might be on a particular day."[1] He proved to himself that his model worked by listing his own broken laser pointer on the site. The broken item even got him $14, enough for a couple of lattes and scones at the nearest Starbucks. Omidyar proved that his concept had promise, receiving ten thousand individual bids by the end of 1995.[2]

Making AuctionWeb into a Business

By February 1996, Omidyar's Web site was getting so much traffic that his Internet service provider (ISP) decided he must be doing more than just maintaining a personal Web site. The ISP started charging him $250 per month. To pay his ISP bills, Omidyar started charging the site's users. Whether they would pay—and if so, how much—was a huge leap of faith. Omidyar decided that, for his new revenue model, it made sense to keep the service free to buyers and charge sellers if and only if they successfully made a sale. His "final value fee" to sellers was based on a percentage of the item's sale price.[3] Later, listing fees were added when a seller listed an item, calculated on a graduated scale based on the cost of the item. These various fees were AuctionWeb's revenue.

Unlike other auction Web sites at the time, AuctionWeb never took possession of the goods being sold on its site. And AuctionWeb did not stand in between buyers' and sellers' exchange of money. Instead, the buyers and sellers were responsible for coordinating the payment and shipment of goods.

By the end of 1996, Omidyar quit his day job to focus on AuctionWeb. That year, AuctionWeb took in $350,000 in listing and transaction fees. But

AuctionWeb's costs were minimal, with COGS including only expenses for moving bids and responses—just electrons, really—over the Web and hosting and operating the Web site on which its customers' items were listed. The rest of its costs—office rent, salaries, computer hardware, and software development—were operating expenses and thus didn't impact gross margins. AuctionWeb's gross margin exceeded *80 percent*. Compared with the complexity of a manufacturing business, this gross margin model is so simple—and so lucrative—it hurts!

By using the Web, AuctionWeb eliminated the need to set up a physical store, procure and ship goods, manage inventory, and deal with returns. At the time, Faye Landes, an e-commerce analyst at Sanford C. Bernstein & Co., said, "AuctionWeb is the only e-tailer that really fulfills the promise of the Web. And the key is its virtuality."[4]

eBay's Gross Margin Revolution

Let's compare AuctionWeb's virtual business with its rival at the time, Onsale. In 1996, Onsale was the biggest online auction site. Onsale had a solid revenue model, charging sellers both for transactions and a percentage of the sale itself.[5] But, unlike AuctionWeb, Onsale took possession of the auctioned goods to inspect and ship them. In doing so, Onsale had a lot of COGS that AuctionWeb did not: payroll for employees managing the inspection, shipping, and receiving, the shipping costs themselves, and so on. These expenses made Onsale far less profitable than AuctionWeb—while AuctionWeb's gross margins were hovering around 80 percent, Onsale's were just under 10 percent.[6] Onsale was using the wrong gross margin model.

In 1997, AuctionWeb received its first and only round of venture funding. Benchmark Capital invested $5 million for 21.5 percent of the company, one of the best venture capital investments ever made. That year, the AuctionWeb name was retired and eBay (for Echo Bay Technology Group) was born. Growth took off—by the first quarter of 1998, eBay was collecting $3 million per month in revenue!

Almost two years after Omidyar sold his laser pointer, eBay went public, valued at $2 billion on the day of its offering (Omidyar wouldn't have to worry about the price of lattes any more!). At that time, eBay had gross margins of 88 percent; Amazon.com, the other "big" Internet company, had 22 percent gross margins. In 1999, three years after its inception, eBay employed fifteen hundred people and supported $5 billion in transactions. By comparison, it took Microsoft nineteen years and sixteen thousand employees to generate that same amount of economic activity.[7]

Like any smart company, eBay continued to find new ways to generate revenue and a stellar gross margin. To increase its average selling price, eBay launched eBay Motors. Although it seemed hard to believe at the time, people felt comfortable buying and selling cars online. For $25, a seller could list a vehicle on eBay. If it sold, eBay collected another $25. Simon Rothman, who was in charge of eBay Motors, said, "Our profit margins are so high it's almost impossible to have higher margins."[8] After all, it didn't cost eBay any more or less money if a seller was listing a toaster oven or a Lamborghini. However, the revenue generated from the two listings was totally different. eBay's gross margins, in both percentage and absolute terms, grew better still!

By the end of 2000, eBay's revenue—from listing and transaction fees— was $431.4 million, a 92 percent increase over 1999. The company had 22.5 million registered users and $1.6 billion in merchandise sales. And, unlike brick-and-mortar companies, eBay's COGS were minimal. The only costs eBay incurred to make a sale were for payment processing—which eBay had begun to facilitate—plus customer support and Web site operations.[9] As CFO Gary Bengier put it, "I've been in technology for nineteen years, and I've never seen a business model as simple or as elegant as this one. How many companies can say their business model is characterized by the things they don't have to do?"[10]

Lessons Learned from eBay

From the eBay story, we've seen the sheer power of a gross margin model where COGS approaches zero. Best of all for Pierre Omidyar, its Plan A was right on the money from day one, and iteration—to eBay Motors, with even higher gross margins, for example—came much later, after success was already in hand. The Internet makes this possible, though, for far more than trading the unwanted goods in your basement. By enabling the transmission of books, music, and who knows what else as mere bits and bytes of digital data, sellers are now able to sell all kinds of things with a cost of goods sold far less than if these things were sold in their more physical form. That's exciting, on one hand, if customers prove willing to pay physical prices for digital goods. On the other hand, in competitive markets, sooner or later, high gross margins inevitably come under pressure, as later entrants join what looks like a profitable party, driving prices downward toward cost. Will the Internet create new high-margin opportunities? Or will it ultimately simply make buying and selling more efficient in category after category? Perhaps your company will make its mark in one of these ways.

Not every business is so simple in concept, though. Most are considerably more complex, especially companies that are well established, with traditions in place about how "we do things around here." We turn now to Toyota—a company that also did something revolutionary with its gross margin model, though in a quite different manner.

Case 2: Toyota Goes Upscale

Here's a quiz for you.

Question: What do the following terms mean?

a) *Kanban*

b) *Jidoka*

c) *Muda*

d) *Kaizen*

We wouldn't be surprised if those of you familiar with manufacturing or who have received an MBA in the last twenty years knew one or two of the four. These terms turned out to be a recipe for manufacturing acumen and a superior gross margin model. In this section, we explore how these four words formed the basis for Toyota Motor Company's success, in which a crucial element has been a gross margin model that far surpasses others in its industry. As a result, Toyota has become one of the automotive industry's star performers and the most profitable automaker in the world.

At the dawn of the twentieth century, Sakichi Toyoda formed a company to make looms for the Japanese weaving industry. In 1929, Toyoda sent his son Kiichiro Toyoda to Europe to sell the patent for the new power-driven loom his company had developed. The £100,000 raised in the sale of the patent funded the launch of the Toyota Motor Company.[11] Less than seventy-five years later, in 2003, Toyota Motor Company had become the world's most profitable automobile maker. And in 2007, Toyota became the world's largest seller of cars and trucks, outselling former leader General Motors.[12] How Toyota attained this leadership position is a lesson in how to be laser-focused on efficiency, productivity, and profitability, and how to seize a significant gross margin opportunity. The Toyota tale provides lessons for how to manage a business meticulously.

Toyota's Gross Margin Focus: Attacking Costs

In virtually any manufacturing company, there are two key components of cost of goods sold: parts and labor. Building a superior gross margin model often means, among other things, driving down these costs. Toyota followed this diet by designing efficient processes to minimize the direct costs of manufacturing automobiles. Toyota's efficiency objectives guided decisions for decades to come. In 1950, chief production engineer Taiichi Ohno still had the same focus. Ohno's Toyota Production System (TPS) focused, in his view, on "shortening lead time by eliminating waste in each step of a process."[13]

TPS had three pillars: *kanban,* the just-in-time system; *jidoka,* built-in quality; and *muda,* eliminating waste. Whether it was workers waiting around for the next process to begin, unnecessary transport (such as carrying raw materials or work-in-process items long distances), or workers having to walk from one place to the next to do their job, rooting out and eliminating waste, in all its forms, was key.[14]

Measurable Results

Ohno and his successors delivered on their promises. By improving manufacturing processes, making them more "lean" and more productive, Toyota reduced overtime and improved worker productivity. By the 1980s, it took Toyota an estimated thirteen man-hours to assemble a car, compared with some nineteen to twenty-two hours for Honda and Nissan.[15]

But for gross margins to actually improve, you also need revenue that yields a growing spread between the selling price and your declining cost of goods sold. Fortunately for Toyota, the benefit of meticulous management and lean manufacturing was not just lower costs. Toyota was producing better, more reliable cars as well. Its twin focus on costs and quality allowed Toyota to sell cars at gross margins that exceeded their competitors', yet at prices that were both attractive to consumers and very competitive. Toyota's growth exploded. By 1984, Toyota had won a 40 percent share of the Japanese auto-mobile market. Nissan, in second place, held only a 27 percent share. Honda, a laggard at the time, had only 8 percent.[16]

So by the mid-1980s Toyota's Plan A was really humming. Revenue was growing, COGS was managed effectively, and gross margin was continuing to improve. Shoichiro Toyoda, grandson of the founder and then Toyota's president, thought Toyota could do even better, as called for in the fourth of the company's guiding concepts—*kaizen*, to constantly improve. He saw that his company's successful car models were predominantly small to midsized vehicles. And those types of cars had lower overall profit margins than bigger cars, especially in Toyota's export markets, like North America, where it was also making steady inroads. Was there a Plan B that could take Toyota to new heights?

Toyota's Luxury Plan B

Toyoda decided that to reach its potential in the worldwide automobile marketplace, his company needed to turbocharge its growing penetration of the American market. He realized that Toyota had a growing army of loyal customers who had owned Toyotas for years, but were seemingly ready to move up to higher-priced luxury cars. But could Toyota, with its reputation for reliable but somewhat boring cars, complete in the luxury segment? It was a real leap of faith.

Ichiro Suzuki was charged with fixing Toyota's boring image. At the same time, he was asked to produce a luxury line of vehicles that could beat Mercedes and BMW in four predefined areas: fuel consumption, noise, aerodynamics, and vehicle weight. As he and his team got to work, word of Toyota's plans got out. As a writer for *Automobile* magazine put it, "The fox is about to find his way into the henhouse." *Car and Driver* added, "The long-awaited clash between the Japanese and the big-buck Germans is on the horizon."[17]

The sun rose in the form of Lexus. Suzuki was chief engineer of Lexus, but there wasn't much to engineer. The ES250, its sporty model, was based on the Toyota Camry, but with leather seats, maple interior, and other lux-ury touches.[18] The luxury elements added some cost, to be sure, but they permitted Toyota to go head-to-head with Mercedes and BMW at prices far higher than a mere Camry could command. Adding a bit of cost added much more to the car's price, hence widening gross margin.

The 1989 launch of Lexus was, by all accounts, an unbelievable success. At that time, Mercedes-Benz sold three models in the United States, the 300E, 420SE, and 560SEL. In its first year, with just two models, Lexus sold 2.7 times the number of all three of the Mercedes models combined. By 2000, Lexus was the biggest-selling luxury car line in America.[19]

With its efficient manufacturing processes, Toyota produced luxury sedans whose quality matched or exceeded its German rivals using one-sixth the labor.[20] Toyota's Plan B was brilliant: less labor expense, skinnier raw material costs, fewer defects to contend with, and higher priced vehicles. Mercedes prices for a souped-up Camry? Talk about a killer gross margin model! In fact, partly as a result of the Lexus product line, Toyota's gross margins reached 20 percent by 2002, 25 percent mark by 2006, and 27.49 percent by 2007 (compared with General Motors' 16.36 percent).[21] And in the first quarter of 2007, Toyota's worldwide sales passed those of General Motors, making Toyota the number one seller of automobiles worldwide. Generations of Toyodas have woven quite a record, indeed!

Lessons from Toyota

It's easy to forget, in this dot-com age, that old-economy companies like Toyota can wreak havoc on their industries through effective exploitation of superior gross margin models. But that's exactly what Toyota has done. One might think of what Toyota has done as its industry's Plan B, disruptive as it's been. Toyota built its industry-leading gross margin model the old-fashioned way, through relentless focus on efficiency, the elimination of waste, and cutting cost of goods sold to the bone. It's not uncommon for companies to believe that cost and quality must be traded off. But four generations of Toyodas at Toyota's helm have not bought that argument.

Toyota has shown the world that low cost and high quality and reliability can go hand in hand, and that once quality is in hand it's possible to repackage that quality for upscale markets with sharply higher gross margins. Adding small touches of class at modest cost can add much higher perceptions of value for which customers are willing to pay. For those of you in manufacturing industries, what could your company do to emulate Toyota's success? Is there an analog here for you, on either the COGS or the revenue side of the gross margin equation?

There's also another lesson about gross margin models from the Toyota story. Earning fatter gross margins in one part of your business enables you to apply competitive pressure in another part of your business if you choose. Toyota's strong gross margins in its midsize and luxury lines enabled it to be vigorously competitive in the compact car segment, making it extremely difficult for General Motors and Ford to compete therein.

In the eye of some observers, however, Toyota's quest to become the world's best-selling automaker caused it to take its eye off the historical strength of its gross margin model. By 2009, dealers were complaining that some of Toyota's cars were becoming too expensive, due in part to an expensive new paint process and high-tech features like solar-powered cooling systems. Worse, margins were suffering. As the troubled global economy took a bite out of all automakers' sales, Toyota found itself with too much manufacturing capacity and a looming net loss for its fiscal year ending March 2009. Out went three top executives to retirement, and into the presidency rose Akio Toyoda, the fourth family member to lead the company. His key challenge? Overhaul Toyota's new manufacturing and design methods and cut costs, including cost of goods sold.[22]

We've seen in the Toyota story its relentless focus on both cost and quality. Next up is the story of an entrepreneur whose equally passionate focus was directed in an entirely different sort of direction.

Case 3: Patagonia Puts Its Values First

Yvon Chouinard never set out to become a businessperson. In fact, he simply wanted to make the world a better place. So it was surprising—even to him—when he founded Patagonia in the 1950s. Even today, the company that Chouinard leads is not as much a business as a vehicle for doing other things Chouinard finds important. As he recently put it, "Patagonia is a private company, and the sole stockholders are me and my wife, so we can do anything we want."[23] What Chouinard and his wife wanted was to sustain a company that lived up to a strong moral code, which contributed to society and put environmental protection and conservation atop its list of priorities.

When Chouinard was a child, he and his family moved from Maine to Southern California. In his new surroundings, he fell in love with the great outdoors. He started rock climbing at the age of fourteen, becoming an avid and renowned climber in his late teens. In 1957, he taught himself to be a blacksmith so that he could fabricate his own climbing equipment. Soon, Chouinard began selling his homemade climbing gear to support his climbing fetish, launching Chouinard Equipment in the late 1950s. By 1970, Chouinard Equipment was the largest supplier of climbing equipment in the United States. But Chouinard and his climbing partners had an unsettling realization. They all loved the outdoors; climbing was their way of being close to nature. Yet the hard steel pitons Chouinard Equipment produced were damaging the rocks they climbed. Although pitons accounted for 70 percent of Chouinard's revenue, he decided to phase them out and introduce in their place aluminum chocks that were far less damaging to the rock face. This was the first example of Chouinard's commitment to the environment and the beginning of a professional life marked by putting profits at risk for his environmental values.

Chouinard's pro-environmental philosophy, his Plan A, served him and his business well. In 1977, Chouinard introduced the famed fleece jacket, made of polyester, a fabric ideal for the outdoors, which kept moisture out and heat in.[24] To be more environmentally conscious, Chouinard soon changed the manufacturing of the fleece, using recycled plastic soda bottles to construct the fabric.[25] The fleece jacket became one of Patagonia's defining products, attracting both outdoor enthusiasts as well as fashion-conscious consumers. By 1990, the company was bringing in $100 million in sales.[26]

But Patagonia's growth was unmanaged and out of control. Chouinard recalled those wild and heady days: "It was back in 1990 or so and we were growing the company by 40 to 50 percent a year and we were doing it by all the textbook business ways—adding more dealers, adding more products, building stores. And I realized that I was on the same track as society was—endless growth for the sake of growth."[27]

Patagonia Loses Its Foothold, Turns to Plan B

In 1991, when the U.S. economy fell into recession, Patagonia hit a wall. Sales slowed considerably, and its bank called in its revolving loan. The company was forced to file for bankruptcy. Patagonia's near-death experience taught Chouinard two big lessons about his business model. First, to stay in business he would have to manage the company's growth rather than let it get out of hand. Second, he firmly rejected the growth-for-growth's-sake pattern—now an antilog—that had gotten his company into trouble.

Postbankruptcy, Chouinard decided that his company's environmental values were paramount: "The reason we hadn't sold out and retired was that we were pessimistic about the fate of the world and felt a responsibility to use our resources to do something about it."[28] Businesswise, however, it was time for Plan B. His leap of faith was that Patagonia customers would pay higher prices, giving Chouinard the gross margins he needed to support his high internal cost structure and his company's pro-environmental creed.

Years of unmanaged expansion had taught Chouinard an important lesson. Now he would keep a watchful eye on revenue growth, and one foot on the brake. Prices—and gross margins—were raised, especially on Patagonia's most environmentally friendly products, and growth settled down to a more manageable pace. The measured pace gave Chouinard the opportunity to focus more of his attention on what mattered most—the environment. Soon after the company emerged from bankruptcy, Patagonia conducted an environmental impact assessment on its products and found that regular cotton was among the least environmentally kind fabrics: the pesticides used to cultivate cotton damaged soil and water and were harmful to workers in the field. In 1994, Chouinard mandated that Patagonia only use organic cotton: "I gave the company eighteen months to completely get out of making any product with industrially grown cotton."[29] By 1996, all Patagonia cotton sportswear was made of organic cotton. Fortunately for Patagonia, its consumers loved the organic cotton, and sales of its cotton clothes increased by 25 percent.[30]

Next, in an effort to reduce waste, Patagonia changed the packaging of its long underwear. Chouinard explained, "We were using a thick, wraparound cardboard header inside a heavy Ziploc plastic bag. Instead, we decided to hang up the heavier long underwear like regular clothing and simply bundle our lighter underwear with a rubber band. The first year after the change, we saved twelve tons of material from winding up in a landfill, saved $150,000 in packaging, and boosted sales by 25 percent."[31]

Both the organic cotton initiative and the long-underwear packaging were decisions made to reduce impact on the environment. Yet both initiatives had positive impacts on the company's gross margins and revenue! Next, in what seemed like an unprecedented effort, Patagonia started recycling its fabrics. The company asked customers to send back their worn-out polyester underwear. Using recycled fabrics was another win for the company's bottom line, reducing the amount of energy and cost spent to produce its flagship fleece products.[32]

Not only did Patagonia play its part in reducing its own environmental footprint, it was also able to contribute to other environmental causes. With its cost-saving and revenue-generating efforts and its high gross margins, Patagonia provided grants to organizations protecting habitat, wilderness, and biodiversity. Between 1985 and 2006, Chouinard and his company donated $26 million to environmental organizations.[33] In 2001, Chouinard created 1% for the Planet, encouraging Patagonia's partner organizations to donate 1 percent of revenue to environmental efforts.

Chouinard described his newfound business philosophy, "In many companies, the tail (finance) wags the dog (corporate decisions). We strive to balance the funding of environmental activities with the desire to continue in business for the next one hundred years. Managing our finances this way helps the company remain *yarak*, a falconry term derived from Persian and meaning 'superalert, hungry but not weak, and ready to hunt.'"[34]

At the heart of Chouinard's success in turning Patagonia into a financially sustainable environmental advocate was Patagonia's gross margin model, which (with its lofty prices providing high gross margin) provided the funding for his environmental efforts. As things turned out, Chouinard's leap of faith had proven to be right on target. A large enough market of quality-focused, price-insensitive outdoorsmen and -women were willing to pay premium prices to get their hands on Patagonia's goods. By 2001, the company crossed the $200 million mark in revenue, double its prebankruptcy level of eleven years earlier.[35] By 2006, the company had thirty-nine stores in seven countries and $270 million in revenue.[36] Not bad for someone who never wanted to be a businessperson!

Lessons from Patagonia

There are lessons from Patagonia's inspiring story about more than gross margin models. First, Chouinard's laserlike focus on his company's environmental values prompts us all to consider why we are in business. Chouinard was clear about this question. "The reason we're in business is to be in politics; it is to change the world, not to make clothes. I decided that if I was going to be a businessman, I was going to do it on my own terms. And I wasn't going to act like a lot of the other businessman. And

I wasn't going to be bottom-line oriented. I believe that if you do every-thing correctly in business, the profits will happen. But you don't focus on it. My bottom line at the end of the year is how much good we've done, not how much money we've made."[37]

On the front door of the Patagonia headquarters reads a famous quote from the Sierra Club's David Brower, "There is no business to be done on a dead planet."[38] Chouinard's principled, focused mission drove Patagonia to take extraordinary strides toward bettering the world, making tough decisions in order to do what Chouinard saw as the right thing.

Second, as Chouinard would probably be the first to say, it's the gross margins that made it all possible. Once Chouinard found his Plan B, there were no longer rocks nor hard places between which his cost structure had to squeeze. Why are Patagonia's customers willing to pay the prices that his gross margin model commands? Because they love Patagonia quality and they buy into its environmental creed. In short, they value what Patagonia offers.

There's also a lesson here about pricing decisions, which smart decision makers base on the value the customer derives from the purchase, not a simple markup on cost, as far too many companies do. Pricing his goods as customers valued them gave Chouinard the ability to do more and more of what his customers wanted. It was a virtuous circle. Satisfying for Patagonia, and for its customers, too.

Finally, Patagonia warns us about growing too fast. If growth in your company is threatening to spin out of control, one good way to take your foot off the growth pedal is simply to raise your prices, probably not across the board, but where customers particularly value what you offer. Strengthening your gross margin model in this way can put you in a very good place from which to compete.

Lessons Learned About Gross Margin Models

As we noted at the outset of this chapter, building breakthrough gross margin models is all about managing the spread between the price at which you can sell your wares—whether Web site listings, automobiles, or fleece jackets—and your cost of goods sold, ignoring for now your other costs of being in business, your operating costs. Thus, effectively managing COGS, as Toyota has done, is only half of the story; making good pricing decisions, as Patagonia has done so well, is the other half. We've seen three companies build their gross margin models in quite different ways.

There are three key messages we hope you have grasped about building gross margin models:

- New digital technologies are enabling new gross margin models in which COGS approaches zero (and gross margins approach 100 percent!). Can you apply any of them in your business?

- Building a gross margin model that's superior to others in your industry provides incredible leverage that you can apply wherever you choose, putting pressure on your competitors, perhaps, where they are most vulnerable.

- Your products' pricing need not—and should not—be driven simply by cost. Your pricing decisions should be value-based, according to the value your customer perceives—or can be led to perceive—in what you sell. Thus, your gross margin and revenue models are intimately linked through your pricing decisions. The dashboarding process can help you discover just how much your customers are willing to pay!

Let's dig a bit deeper into each of these messages.

Gross Margins Can Now Approach 100 Percent

Let's explore what these themes mean beyond the three examples we've just examined. First, the eBay gross margin model is by no means the only compelling gross margin story starting to play out on the Web. We caught a brief glimpse of another one in the Shanda story in chapter 3: the sale of virtual goods, such as virtual weapons and costumes for avatars in multiplayer games. In this fast-growing market, research firm Gartner Media estimates that by 2011 a whopping 80 percent of all Internet users globally—not just gamers—will have avatars. Mike Everest, an eighteen-year-old virtual trader working from the small mountain town of Durango, Colorado, made $35,000 in four summers selling virtual animal skins and weapons in a Web-based fantasy world called Entropia Universe.[39] While his goods exist only in the virtual world—with cost of goods sold of essentially zero—his profits are real. It sure beats flipping burgers at the local McDonald's!

Other virtual-goods entrepreneurs with similar computer skills work as architects, land developers, fashion designers, and in other roles in Second Life, another virtual world. On a typical day, players in Second Life spend nearly $1.5 million in real-world cash on virtual real estate, cars, clothing, and more. Says Claudine L'Amoreaux of Linden Lab, the originator of Second Life, "It's an incredible environment for young entrepreneurs. The ones who are really successful at it are beginning to make that their main work."[40]

Your Gross Margin Model: A Tool for Havoc

Second, in what industries will new gross margin models wreak havoc next? Toyota now has its way in automobiles. Nokia seems to keep coming out on top in cell phones, in part due to manufacturing efficiency it has learned by serving the rapidly growing but low-priced markets in the developing world. Which industries will be next on the list? Will yours, and will you be the driver, or a victim?

Value-Based Pricing

Finally, value-based pricing depends heavily on delivering real value, of course. Viewed from the perspective of the revenue model questions we explored in chapter 3, this means either resolving some serious customer pain, or providing so much customer delight, as Patagonia does, that your premium price is worth paying. The four-dollar latte from Starbucks or Peet's provides a completely different customer experience from the under-a-dollar cup o' Joe at the neighborhood diner. A better gross margin model? It sure is.

Q&A with John and Randy

With the key gross margin model principles now in hand (see the checklist at the end of this chapter for a concise reminder of the building blocks for which evidence is required), what questions remain about building your gross margin model? Four come to mind:

- How should you decide in which parts of your product mix you can get superior gross margins?

- Where should you start if your strategy, like Toyota's, is to drive COGS downward?

- What should the evidence underpinning your COGS building blocks look like and how can you find it?

- How can you evaluate whether or not a possible analog or antilog really operates a solid gross margin model?

Where Can You Generate Superior Gross Margins?

At the end of the day, where your more generous gross margins can be earned isn't really your decision at all. It's your customer's decision. Just because you ask a high price doesn't mean you can get it. So underlying your gross margin model is a familiar theme that underlies your revenue model, too. What's the customer pain you resolve or the delight you provide? Only by understanding these issues—based on studying your analogs, antilogs, and identifying the leaps of faith that follow—can you discover what sort of pricing your customers will bear. Your experimental mindset will serve you well as you do so.

Where Should You Start Your Strategy to Drive COGS Down?

There are no easy ways to drive your COGS down, especially to press it lower than others in your industry as Toyota has done. If other automakers could match Toyota's costs, they would do so! But there are some patterns from which we can learn. In some industries, economies of scale can kick in as you grow. So sometimes you must bite the bullet in your early days, trimming your gross margin now in order to grow bigger tomorrow. In other businesses, greater volume means greater clout in buying the goods and services you need. In still others, it's simply a matter of pressing every last ounce of efficiency into each of your processes, à la Toyota. Here, too, analogs and antilogs can provide the necessary inspiration and a good place to start.

What About Finding the COGS Evidence You Need?

One way to do this is with analogs. Simply take typical revenue mix and gross margins that apply in your industry, or the figures of one analog company therein (or elsewhere, if you aim to turn your industry upside-down), and apply them as an analog to the top-line revenue that your revenue model generates, or intends to.

The other, more detailed (and sometimes more credible) approach is to build your COGS one brick at a time, either with more detailed analogs or with more precise estimates of costs. There are two key components:

- *Cost of materials:* If you will be assembling or manufacturing something, as Toyota does, you'll need evidence that shows what it will cost to buy your components, what accountants call your bill of materials. What are the parts and materials you will need, and what will they cost? For other kinds of businesses—if you are simply buying and reselling as retailers do, for example—you'll need analogs or other tangible evidence to show what you'll pay for what you resell. As we saw in the Apple story in chapter 1, striking deals with the record companies over the price iTunes would pay per tune was a crucial leap of faith that Steve Jobs had to identify—and ultimately prove or refute by testing his hypotheses—in determining whether or not the iTunes gross margin model would actually work.

- *Labor:* The labor entailed in COGS is a crucial element in manufacturing industries and, especially, in services. How much labor will you need for COGS, what will it cost, and where is the evidence that underlies your answers? Analogs can help you here, too.

How Can You Assess the Gross Margin Models of Analogs?

In theory, this is a straightforward matter. Just look at their reported gross margin percentage and the breakdown thereof on their income statement—materials and labor, for example—and there you have it. In practice, though, things aren't always so simple. Many companies, especially public companies when reporting their results, bury all kinds of things into cost of goods sold that really aren't COGS in the sense we use the term and most businesses think of it. Most people would not think of retailers' store rent or store labor as COGS, for example, but some retailers include it there—perhaps to disguise the lofty markups they take on their merchandise! So you need to be careful about using reported data. As we noted at the end of chapter 3, using your network to help you learn the details that lie beneath the reported financials can make a big difference in the depth of the insights your analogs give you. Dashboarding to examine the leaps of faith about your gross margin model will help ensure that you get the answers you need.

What's Next?

So far in chapters 3 and 4, we have examined how innovative revenue models and great gross margin models can conspire to create runaway successes. Working hand in hand, well-chosen revenue and gross margin models can provide a strong cash flow foundation for your business, from the best possible source, your customers. Together they comprise the starting point for nearly every successful businesses model. You cannot ignore them.

But revenue and gross margin are only a part of any company's overall profitability and cash flow. Indeed, for many companies, it is operating costs that they really worry about. We now turn to your operating model.

John and Randy's Gross Margin Model Checklist

The quickest overview to remember is this:

Gross margin = Revenues − Cost of goods sold

Your goal is ensuring sufficient gross margin so that your firm has the financial freedom—the breathing room—to expand, to pay investors, to cover other costs, or to fund your next vacation. There are three key building blocks from which to construct your gross margin model:

✓ **The spread between price and COGS, in both absolute and percentage terms:** How low can you drive COGS? How high can you drive your pricing, customers willing?

✓ **Managing your gross margin mix:** What are the gross margin percentages you will earn on the revenue generated from the various portions of your product mix? What are the relative proportions of revenue you expect the high-margin and low-margin portions of your product mix to account for?

✓ **Your strategy:** Thinking strategically, on which products or product lines will you choose to take a higher spread? Why? On which of them will lower gross margins pay strategic dividends and help enhance your competitive advantage?

You will need clear strategic thinking to underpin your gross margin model, as well as evidence to support it—hard, cold facts rather than hopes or dreams. This evidence will come either from analogs you know and trust; from careful research into the costs associated with procuring, producing, and delivering your goods or services; or from identifying leaps of faith about the revenue and costs (the right-hand side of the COGS equation) and testing the hypotheses that grow out of them.

CHAPTER 5

Trimming the Fat

Your Operating Model

Let's return to Johnny's lemonade stand. Surprisingly, Johnny stuck with it. By the time he was sixteen years old, he was targeting $500 in revenue from stands all over town. His gross margins had grown to 70 percent. One of the ways Johnny increased his gross margin was by asking his genius friend Louise to devise a new recipe for his lemonade. Her goal? Reduce the number of lemons and sugar needed (i.e., reduce COGS).

Louise delivered. At the same time, she vastly improved the lemonade's taste. Johnny's lemonade was a hit! Johnny was ecstatic—until Louise sent him an invoice for $150 for the time she spent researching the properties of lemons and sugars and developing the new recipe. Foiled again! Johnny's gross margin had been looking up, but with Louise's charges for research and development, Johnny went from his planned $325 before paying his friends to staff the other locations to a mere $200. After he paid his friends, there was no chance he'd be able to buy the new mountain bike he coveted.

Operating Costs Defined

Operating costs are all the other day-to-day costs that must be incurred in addition to cost of goods sold. They are not glamorous. Together they comprise your operating model. They are "below the line" so to speak, getting less attention sometimes than they should. But operating expenses, if not kept in check, can bankrupt a company. Just look at the airline industry, constantly in the news for yet another bankruptcy.

The foundation for building your operating model is what accountants call a *chart of accounts*. Every industry has one, with operating expense categories that fit that industry. Mail-order marketers have an expense category called fulfillment, for example. Airlines have landing fees. Technology companies have research and development (R&D). If your company already exists, its financial statements will be structured with these expense categories.

With your chart of accounts in hand, there are three strategic questions that will drive your operating model:

- In order to deliver on your planned strategy and once revenue begins to flow, what level of cost, expressed in absolute or percentage of sales terms, will your company incur in each of the operating cost categories (that is, all day-to-day costs other than cost of goods sold)?

- Which of these costs can be reduced or eliminated entirely?

- Which of them should be increased in line with your planned strategy?

How will you address these questions? By now you know the answer. You'll look for analogs and antilogs and you'll start dashboarding as you identify any leaps of faith that you need to examine.

Goal for Chapter 5: Use Analogs and Antilogs to Rethink Your Operating Costs

Your strategic thinking must be intimately linked to the operating costs that will be necessary to do whatever your company does. Are there costs your competitors incur that you can live without? If so, you'll have the happy choice between undercutting your competitors' prices, earning better overall profit margins, or both. Are there costs you can add to make your customer experience more compelling? As we'll see from the cases profiled in this chapter, these questions are crucial. These companies built operating models that became primary ingredients in their success:

- Ryanair utilized an analog exceptionally well. In doing so, the no-frills airline drew bold red lines through typical airline operating costs, creating a cost structure that was far lower than those of its European competitors.

- Oberoi Hotels, which we study more briefly, shows how, in contrast to Ryanair, *increased* operating costs can propel a company's strategy. Indeed, trimming operating costs to the bone is not the only way to build a successful operating model. Many of Oberoi's luxurious hotels are set in exotic destinations and offer copious amenities to attract discerning guests and pamper them during their stay.

- We take two lessons from ZoomSystems. One is the classic cost-saving replacement of labor with a machine, in this case quite an elegant and sophisticated one. The second is about finding ways to minimize the use of scarce and expensive resources—retail real estate, for ZoomSystems—and thereby serve new kinds of locations in potentially more productive ways.

For both Ryanair and ZoomSystems, there's also a common theme. The operating models that emerged only did so after Plan A had not worked. As always, key analogs, antilogs, and leaps of faith led the way in iterating toward a more compelling, more viable Plan B.

Case 1: Ryanair Takes Its Analog to New Heights

Let's recall how it was to fly circa 1995. You first called a travel agent to check flight schedules and book your flight. The agent then mailed you paper tickets. You arrived at the airport forty minutes before your flight and checked your baggage with a ticket agent. Your spouse walked you to the gate to bid farewell. As you boarded the plane, you grabbed a pillow and a blanket. Midway through your three-hour flight, you were served snacks, beverages, and a multicourse meal by a flight attendant in her airline-issued uniform.

My, how things have changed! Today, most flights are booked online, up from virtually none a decade ago. Post September 11, 2001, you can no longer arrive forty minutes before a flight and expect to check luggage. No longer can your spouse walk you to the gate. On board, you cannot expect to have the airline experience you once had. Lunch on a three-hour flight? Not a chance! A bag of peanuts and a Pepsi? You'll probably have to pay. Many of these amenities were cost of goods sold, now long gone from most airlines' cost structures due to the cost pressures inflicted on them by their no-frills brethren.

But the real revolution in the airline industry goes deeper than peanuts and pop. It's what has happened to wipe out huge swathes of operating costs, many of them incurred on the ground. Beyond the cost of goods sold to take a passenger from one destination to another, there's an array of costs that are incurred before a plane ever takes off: aircraft leases; labor at airports, in maintenance facilities, in call centers, and at headquarters; maintenance materials and repairs; marketing and distribution; and airport landing and gate fees, to name just a few. Such costs have run many large airlines into the ground. Just consider many of the top U.S. airlines from the 1980s. United, Delta, Continental, and US Airways have all been in and out of bankruptcy.

We have yet to see an industry that's more brutally competitive, with such consistently poor performance. Still, most people have heard of Herb Kelleher's Southwest Airlines. Kelleher made Southwest into one of the most consistently profitable airline companies in the world by ratcheting down operating expenses and doing some other things very well. Not as many people outside Europe are as familiar with Southwest's European protégé—Ryanair. Though it's hard to believe, Ryanair's improvements on Southwest's operating model have made the latter's operating-cost waistline look plump by comparison. Couple that with Ryanair's creative ways to enhance its revenue model and you have an airline with a truly impressive business model.

Ryanair's Plan A

Christy Ryan, Liam Lonergan, and Irish businessman Tony Ryan founded Ryanair in 1985.[1] Their Plan A for the airline was nothing special. They started offering service between Waterford, Ireland, and London with a goal of competing with the duopoly that existed at the time between British Airways and Aer Lingus, the then government-owned flag carriers. In 1986, they added a route between Dublin and London. Harvard professor Jan Rivkin said, "In the early days the company was trying to be everything to everybody—they were trying to provide service and amenities comparable to Aer Lingus and British Airways, but at a lower price."[2]

By 1991, though, it was clear that the Ryanair Plan A was not working. With two routes and two airplanes, the company was not profitable. The

Ryanair founders brought in new leadership—Michael O'Leary, an Irish accountant with a ferociously competitive streak. O'Leary was charged with fixing the unprofitable company. One of the first things O'Leary did was to meet Southwest founder Kelleher. Over dinner, Kelleher provided O'Leary with a few secrets to his success: "Fly one type of plane to keep down engineering costs; drive down costs every year; turn around aircraft as quickly as possible," and more.[3] The meeting with Kelleher provided the inspiration O'Leary needed. Southwest would be O'Leary's analog. Aer Lingus and British Air would be antilogs.

Michael O'Leary's Plan B

O'Leary followed Kelleher's advice scrupulously, leading Kelleher to later dub Ryanair, "The best imitation of Southwest Airlines that I have seen."[4] O'Leary returned the compliment: "Southwest set the example for disciplined growth by a low-fare, no-frills carrier. All we're trying to do is copy the master and pay homage to the Southwest model in Europe."[5]

Europe's evolving airline policies aided Ryanair, too. In 1997, carriers in the European Union were allowed to more freely operate across the borders of the EU states. That same year, Ryanair went public. With a new trove of cash, Ryanair ramped up its network, flying short-haul, point-to-point routes between Ireland, the United Kingdom, and continental Europe. Ryanair expanded its service and its low-price reputation across Europe, while keeping its costs, operating and otherwise, to a bare minimum. Let's look beyond the peanuts and Pepsi to see how Ryanair kept its operating model lean.

First, following Southwest's lead, O'Leary decided that Ryanair would fly only one model of airplane, a stripped-down Boeing 737. This way, Ryanair spent less to train its maintenance staff and simplified its inventory of parts for repairs. Then the September 11, 2001, tragedy put the airline industry into a tailspin, and many airlines cancelled their Boeing orders. O'Leary approached Boeing to negotiate a deal. Ryanair received massive discounts on one hundred next-generation Boeing 737-800s and on options for another fifty planes. The $9.1 billion order tripled Ryanair's capacity and soon made it Europe's largest and most fuel-efficient airline. The outspoken O'Leary, understated for once, said, "This order eliminates some uncertainty which hung over Ryanair's growth plans."[6] And, with fuel prices set to skyrocket, the attractive pricing on the planes was just part of the bargain.

Second, rather than flying in and out of large metropolitan airports, O'Leary believed passengers would accept flying to and from smaller, regional airports outside of major European cities in exchange for lower fares. It was a leap of faith that would reshape not only European air travel but economic development in some smaller communities for a decade or more. Many of these airports were former military bases with little commercial traffic—Charleroi, Belgium (south of Brussels), for example, rather than Brussels National.[7] Eager for Ryanair's traffic, Charleroi charged Ryanair one euro per passenger ($1.12 at the time) to land its aircraft, half the normal landing fee charged at other airports, plus another euro for ground handling, one-tenth the typical rate.[8] The local government also spent millions in advertising and other support to help Ryanair grow its Charleroi traffic. By 2003, Ryanair was flying 1.7 million passengers a year through Charleroi, an airport that had been all but deserted in 1997.[9]

O'Leary's second leap of faith counted on the growing Internet savvy of his customers. Customers would happily buy their tickets online instead of over the phone, O'Leary believed. In 2000, Ryanair launched its Web site, cutting out both the travel agent and the call center. Ryanair would save both commissions and operating costs. O'Leary, ever the promoter, promised the lowest fares or double your money back. Consumers voted with their feet, and distribution costs fell from €7 (about $8) to €1 per booking. The Web site also saved the company marketing spending. "It [the Web site] is transforming the business model," O'Leary said in 2000.[10] By 2003, more than 90 percent of Ryanair tickets were purchased online, compared to Southwest's 59 percent.[11] Ryanair's Plan B was not just mimicking its analog, it was bettering it!

Turning airplanes around quickly was O'Leary's next task. A Boeing 737 is a $50 million chunk of aluminum, and it's not making money when it's sitting on the tarmac. By using smaller airports that had less congestion, Ryanair was able to get its planes back in the air twenty-five minutes after landing, half the turnaround time at busy major airports.[12] But O'Leary took two additional measures to ensure a quick turnaround. O'Leary saw that pushing shades up and cleaning out seat-pockets in preparation for the next flight was a waste of critical time for his ground staff. So he ordered his next batch of 737's without window shades and seat-back pockets. By 2006, Ryanair's aircraft were in the air for an average of eleven hours per day, compared with British Airways' eight hours.[13] And no shades and no seat-back pockets meant slightly less weight, hence less fuel, an added bonus.

O'Leary was maniacal about keeping operating costs down. "We want to be known as the Walmart of flying," he said.[14] As he said in 2006, "Our average fare has fallen by almost 20 percent from €50 in 1997 to just over €40 today. Ryanair will continue to pursue lower costs and pass on these savings in the form of lower fares to the traveling public of Europe. Ryanair is the only airline in Europe which commits to offer the lowest fares in every market in which we operate."[15]

But offering the lowest fares did not necessarily mean that additional revenues couldn't be pried out of its passengers' wallets, so O'Leary tinkered with his revenue model, too. Passengers could pay, if they wished, for priority boarding, assigned seating, and checking a bag. Snacks and beverages, O'Leary reasoned, weren't free of charge on European trains, another analog. Why shouldn't passengers pay for peanuts and Pepsi on Ryanair? Not only did flight attendants sell food, but they also sold items like cameras, lottery tickets, and rental car and hotel reservations. And while passengers sat back and scratched their lottery tickets, they stared at seat backs plastered with ads. "Every chance they get, Ryanair tries to squeeze just that little bit of extra (revenue) out of its passengers," said Tim Jones, of London consulting firm Innovaro Ltd.[16] And what, might you imagine, is Michael Ryan's latest revenue idea? Putting a coin slot on the toilet door![17]

Ryanair's Plan B not only revolutionized its own performance, but it is rewriting the rulebook on how to run a low-cost airline. In its 2007 fiscal year, Ryanair reported profit of €435 million on revenues of €2.2 billion, or 20 percent of sales, a profit margin practically unheard of elsewhere in the airline industry.[18] Southwest reported $1.05 billion in pretax profit, or 10.6 percent of sales, half the Ryanair percentage, on $9.8 billion in revenues.[19] In 2008, Ryanair's passenger count surpassed the European traffic of Lufthansa and Air France/KLM, making it Europe's biggest short-haul airline, handling 57.7 million passengers.[20] "O'Leary and his management team are absolutely the best at adopting a winning strategy and sticking to it relentlessly," Ryanair's chairman David Bonderman says.[21] O'Leary touted, "We weren't the first to figure this out . . . But we do it better than everybody else."[22] O'Leary had learned the analog's lessons very well, indeed!

Lessons from Ryanair

Let's consider what Kelleher and O'Leary did to the airline industry. In essence, they said, "Who needs all these operating costs? We—and our customers!—certainly don't." By leaving no stone unturned to take ever-increasing swathes of operating cost out of their businesses and by lowering their prices, they brought hordes of new passengers to air travel.

So, which competitors in your industry have operating costs through which you could strike a bold red line? They are your antilogs. Where are the analogs that you can follow? For O'Leary, the Southwest Airlines analog was obvious.

Are strategies like Ryanair's sustainable? O'Leary said in mid-2008 that, in the face of soaring fuel prices, Ryanair would probably only break even in its year ending March 2009.[23] But then fuel prices plummeted. Never at a loss for words, O'Leary was pugnacious. "I hope oil stays high for the winter so a lot of crappy airlines go out of business."[24] If that had come to pass, he would probably have bought their planes for a song and Ryanair would have grown some more. In theory, at a point where processes are almost perfectly efficient and components or parts are totally commoditized, relying on operational efficiency should not be enough to maintain competitive advantage. But Southwest Airlines has achieved a string of unbroken profitability unmatched in its industry. Until recently, the same was true for Walmart in retailing. Both of these companies have low-cost operating models in brutally competitive industries, but they seem to have survived just fine. Difficult, yes. Impossible, no.

Taking costs out of your industry's operating model is one path to a disruptive Plan B. But not all operating models are of the low-cost variety. Let's now look to the foothills of the Himalayas for an operating model that's the antithesis of the one Michael O'Leary built at Ryanair. Here, we take a brief look at a company where managers struck gold by *increasing* operating costs in new and ever more exotic ways.

Case 2: Oberoi Hotels Raise the Bar

At an Oberoi hotel, a night's lodging involves much more than a bed and a hot shower. Oberoi's hugely successful operating model makes for a very different kind of travel experience than flying Ryanair.

Take the Oberoi Cecil in Shimla, India, for example. Perched at an elevation of seven thousand feet in the Himalayan foothills, the Cecil offers an extensive menu of relaxing and reviving massages and beauty treatments. Would you prefer an ayurvedic, Balinese, Hawaiian, or Thai massage? Specialists are on staff waiting to serve you. How about a Chakra head and shoulder massage to ease stress?

In the 1990s, Oberoi's designers saw extraordinary potential in Shimla. A dilapidated colonial hotel, dating to 1884, offered stunning views of the mountains and valleys. Oberoi decided to restore the Cecil, a part of Shimla's colonial history, to its original grandeur. A heated swimming pool, billiards rooms, and a children's activity center were added, complementing the customary assortment of fine restaurants, luxurious rooms, and virtually every amenity you can think of. And then some.

Let's consider the sort of operating model such a hotel experience requires. Rather than seeking ways to trim operating costs, as Ryanair does with relentless fervor, Oberoi constantly looks for ways to add more luxurious amenities to its guests' experiences. Each of these amenities adds costs to its operating model in at least two ways. First, many of them require a specially designed space—a spa, for example. Thus, there's the cost of the space that could be put to a variety of other uses, and the cost of keeping the space heated and cooled, well lit, and up to date. These day-to-day operating costs are fixed costs, incurred regardless of the number of guests who choose to have a massage.

Second, most of the amenities require trained staff to deliver treatments, all of which makes a stay at the Cecil quite special. These costs are variable, depending on the level of customer demand. Cecil's discriminating guests request such services and are willing to pay top rupee or dollar for the latest and most lavish treatments—so Oberoi does not cut corners.

Oberoi's luxuries have not gone unnoticed. *Condé Nast Traveler* rated Oberoi Hotels and Resorts as the best hotel chain outside the United States. In the magazine's 2008 Reader's Choice Awards for the best hotel in the world, Oberoi took three of the top ten places for its properties in India: in Ranthambhore (second), Udaipur (fourth), and Agra (eighth).[25] Even the luxuries of the Oberoi Cecil were no match for Oberoi's even more extravagant properties!

Lessons from Oberoi

The Oberoi example demonstrates that the design of your operating model is central to the customer experience you seek to deliver. Thinking about what costs you can add to your operating model in order to deliver a more meaningful customer experience is not second nature to most entrepreneurs or executives. But for some target customers, it makes all the difference in attracting them and encouraging them to return again and again.

Ryanair and Oberoi are familiar brands to many travelers, though the details of their operating models are not so evident to the casual observer. For quite a different approach by a company that's flown largely under the radar to date, we now turn to ZoomSystems.

Case 3: ZoomSystems—Not Your Parents' Vending Machine

There you are, in the middle of the Hartsfield-Jackson Atlanta International Airport. You have forty-five minutes to kill before your next flight. You wander the terminal, looking for a halfway nutritious snack. Out of the corner of your eye, you catch a glimpse of an oversized vending machine. It's flashier than the normal vending machine. Interesting, you think: no candy bars or Diet Cokes in this machine. Instead, it's chock-full of iPods, iPod accessories, and cell-phone headsets. "Wow," you think, "I remembered to bring my iPod, but I forgot my charger, and my iPod is almost out of juice." On the touchscreen you read about the charger, ensuring that it is compatible with your now-obsolete iPod mini. Within a minute of arriving at this machine, you pop your credit card into the slot, agree to pay $24.99, and walk away with a brand-new charger.

This experience may sound unlikely to many of you, but for those living in Japan or South Korea, it's closer to the status quo. If ZoomSystems has its way, such stores could transform western retailing by using retail's most crucial resource—space—in a new and more productive way and by replacing labor-intensive activities with more efficient mechanized ones.

Founded in 1998, ZoomSystems developed and patented a software platform that has evolved to enable robotically automated retailing.[26] As CEO and founder Gower Smith described it, Zoom's Plan A was "an automated supply cabinet of sorts."[27] But Plan A was slow to gain traction. In March of 2005, Smith embarked on Plan B by combining his software platform with a Japanese company's robotic technology to develop its first truly robotic store.[28] "We wanted to take that a step further and incorporate an electronic salesperson to give consumers information about each product and to aid in the purchase process. By implementing [it] with a robotic store, we've created a stand-alone retail channel."[29]

Zoom's Leaps of Faith

Smith's first leap of faith in developing his Plan B was that the combination of his software and the robotic technology would create a more attractive and convenient user experience for small but high-value products—at sharply lower costs than conventional, full-service, location-based retailing could deliver. Zoom's robotic store would be a cross between a vending machine and a retail experience. Like typical vending machines—one analog—Zoom's stores would be located in hotels, airports, and other high-traffic locations. Like a vending machine, customers would visually browse the merchandise. But, unlike a vending machine—now an antilog—the customer would then use the touchscreen to learn all about the items in the store. Zoom's stores would peddle items costing $10–$200, including electronic devices such as iPods and cell phones.[30]

To be certain that the customers got what they paid for—unlike the annoying mechanical vending machine that sometimes leaves your candy bar hanging in thin air after you have paid your 75 cents—Zoom would include optical sensors that would verify that a customer had taken the purchased item. Only at that point would the customer's credit card (Zoom's merchandise requires more than pocket change!) be charged. "Zoom Shops are not your parents' vending machine," says Gower Smith. "It's like shopping online, but consumers have the instant gratification of getting their product immediately."[31]

There were other questions that generated additional leaps of faith, each of which had to be empirically examined. Where should Zoom stores be located: Airports? Shopping malls? Colleges? Hotels? Different kinds of locations would probably call for different kinds of merchandise. Airports might have a collection of relatively high-priced items, such as electronics and unique gifts. A hotel store might include lower-priced convenience items such as toothpaste, razors, or Tylenol. As Brian Hughes, general manager of

San Francisco's four-star Argent Hotel, an early Zoom adopter, said, "As hotel gift shops become less and less viable in today's high-labor-cost environment, the opportunity presented with the Zoom Shop was quite simply an opportunity to not say 'no' to our guests when asked if we have a venue to purchase essential and convenience-based products."[32]

But Smith also had another—quite different—leap of faith he thought had potential. Rather than restricting the marketing of his technology to hotels and airport concessionaires, he believed manufacturers would buy or lease a Zoom store to display, promote, and sell their line of products exclusively, thereby eliminating the retail middleman. Initial results were promising. Motorola tried Zoom as a "way to directly connect with consumers in places and at times where convenience is needed most."[33] Sony's senior manager of new business development, Bruce Schwartz, saw potential as well: "We believe that there are incremental sales that we are not capturing out there in the marketplace [and Zoom] will be able to capture them."[34]

To Smith, the possibilities for his technology were endless. One more analog pointed the way. "Just as ATMs [automatic teller machines] extended banking services to locations far beyond the teller window," Smith says, "Zoom is extending the retail experience to thousands of locations where transactions weren't possible before."[35]

Will Zoom's Leaps of Faith Pan Out?

Let's compare Zoom's operating costs at an airport such as Atlanta's Hartsfield with those of a normal retail electronics store. In 2005, in an average U.S. electronics and appliance store, salaries, wages, and benefits accounted for 12.1 percent of revenue.[36] By eliminating the need to pay wages and benefits to an actual salesperson, Zoom was looking at far lower labor costs. Zoom's automatic inventory system also reduced costs, as there was no longer a human needed to track or manage inventory, although Zoom still had to pay for staff to monitor the equipment and restock the store.

But labor productivity is only part of the Zoom story. With retail, the saying goes, location is everything. U.S. electronics retailers spend an average of 2.3 percent of their revenue on rent.[37] Zoom only required a very small space to operate. Said Zoom's lead investor, Peg Jackson of Neo Carta Ventures, "Zoom can transform forty square feet into a profit center that generates thousands of dollars in annual revenue per square foot."[38]

Further, unlike traditional retailers for which rent typically had a fixed cost component regardless of sales, Zoom proposed a profit-sharing model, paying the property owner a portion of the revenues (between 5 and 10 percent) for the physical space it used.[39] While the profit-sharing model didn't necessarily decrease Zoom's operating costs, it did lessen Zoom's risk and its breakeven point. By moving a potential fixed cost (rent) to variable cost (the landlord's share of revenue) Zoom reduced the costs of testing its leaps of faith too. If the Zoom store didn't generate enough revenue, Zoom could simply move it to a more promising location.

As its early results soon demonstrated, Zoom's revenues per square foot had the potential to be much greater than those of a traditional retail store. In 2005, mall retail stores in the United States averaged $33 per square foot, per month.[40] By the end of 2008, Zoom had placed 790 machines in stores, airports, and shopping malls. According to the company, its typical twenty-eight-square-foot units were generating $3,000 to $10,000 per square foot per month.[41]

Will Zoom's new operating model, its Plan B, work in the long term? It is still early days for Zoom's Plan B, but Smith and his team have developed proprietary technology and an efficient cost structure, enabling Zoom to sell high-end items in what might otherwise be expensive, unreachable, or cost-prohibitive places. And, because Zoom has a lower-cost operating model than conventional retailers, it could earn potentially fatter margins than its brick-and-mortar or online cousins. "We're doing for retail what ATMs did for banking," says Smith.[42] Automatic teller machines (ATMs) have transformed banking as we used to know it. Will Zoom's low-cost operating model do the same thing to retailing?

Lessons from Zoom

The Zoom story is one of enhanced productivity. And it offers two lessons for building disruptive operating models, one classical, one new. The classical lesson is that dramatic increases in productivity are possible by replacing labor with more efficient capital—a robotic machine with touchscreen software. It's a twenty first-century version of the industrial revolution applied to the retailing industry. The newer lesson is that for operating models that create ways to use other critical resources far more efficiently— retail real estate, in Zoom's case—significant productivity gains are also possible. Though ZoomSystems is still finding its way, its productivity potential should find application somewhere. One or more of its leaps of faith may yet pan out.

Lessons Learned About Operating Models

Who says you can't teach an old dog—or an existing industry—new tricks? Airlines do not all have to operate in the same way. It's okay to increase operating costs to meet a customer need for luxury. Vending machines don't have to be coin-operated and carry only items ranging from 50 cents to a dollar or two. Take that old dog—the vending machine—teach it to be robotic, combine it with a touchscreen and credit-card payment capability and—voilà!—a new kind of retailing is born.

To begin this chapter, we identified the three strategic questions that drive operating models: the levels of costs in each operating expense category in your industry's chart of accounts, your strategic thinking about which of them should be reduced or eliminated, and third, which, if any, should be raised. In the examples we've explored, we've seen an operating model that cuts operating expenses to the bone; another that raises them at every turn; and a third that pursues greater productivity from at least two elements—labor and space—of the traditional cost structure in the retailing industry. From these examples, three themes have emerged:

- In some industries there are huge swathes of costs that your operating scalpel can eliminate, simply by doing things differently. Where high prices are sources of customer pain, cost cutting can be an answer.

- Some groups of consumers want the very best. To serve such high-end markets, *adding* costs to your operating model to enhance the customers' experiences can keep your customers coming back. If customer delight is what you are offering, being penny wise and pound foolish by cost cutting is probably *not* the answer.

- Using technology or mechanization for productivity gains is a time-honored gambit most of us learned in Economics 101. Such gains can be found in the unlikeliest of places. What can you do to make the most costly or scarcest resources in your industry or in the market you serve—such as labor and space in retailing—dramatically more productive?

Let's consider the wider implications of the examples—each a potential analog for you—we have examined in this chapter.

Scalpels and Machetes

It is our view that many industries are chock full of inefficient—sometimes bloated—antilogs, just waiting for your cost-cutting scalpel or machete. Ryanair found ways to cut costs in numerous areas, and then kept on trimming, in keeping with the customer pain it was addressing, the high cost of travel. Similarly, in hotels, Accor cut out the meeting rooms and fancy restaurants to provide clean, comfortable rooms at bargain prices. Dell cut out the middlemen and most of the R&D to sell low-priced PCs; in 2007, Dell spent one-sixth of what HP spent on R&D—and one-tenth IBM's figure.[43]

Adding Value with Featherbeds

Oberoi, in contrast, took the opposite approach, adding costs—for fancy bedding, massage facilities, and much more—to its operating model that would add value to its customer experience. This approach was in keeping with the consumer delight it sought to provide. Doing so can also keep you one step ahead of your more lead-footed competitors. If your target market wants something special, think what new elements you can add to your operating model to spice up your customer's experience. Then do it again. And again.

Productivity Gains

Much economic progress—not to mention competitive advantage—arises from the efforts of innovative companies putting some kinds of resources to work more productively. Doing so effectively can wreak havoc with your competitors and create long-lasting competitive advantage for you. As we've seen from ZoomSystems, such a strategy is not necessarily about replacing labor with capital. Identify in your industry the crucial resources that, if deployed more productively, might enable you to create your own breakthrough operating model.

Finally, though your operating model constitutes a crucial ingredient in your overall strategy and business model, there is no reason that your operating model or overall business model has to be unique. In fact, the examples in this and the earlier chapters have shown that, most of

the time, there's already something out there—an analog or an antilog—
ready to be copied or adapted to your situation. Your task, when it comes
to choosing an operating model, is to find somebody's operating model
that's right for what you want to do. Once you've found it, copy it, then
add your own twist and do it even better. O'Leary the apprentice has,
arguably, crafted his operating model better than did Kelleher, the master
craftsman.

The Ryanair and Oberoi examples offer another insight as well, besides
serving as exemplars for low-cost and high-cost operating models. They
show us that some of the costs of providing what you offer can be bundled
or unbundled in various ways and, to at least some degree, moved back
and forth between operating expenses and cost of goods sold. Ryanair
charged its customers for things that airlines had long bundled into what
came with a ticket: peanuts and a Pepsi and a baggage allowance, for
example. By unbundling baggage from the price of a ticket, Ryanair
was able to lower its ticket prices and move some of its baggage handling
costs into COGS and generate revenue accordingly, from customers who
wished to check baggage when they flew. Oberoi did the opposite,
bundling more and more luxuries into its offering, thereby permitting it
to charge higher prices for its rooms and enhancing its ability to add to
gross margin through higher prices. What can your company do to
enhance your operating model—or another element of your business
model—by bundling or unbundling operating costs differently than your
competitors?

Q&A with John and Randy

By now you should have a good idea about what sort of analogs and
antilogs you need to find to craft your operating model (see the checklist
at the end of this chapter for a concise reminder of the things for which
evidence is required). But there are probably at least two questions that
remain in your mind:

- Analogs are fine, but if not sourced with care they may be mostly
  words and ideas. I'll need real numbers. Where will I find them?

- Some operating costs stay the same over time and some vary with
  my sales. How should I plan for this reality?

Finding Real Numbers

Yes, it's actual evidence—quantitative data—you will need. To build your operating model, you'll have to use your analogs and antilogs to quantify what you expect to happen, perhaps generating one or more leaps of faith that will lead to hypotheses that you can then test empirically through your dashboarding process. If Plan A does not pan out, as was the case for both Ryanair and ZoomSystems, you'll then iterate toward Plan B. But where, besides another company you may know well, might you find the data you need?

In the United States, two handy sources are the Risk Management Association's Annual Statement Studies and BizStats, both of which provide a plethora of data on industry averages for the various categories of operating cost in practically any industry.[44] In the United Kingdom, all incorporated companies, whether public or private, are required to report their financial performance to Companies House. This data is made public for all to see—including you![45] While you cannot be certain about exactly what's included in the categories reported—and what's not—these resources provide a good place to start. A few interviews with industry experts can be used to interpret these kinds of data more effectively. If you are somewhere else in the world that does not publish such data, the American or British data may be the best you can get.

How Can You Plan for the Vagaries of Operating Costs?

As you develop your operating model, you'll find that your operating costs will follow one of two patterns:

- *Fixed:* Some operating costs will be fixed costs that don't vary with the level of revenue you generate, at least not over some range you expect to achieve during some finite period of time. Rent for your factory or office is a typical example. Your salary, if you plan to take one, is another.

- *Variable:* Some costs may be variable, expressed as a percentage of revenue that your revenue model will generate. For retailers, supplies used in the store are likely to vary with sales—the more you sell, the more packaging, bags, and so on you'll need. For airlines, baggage-handling expenses are a variable cost. The more flights you operate and the more passengers who fly with your airline, the greater your bill for these and other ground services will be.

Whether fixed or variable, each line of expense in your chart of accounts requires evidence that will tell you and others what your costs will be in that expense category. By searching out analogs and antilogs, identifying your leaps of faith, and then testing your hypotheses with one or more dashboards guiding the way, you'll soon have a much clearer idea what it will really cost to run the business you have in mind.

So, there you have it, one more ingredient—your operating model—to add to the growing set of elements that will lead to your overall business model. If you are reading and working sequentially, your revenue and gross margin models are already sketched out, at least in terms of the leaps of faith you must examine to verify whether your hypotheses are correct. So, what's in place at this point?

- A revenue model that specifies how you expect your revenue to arise

- A gross margin model that—when applied to each dollar, euro, or rupee of revenue—specifies how much money you expect to be left over to cover your operating expenses and contribute to profit and cash flow

- An operating model that fills in the rest of your cost structure

Building on a suitable set of analogs and antilogs, each of these models paints part of the picture that describes the operating cash flow that your business might deliver under your Plan A. Inevitably, though, there remain leaps of faith to be examined. Testing them systematically will lead, over time, to Plan B, Plan C, or Plan Z. And somewhere along this path, you'll probably find an operating model that works!

What's Next?

You might think that developing a business model comprising the three elements we've dealt with so far—your revenue, gross margin, and operating models—completes your business modeling task. Revenue minus COGS minus operating expenses equals profit, right?

Alas, at the end of the day it's not profit that matters, despite what we read in the financial pages. Profit is an accountant's fiction. It's *cash* that counts, the cash flow you generate compared to the cash you must invest to build your cash flow machine.

Thus, two crucial issues remain to be addressed in crafting your business model. First, for your revenue, gross margin, and operating models, we have not yet addressed the *timing* of when the revenue arrives or when the expenses must be paid. Timing of your cash flows is crucial, so we'll turn to that next in chapter 6. We will address your working capital model—arguably, after your revenue model, the most important of all.

Then, in chapter 7, we'll address the remaining issue: how much up-front investment it will take to build your money machine, like the complete makeover of Oberoi's hotel in Shimla or the $20 million in software development that led to Zoom's new robotic stores.

John's and Randy's Operating Model Checklist

To get started on building your operating model, you must first get a copy of a chart of accounts for your industry. To develop the operating model for the strategy you have in mind, you'll need evidence to support the level of cost that you will incur in each of its expense categories. Existing data from your analogs and antilogs will get the ball rolling.

The strategic questions you should ask for each category of your chart of accounts are these (also listed at the start of this chapter):

✓ Once revenue begins to flow, in order to deliver on your planned strategy, what level of cost, expressed in absolute or percentage of sales terms, will your company incur in each of the operating cost categories (that is, all day-to-day costs other than cost of goods sold)?

✓ Which of these costs can be reduced or eliminated entirely?

✓ Which of them should be increased in line with your planned strategy?

You'll be in good shape when you can say which companies' analogs and antilogs, or some other tangible evidence, underpins your thinking about the questions outlined above.

To take your plan a step closer to the reality your business will face, you will probably find yourself identifying a number of leaps of faith. How much will rent really cost? How many employees will you need? What will you pay your employees? What will it cost to keep the lights on and the computers running? And more. Dashboarding will give you the answers.

CHAPTER 6

Cash Is King

Your Working Capital Model

J OHNNY, OF LEMONADE FAME, has a favorite uncle, Ted. Uncle Ted, a native of Wichita, Kansas, has owned and operated Ted's Barber Shop for almost twenty-five years. In that time, the demographic profile of his clients has barely changed. The majority are men in their fifties and sixties with a few younger men, usually the sons of Ted's clients or businessmen passing through town. Ted's clients don't ask for anything fancy: just a trim and a shave. Once in a while, a non-Wichita native will ask to have his gray hair colored.

Fortunately for Ted, it takes very little cash to run his business. He doesn't hold any *inventory*—accounting lingo for goods and materials that you buy (either raw materials or finished goods) to sell later—since he doesn't sell hair products to his clients. His storefront rent is a modest $900 per month. Utilities run $150 per month. His bill for shampoo, conditioner, and shaving supplies costs him less than $50 each month, payable thirty days later. With the price of an average cut only $15, his clients pay in cash at the time of service. Out of the cash he takes in, Ted pays his two employees—Joe and Fran—twice each month for the hours they've worked. Ted pays himself at the end of each month, with the amount of his take-home pay depending on the cash that's left over.

Ted is a man with few worries. He has no investors clamoring for a return on their investment. There are no shareholders pushing him to generate consistently growing quarterly performance. No banker bugs him to repay a loan. Ted has virtually no inventory, no *accounts receivable*—accounting lingo for money that customers owe you for what you have already sold them, when they have not yet paid you—and a well-managed relationship with his main supplier.

Ted's Barber Shop is an example of a company, and an industry, that doesn't need much, if any, working capital. Ted runs his business *on his customer's cash*. He can pay payroll, operating expenses, and anything else that comes up—like the plumber who has to unclog his drains once in awhile—using money from customer payments. Even two years ago, when he refurbished his shop, he covered the costs of his fancy new barber chairs out of the monthly cash intake.

A chapter on working capital? We can see your faces now. You're saying, "I think I'll skip this one. I don't think it pertains to my business." Think again. For if your cash reserves dry up, so too will your company!

You can literally find money by looking at your balance sheet differently. Does that interest you? There are numerous industries—haircutting is but one—that simply don't need much or any working capital. Other industries stand to learn a lot from them. Wouldn't you like to be worry-free, like Ted? As we'll see in this chapter, some savvy entrepreneurs have sharply reduced the gross margins they need by developing working capital models that have disrupted their industries. Could you be the disrupter that does this to your industry? Or are you at risk of having this done to you? If any of these questions merits even a tentative "Yes," stay with us. If you're still on the fence, read "Where Is Your Cash?"

As we'll see in this chapter, working capital models form the foundation for some of today's most interesting, most revolutionary business models. Your business model will not be complete until your working capital model is in place. Unfortunately, addressing their working capital model is an issue too many entrepreneurs ignore in their haste to fill in the spreadsheets that their business plan requires. As we will also see, this chapter is about finding the cash you need from sources that don't ask for equity, your customers and suppliers, unlike investors.

To get started, let's make sure you know why a seemingly innocuous concept like working capital is so important and exactly what we mean by this term.

Where Is Your Cash?

Time and again, as a professor (John), and as a roaming CEO and investor (Randy), we have seen nascent entrepreneurs and many corporate executives focusing their time and energy on their income statements. They spend valuable time evaluating profitability, gross margins, operating costs, and net income. And then they make the debilitating mistake of spending very little time—if any at all—understanding their balance sheets.

Staying in business over the long term—whether getting past infancy in an inevitably uncertain new venture, or steering an established company through times of economic crisis—means not running out of cash. And where is your cash balance found? Not on your income statement. It's on your *balance sheet*.

What's a balance sheet, and why are we so hung up on it? Unlike your income statement, which keeps track of your revenue, expenses, and profits over a period of time such as a year, your balance sheet is a snapshot taken at an instant in time. This picture tells you, in essence, how much you own at that moment, assets in accounting-speak. These include equipment, inventory, and such, as well as obligations that your customers or others owe you. And, all-importantly, cash. It also shows how much money you owe others—liabilities—including things you've bought but not yet paid for, any loans you are paying down, and so on.

All five elements of your business model have implications for the cash your business generates and consumes. But the element that has the most to say about this—by far—is your working capital model. So if you want to significantly improve your likelihood of not running out of cash, this chapter is for you.

Working Capital Defined

Working capital is the cash a company needs to have on hand in the short term to keep the business running—pay its employees, suppliers, and so on. The naked truth about working capital is that it doesn't matter how clever your products, or how keen your customers: if you haven't got cash on hand to keep your business moving, you'll be out of business, as numerous hedge funds and others learned the hard way in the financial crisis that began in 2007. In fact, running out of cash is what drives so many young companies out of business in their infancy. For that reason, we will spend a lot of time in this chapter talking about the *timing* with which cash comes in or goes out.

In a CFO's eyes, working capital at any particular point in time consists of two categories on your balance sheet: current assets and current liabilities, in accounting lingo.

- *Current assets* include money that is (or soon will be) readily available to the company. This includes cash, cash equivalents (like short-term deposits in a money market account), accounts receivable (cash owed by your customers who have not yet paid you), and inventories you can sell.

- *Current liabilities* are the organizational commitments that you will soon have to pay to others, typically in less than one year. These include accounts payable (to your suppliers for things they have delivered, but for which you have not paid), and short-term debt (bank loans, lines of credit, etc.). When you subtract current liabilities from current assets, you end up with working capital. Thus,

$$\text{Working capital} = \text{Current assets} - \text{Current liabilities}$$

In essence, working capital consists of piles of stuff—sometimes piles of paper representing obligations to pay or be paid, sometimes piles of more tangible items, like inventory—plus the cash in your bank accounts.

What we, and hopefully you, are particularly interested in is the *noncash* portion of working capital—in other words the various piles of goods and paper that tie up or free up cash. Some piles may be inventory, tying up precious cash that you've spent to buy it. Some piles, in effect, give you *somebody else's* cash to use for awhile (your accounts payable to your suppliers do exactly this). Some give somebody else *your* cash so you can't use it (your accounts receivable from customers who have not yet paid for what they have bought do this). As its name suggests, the noncash portion of working capital does not include any cash (or cash equivalents like money market accounts) you hold. It does, however, include all the rest of your working capital, all of which either frees up or ties up cash. When we say *negative working capital* later in this chapter, we are referring to the non-cash portion of working capital, as defined above, with the cash and cash equivalents netted out.

Measuring Working Capital in Days

The depth of these piles can be most usefully measured in days. How many days worth of inventory at your current selling rate? How many days worth of *sales* do your accounts receivable represent? How many days worth of *accounts payable* at the rate you are incurring cost of goods sold? And so on. Each of these piles—of paper or inventory—represents cash that you, your suppliers, or your customers hold. Wouldn't you like to manage these piles so that you get the cash and someone else gets the paper? Read on.

Think about it this way. If your business needs lots of working capital, you'll have to raise it from somewhere. Capital always comes at a price. The better a company manages its working capital, the less it needs to raise equity capital from investors or borrow, hat in hand, from a bank. Clearly, then, it's good if you can get by with little or no working capital (that is, your current liabilities are equal or nearly equal to the noncash portion of your current assets, per the working capital formula above).

Even better is to figure out a way to have the noncash portion of your working capital be negative, thereby feeding your pile of cash (more current liabilities than current assets other than cash), and giving the piles of paper and inventory to others. In effect, you'll try to get your suppliers to hold that large pile of inventory and a large pile of (paper) invoices (accounts payable) once they ship it to you; and you'll do your best to get your customers to pay you quickly so you don't hold a large pile of *their* paper (accounts receivable).

As *Fortune* magazine described it:

> *Reducing working capital yields two powerful benefits. First, every dollar freed from inventories or receivables rings up a one-time $1 contribution to cash flow. Second, the quest for zero working capital permanently raises earnings. Like all capital, working capital costs money, so reducing it yields savings. In addition, cutting working capital forces companies to produce and deliver faster than the competition, enabling them to win new business and charge premium*

prices for filling rush orders. As inventories evaporate, warehouses disappear. Companies no longer need forklift drivers to shuttle supplies around the factory or schedulers to plan production months in advance.[1]

We're not done with working capital just yet. Why else is less working capital desirable? It has to do with earning an attractive return on the investment (your invested capital) that you and your backers will put up to put you in business. Because that's something that your investors care deeply about, as should you, developing an attractive investment model is a topic that we examine in considerable depth in chapter 7. For now, though, let's look at one more simple formula that further underlines why working capital is so important:

Return on investment (ROI) = Net cash flow ÷ Invested capital

If you can find a way to let your noncash working capital be small, or even negative (more current liabilities than your noncash current assets), this will free up cash you can use to cover the fixed assets you need, such as Ted's barber chairs. The follow-on result is that invested capital, the denominator in the ROI formula above, will fall, making it possible for the numerator, net cash flow, to fall, too, without reducing the ROI you earn on your capital. As we'll see later in this chapter, minimal or negative working capital can also enable you to add features to your product or drive down prices, thereby trimming your margins, while still earning an attractive ROI. Figuring this out—when others in your industry have not—gives you a license to disrupt your industry with a revolutionary Plan B or earn a higher return on investment (ROI) than everyone else. The choice is yours, and it's a nice choice to have.

As always: there are always a few key strategic questions that drive each element of the business model that you are developing. What are they for your working capital model?

- Keeping your planned revenue model in mind, when (in relation to when you deliver the goods) can you encourage your customers to pay? As we'll see, the timing is important.

- How quickly or slowly (measured in days from when the supplies are delivered or the work is performed) must you pay key suppliers and employees, on average?

- How many days worth of inventory or other prepaid items—current assets, as they are called—must you hold to run your business effectively?

To address these questions, as always, you'll be looking for leaps of faith you can identify which, if borne out in your next experiment, will enable you to dramatically differ, in working capital terms, from others in your industry. Your dashboard will guide your way.

Our Goal for Chapter 6: Make Cash Your King

Our goal in this chapter is to get you thinking, in a strategic sense, about cash and cash flow, rather than profit. From a business model point of view, profits are irrelevant. Why? Failure to earn a profit won't put you out of business, as long as you still have cash. But if you run out of cash, even if you are profitable, you'll be gone in a heartbeat. Cash, as they say in entrepreneurial circles, is king.

From the two companies we profile in this chapter, we'll explore what cash really means:

- First, we'll observe the journey of Dow Jones, the publisher of the *Wall Street Journal* and other publications in both print and digital media. Dow Jones's working capital model provided a much-needed cushion to help the company address the potentially wrenching transition in the late 1990s from the so-called old economy and its print-based Plan A to the so-called new economy and a digital Plan B.

- Costco, the warehouse club chain, provides an example of a Plan A that worked from the start. However, as we'll see, from an industry perspective its business model constituted a disruptive Plan B. Its working capital model gave it the ability to take chunks out of the hides of numerous other retailers, and made traditional profit margins on the sale of its merchandise pretty much unnecessary.

Dow Jones and Costco reinforce the importance of the timing of your cash flows. These examples also share two common themes. First, in both companies, negative working capital is seen as the Holy Grail, just as exciting as eBay's near-100 percent gross margin. Second, we'll see that negative working capital offers real benefits: it makes it easy to get into business and easy to adapt and grow.

Case 1: Dow Jones: Using Customers' Money to Cope with Change

Imagine a working capital model where your customers pay you before your product or service is even produced, not to mention delivered. A good idea, right? Consider the subscription-based periodical publishing industry. From the barebones *Kiplinger Letter* (a subscription-based personal finance newsletter) to the complex workings of the *New York Times*, companies in the periodicals industry historically have had negative working capital.

Why is this? Periodicals publishers—whether they publish newsletters, newspapers, or magazines—tend to have almost no inventory, just some paper and ink. As soon as they print the current edition, out it goes. On the other hand, subscription fees are collected long before the publication is printed and shipped. That's good news if you want to drive working capital down. For the publisher, the cash the subscriber pays up front is what accountants call a liability (unearned subscriptions or deferred revenues, as they are often called on publishers' financial statements), since the publisher now "owes" the upcoming issues to the subscriber. The result of all this: modest current assets (limited mostly to accounts receivable from advertising not yet paid), large current liabilities (the issues due for the rest of the year, for example), and negative working capital.

Dow Jones & Company (Dow Jones)—known best for its newspaper, the *Wall Street Journal*, and its stock market index, the Dow Jones Industrial Average—is a case in point for negative working capital. Its business was based on this working capital model for more than a century. Then along came the digital revolution. Was it time for Plan B?

Let's start at the beginning. Founded in New York City in 1882 by Charles Henry Dow, Edward Davis Jones, and Charles Milford Bergstresser, print media was Dow Jones's bread and butter. The company started off producing daily, handwritten news bulletins called *flimsies*, delivered by messengers to subscribers in the Wall Street area of Manhattan. In 1883 the company started publishing the *Customers' Afternoon Letter*, which six years later became the *Wall Street Journal*. The four-page *Journal* could be purchased for 2 cents a copy. Advertising was sold for 20 cents per line. In 1902, Clarence Barron, who was one of Dow Jones's first employees, purchased Dow, Jones & Company for $130,000. He added a weekly financial publication, *Barron's*, in 1921. Decades later, in the 1970s, Dow Jones diversified, purchasing a number of local newspapers, increasing its circulation and reach and lessening its reliance on the financial markets.

But in the late 1980s, with the advent of digital media like the now-ubiquitous Bloomberg terminals that have sprouted on nearly every desk in the financial world, the *Wall Street Journal* started losing subscribers. Circulation dropped from a high of 2.11 million in 1983 to 1.95 million by 1989. Profits deteriorated.[2] The publishing world was changing, the Internet had arrived, and electronic publishing became Dow Jones's Plan B. But moving from print to digital was no trivial task. That it believed it could do so was a huge leap of faith.

Let's take stock of Dow Jones's working capital model at the end of its old-economy heyday, in 1992. These were the noncash elements of its working capital at that time:[3]

- Current assets (other than cash) = 37 days
  - Inventory: 4 days
  - Accounts receivable: 33 days (subscribers pay in advance, but advertisers pay in arrears; this figure reflects the latter)
- Current liabilities = 109 days
  - Accounts payable: 70 days
  - Unearned subscriptions: 39 days (subscriptions paid for but not yet delivered)
- Net of these elements = −72 days[4]

That's seventy-two days worth of customer cash, or about 20 percent (72 days out of the 365-day year = 19.7 percent) of 1992's $1.8 billion in revenue, that Dow Jones could use for other things. It's like having $360 million of free money, just sitting there, ready to use to buy printing presses, pay wages, or to develop new businesses! By paying its suppliers (of newsprint among other things) in an average of seventy days and by collecting people's subscriptions for its publications and newswires up front, Dow Jones had the ability to literally use other people's money to pay its bills. But the game was changing. Would the working capital model that was central to any publisher's success have to change as well?

Dow Jones Goes Digital

By 1992 the company had already launched DowVision, a news service customized for Dow Jones's corporate customers. DowVision delivered published text from the *Wall Street Journal*, *New York Times*, *Financial Times*, *Washington Post*, and *Los Angeles Times,* together with a premier version of the Dow Jones newswires, directly to corporate desktops.[5] Pleased with its early progress, in 1995 Dow Jones's leadership went public with its new strategy. "We're taking our editorial standards to the Web, where a glut of information often makes searching for the right piece of information time-consuming and fruitless." The company saw two distinct segments for its electronic services: individuals or small companies and large enterprises, both of which it wanted to serve. Dow Jones developed new online services for individuals and small businesses, allowing them to use credit cards to purchase subscriptions or to pay for downloads of specific packages of information such as articles. Large enterprises on the other hand were expected to sign annual contracts for electronic access to Dow Jones's information, paid in advance, of course. The company's leaders had not forgotten what had gotten it this far, paid subscriptions up front!

Soon there was an online electronic supplement to the *Wall Street Journal's* Money & Investing section, known as the "*Wall Street Journal* Interactive Edition" (known later as *WSJ Online* at WSJ.com). This electronic newspaper subscription service allowed individual users to browse articles online. Both DowVision and The Publications Library, a news archive, were made available for Web users, primarily serving large enterprises as research tools, on a subscription basis.

From 1999 through 2006, Dow Jones quickened its digital pace, developing a joint venture with Reuters to create Factiva, a Web-based source of current and archived global news—subscriptions paid up front, of course. NewsPlus, a Web-formatted enhancement of Dow Jones's newswires, and Dow Jones Financial Information Services, which gave financial professionals additional Web access to electronic media, information, and directories, were added.[6] MarketWatch.com, which provided online business and financial news, was acquired.[7] Dow Jones's digital Plan B was well under way.

In 2006, Dow Jones went further, getting rid of some of its paper-based products in favor of online offerings. It launched *Barron's* online and bought Factiva outright, terminating the joint venture with Reuters. In December it sold six of the community newspapers that it had published for years.[8] CEO Rich Zannino said, "This sale and the pending acquisition of Factiva are the latest examples of our commitment to transform Dow Jones from a company heavily dependent on print publishing revenue to a more diversified company capable of meeting the needs of its customers across all consumer and enterprise media channels, whether print, online, mobile or otherwise."[9]

Would Its Subscription-Reliant Working Capital Model Still Work?

The Dow Jones management team consisted of veterans who understood the crucial role that the working capital model played in the publishing industry. When they adopted Plan B and its new digital revenue model, they retained a crucial element of Plan A—the company's working capital model. Take a look at the 2006 Dow Jones numbers to see what happened:

- Current assets (other than cash) = 58 days
  - Inventory: 3 days
  - Accounts receivable: 55 days

- Current liabilities = 135 days
  - Accounts payable: 88 days
  - Unearned subscriptions: 47 days

- Net of these elements = −77 days[10]

The Dow Jones's working capital model had improved to −77 days in 2006 (compared with −72 days in 1992)! The bedrock of the model, paid subscriptions up front, was still in place. The company still charged for traditional subscriptions for the *Wall Street Journal* and its remaining local newspapers, and for *Barron's*, Factiva, and its newswires. Most components of *Barron's Online* and WSJ.com required a subscription, as did some elements of MarketWatch. The Dow Jones indexes were both subscription- and license-based. And *Dow Jones Online News* could be licensed for a fee. Only a few experiments, such as CareerJournal.com, RealEstate Journal.com and OpinionJournal.com, came subscription-free.

The business had been transformed without going hat-in-hand to investors, funded largely by its customers' cash, and its precious working capital model had remained intact. The results for Dow Jones shareholders? Net income more than tripled on virtually the same $1.8 billion in revenue, rising from $107 million in 1992 to $386 million in 2006. And, perhaps with a nod to the company's successful transition to the digital age, Rupert Murdoch's News Corporation purchased Dow Jones for $5 billion in August 2007. Notably, and probably with thanks to Dow Jones's veterans, Murdoch, who indicated before the acquisition that he would make *WSJ Online* free and ad-based, has left its subscription-based, negative working capital model in place.

Lessons from Dow Jones

Dow Jones & Company shows us that negative working capital is helpful in coping with dramatic changes, such as those it faced in the digital revolution. Such a model provides customer cash with which to develop new products and strategies to iterate toward Plan B. Equally important was its management team's ability to identify new kinds and forms of content— new products, each of which was a leap of faith until proven—that consumers and business customers would value and pay for.

By itself, a better working capital model is not enough. Indeed, this point is evidenced by the cash infusion the *New York Times* needed in January 2009 from Carlos Slim, the Mexican billionaire, in order to remain afloat.[11] The *Times* had not been nearly as inventive as Dow Jones in developing cash-generative digital offerings to make its own digital transition. While Dow Jones largely maintained its subscription-based model as it went digital, the *New York Times* did otherwise in making the *New York Times Online* free.

Dow Jones & Company also shows how a powerful working capital model, common to an entire industry in this case, can enable changes in other parts of one's strategy and make seemingly wrenching changes appear as smooth as silk. Though sailing was not always easy for Dow Jones—there were a couple of loss-making years along the way—its transition to the digital age was, for the most part, successful. Sometimes, though, it takes innovators to bring new and different working capital models to an established industry. When they do, watch out!

Thus we next examine the story of Costco and the disruption it and others brought to general merchandise retailing in the United States.

Case 2: The Costco Model Disrupts Retailing with an Industry Plan B

Those of us in the United States are familiar with warehouse club stores. With names like Sam's Club, BJ's, and Costco, these enormous stores make their presence felt in or on the outskirts of every sizeable American city. Whereas Dow Jones relies on its subscription-based revenue model, the warehouse stores' working capital model relies on membership fees, quick inventory turns, and strict management of accounts receivable and payables.

Costco has become the preeminent warehouse club retail chain, largely because its management designed its working capital model to gain competitive advantage. In so doing, Costco has taken a chunk out of the hides of other general merchandise retailers.

Let's first examine Costco's roots. While Costco's working capital model was revolutionary, it was by no means original. It followed an analog nearly lock, stock, and barrel. Its model was based largely on Price Club, its progenitor. Price Club was created in 1976 by Sol Price in San Diego, California. Price's original and prescient leap of faith was that, by changing the working capital model in retailing to permit vastly lower prices, he could charge customers for the privilege of shopping at his stores. Audacious? In spades.

By 1982, Price had begun to roll out his strategy. It was Plan A for him, but it would take retailing by storm, serving as the industry's disruptive Plan B. He'd opened ten warehouse club stores, each doing an average of $36 million in revenue, several times the volume of a typical Walmart back then and more than ten times the volume of a high-volume supermarket.[12] The key to Price's early success was his counterintuitive credo, his refusal to try to squeeze an extra dollar out of his customers.

As Goldman Sachs retail analyst Stephen Mandel Jr. would later describe its model, Price Club was the industry's best practitioner, turning its inventory about twenty times annually, while possessing negative working capital of about $3 million per warehouse.[13] Move inventory quickly and charge a membership fee? It held the makings of a working capital model that was little short of spectacular!

Costco cofounder and CEO James Sinegal recalls—and lives by—Sol Price's principles. "Many retailers look at an item and say, 'I'm selling this for ten bucks. How can I sell it for eleven?' We look at it and say, 'How can we get it to nine bucks?' And then, 'How can we get it to eight?' It's contrary to the thinking of a retailer, which is to see how much more profit you can get out of it. But once you start doing that, it's like heroin." There was another element, too. "You had to be a member of the club. People paid us to shop there."[14]

Price Club Begets Costco

Enter Jeffrey Brotman. In 1981, Brotman recruited James Sinegal away from Price Club, where Sinegal had worked since his teens, rising rapidly through Price Club's ranks. In 1983, they launched Costco Warehouse in Seattle. At the heart of the Costco strategy was the Price Club working capital model, an analog Sinegal knew intimately.

First, there was the membership fee. Customers had to pay for the privilege of shopping at Costco. For families the fee was $50 per year; corporate customers paid up to $100, collected before the customer ever started shopping.[15]

Second, Costco collected cash from its customers almost immediately—no credit cards, thank you, but cash, a check, or your debit card (which gave Costco instant cash)—maintaining just three days of accounts receivable.[16] And, as Costco later proclaimed, "Because of our high sales volume and rapid inventory turnover, we generally have the opportunity to sell and be paid for inventory before we are required to pay many of our merchandise vendors, even though we take advantage of early payment discounts. As sales increase and inventory turnover becomes more rapid, a greater percentage of inventory is financed through payment terms provided by vendors rather than by our working capital."[17] With its customers providing the cash it needed to grow, Costco took off. By 1996, Costco was generating $19 billion in sales and $423 million in pretax net income. Let's look at the working capital numbers that were making this possible:

- Current assets (other than cash) = 35 days
  - Inventory: 32 days
  - Accounts receivable: 3 days

- Current liabilities = 41 days
  - Accounts payable: 27 days
  - Membership dues: 14 days (half of membership dues was taken in income in the current year, and half stayed on the balance sheet to be taken in year two)
- Net of these elements = −7 days[18]

Sinegal wanted to have more than his working capital cake, however. He wanted to eat it too. Costco's working capital model let it get away with razor-thin overall profit margins, since earning an attractive return on investment when your investment is near zero (thanks to negative working capital) can be accomplished with very modest profits (recall the ROI formula at the outset of this chapter). So Sinegal passed on to his customers the benefit—in lower prices—of the lower margins he could afford. He was underselling his competition, all the while growing the business on its customers' cash. How did Sinegal and his team take the fat out of margins?

The Rest of Costco's Story

Sinegal pulled no punches: "We'd like it to be known that we are the toughest negotiators in the business. And that we're gonna come after [vendors] for every nickel we can, and we won't let up until we think we've got the price right on the merchandise."[19] Costco negotiated better pricing from its suppliers by ordering in very high volume. In 1998, for example, Costco sold skin-on, bones-in salmon fillets for $5.99 per pound. At this price, Costco sold $100,000 worth of salmon per week. With such high volumes, Costco's buyer had leverage over his vendor, convincing the salmon supplier to remove the skin and debone the fish and charge even less for the fillets. In 2003, the fillet was sold for $4.39 per pound, spurring sales to $2 million per week![20]

Costco also convinced its vendors to package things in volume (e.g., a half-gallon jar of mayonnaise and a twenty-four-pack of toilet paper rolls). By packaging in volume, vendors could bring their wholesale prices down further still. Oh, and one more thing, said Costco to its vendors, "We need better payment terms, too."

But getting low prices from vendors didn't mean that Costco would fatten its margins. On the contrary. Sinegal insisted that no item could be

marked up to a gross margin over 14 percent (contrast that with supermarkets and department stores, which carried 20 to 50 percent gross margins across their various categories of merchandise, maintaining average
gross margins between 20 and 25 percent).[21] Discount stores like Kmart
and Target had even greater average gross margins across their product
mix, ranging from 25 to 30 percent. These were the antilogs Sinegal
wanted to beat.

To turn inventory quickly, Costco carried just 4,000 items. A typical
supermarket, Sinegal explained, carried 40,000 items, while a Walmart
supercenter would stock some 150,000.[22] With only 4,000 items at rock-
bottom prices, Costco could pick items that it knew would move off the
floor quickly.[23] Items were transported straight from the vendor to the
sales floor. No costly warehouses full of expensive inventory tying up precious cash.

There was one key element, though, on which Sinegal parted ways
with Price Club. Price Club targeted small businesses and working-class
families—something that rival Sam's Club mimicked. For Costco, Sinegal
targeted small businesses and more upscale families, more than a third of
which had household incomes greater than $75,000.[24] As retail consultant
and author Michael Silverstein explains, these consumers are happy to pay
for upscale items that "make their hearts pound" and for which they don't
have to pay full price. Then they trade down to cheaper private labels for
things like paper towels, detergent, vitamins, and other household staples.
"It's the ultimate concept in trading up and trading down," says Silverstein.
"It's a brilliant innovation for the new luxury."[25] As Berkshire Hathaway vice
chairman Charlie Munger—a Costco shopper, investor, and director—
notes, there are lots of people who don't have to pinch pennies who shop at
Costco. "I like bargain securities, why shouldn't I like bargain golf balls?"[26]

Three-quarters of Costco's assortment was basic, from twenty-four-count
packages of toilet tissue, Costco's top-selling item, to a lifetime supply of
panty shields. The excitement that brought customers back, however—
returning once every seventeen days on average, lest they miss out on a bargain[27]—came from the other 25 percent. From $800 espresso machines
this week to $29 Italian-made Hathaway shirts next week to $1,999 digital
pianos the week after, Costco's stores offered something for everyone, and
at bargain prices other merchants simply could not touch. "We always
look to see how much of a gulf we can create between ourselves and the

competition," says Sinegal. "So that the competitors eventually say, 'F***
'em, these guys are crazy. We'll compete somewhere else.'"[28] He also notes,
"Our customers don't drive fifteen miles to save on a jar of peanut butter.
They come for the treasure hunt."[29]

Costco Takes Its Toll on the Retailing Industry

By 2006 Costco had 48 million members and its stores were generating an
average of $120 million in sales per year. Best of all, its working capital
model had grown even better:

- Current assets = 35 days (no change from 1996)
  - Inventory: 32 days (half that of Target, its discount store
    competitor)
  - Accounts receivable: 3 days
- Current liabilities = 46 days
  - Accounts payable: 32 days (improved by 5 days against 10 years
    earlier)
  - Membership dues: 14 days
- Net of these elements = −11 days[30]

Costco's eleven days of free customer cash amounted to nearly $3.6 mil-
lion per store, more than enough to build another store for each one currently open. With cash like this to fund your growth, who needs outside
investment, a topic we address in the next chapter? Given a choice between
cash from your customers and suppliers and cash from investors, which
would you prefer?

What was the impact of Costco and its warehouse club brethren on the
rest of retailing? Long-suffering Kmart went into bankruptcy in 2002, and its
2004 merger with Sears held out little hope that either chain could compete
with the likes of Costco, or with Target and Walmart, which continued to
thrive. But discount and department store chains weren't the only retailers to
feel Costco's bite. Costco's $2 million per week in fresh salmon sales took a
chunk out of supermarkets' fresh seafood sales and brought shoppers to
Costco for more groceries than seafood or toilet tissue. Its fast-changing
assortment of durable goods—from apparel to electronics—helped slam the
brakes on retailers in other categories, too.

For Costco, though, the results were as impressive as a 64-ounce jar of mayonnaise. In 2006, the average Costco store generated almost twice the revenue of Walmart Sam's Club stores. Compared with Sam's Club, Costco had eighty-two fewer outlets, but generated about $20 billion more in sales—some $59 billion. Its pre-tax profit of $1.7 billion, of which nearly $1.2 billion was membership fees, was a slim 3 percent of sales.[31] With customers paying for the privilege of shopping, thereby providing the cash needed for running and growing the business, who needed high profit margins? It's exactly how Sinegal wanted it. "I hate to sound so simple," he says, "but all we're trying to do is sell the best quality merchandise for a better value than anyone else."[32] Costco was ranked number 29 in the *Fortune* 500 in 2008 and was the world's fifth-largest retailer.[33] Do working capital models matter? Costco's story speaks for itself.

Lessons from Costco

We've seen how rapidly Costco has grown, thanks to the cash its members keep giving it up front and to its quickly turning inventory. Each existing store's negative working capital provided enough cash to build another new store! Charging a membership fee for the privilege of shopping is a brilliant hedge against cash flow difficulties, too. But customers need a powerful reason to part with that cash, so building the rest of your model to deliver value that's not available anywhere else—rock-bottom prices and a treasure hunt is Costco's customer delight—is necessary if this is to happen.

Finally, we've seen that if you don't really need much in the way of profits, you can drive your competitors—who probably rely on them to earn their ROI—crazy. A negative working capital model drives down the denominator of the ROI formula, thereby enabling you to live with a smaller numerator as well.

Lessons Learned About Working Capital Models

To open this chapter, we noted that thinking strategically about your working capital accounts—who holds the cash versus the paper, and for how many days?—may be considerably more important than what accountants call profit. Costco, with its razor-thin profit margin, makes this point with a bang!

Generally, negative working capital is an attractive route forward if you can find a way to achieve it in your business. What are the lessons for building your own working capital model?

- For many savvy businesspeople, negative working capital is their Holy Grail, equally important as eBay's or Shanda's near-100 percent gross margin: gross margin nirvana, as we called it in chapter 4.

- The negative working capital model offers significant benefits that are well worth striving for.

Let's recap these themes here to be sure these points have hit home.

The Holy Grail of Negative Working Capital

That negative working capital is a key objective in some companies should be clear from both the Dow Jones and Costco stories. But the quest for more efficient working capital models is more widespread by far. And it's nothing new, as the origins of warehouse club chains in the 1970s and 1980s indicates. In the 1990s, the manufacturing industry got into the game. Companies like American Standard, Whirlpool, General Electric, and more sought to move from the *Fortune* 500 average of 20 cents in working capital for each dollar of sales to zero working capital. As managing director Eric Nutter of Wabco UK, a British automotive subsidiary of American Standard, saw it, "In business, it isn't over till the fat lady sings, and I say she doesn't sing till you're at zero working capital."[34] In the 2000s, retailers other than the warehouse clubs began singing the same tune. Between 2000 and 2004, Tesco, the leading grocery chain in the United Kingdom, began stretching the payables terms it obtained from suppliers, freeing up £2.2 billion (nearly $4 billion at that time) in cash that it could use for growth.[35] The trend toward negative working capital will continue, though it will be tested in the aftermath of the global credit crunch that began in 2007. Will your company drive it in your industry, or will you be its victim?

Why Negative Working Capital's Benefits Are Worth Striving For

For aspiring entrepreneurs and for businesses already up and running in other more capital-intensive industries: a negative working capital model is worth searching and working for. Why? It makes it easier and less costly to get into business in the first place. And it makes it much easier for your business to grow. Consumer services businesses—haircutters, landscapers, tax preparers, and the like—seek and find it by nature, since they get paid in cash and have little need for inventory. It is no wonder that some of these formerly fragmented industries are increasingly dominated by fast-growing chains, as savvy entrepreneurs have realized that these businesses are easy to get into and easy to grow, from a working capital perspective.

The Costco and Dow Jones stories offer an additional—and perhaps unexpected—lesson for aspiring entrepreneurs. If you aim to start a new venture, why not do it in an industry whose working capital requirements can be modest, or even negative? Periodicals publishing is but one example of such an industry. Trade show operators, cable television companies, payroll processors, and other human resources outsourcers are other examples. You'll need much less capital to get started, and less capital to grow, than in other industries.[36]

Q&A with John and Randy

With the power of an attractive working capital model now seared indelibly in your brain, what questions might remain?

- What are the implications of your working capital model for the other four elements in my overall business model, and vice versa? Aren't these elements interlinked?

- How might you convince suppliers and customers to play your working capital game? Aren't their interests in this regard opposed to yours?

- Can a company stretch its working capital model too far?

- As you look for analogs and antilogs of your own to build your company's working capital model, where, specifically, should you look to gauge a company's working capital performance?

Links Between Working Capital and the Other
Business Model Elements

In today's hotly competitive, increasingly globalized economy, the world is awash with overcapacity in many industries. As we have seen, companies that achieve negative working capital can take liberties with the other parts of their industry's business model that competitors cannot. Razor-thin profit margins? Not a problem for Costco. It takes pressure off of margins and provides cash to grow, whether through new product development, overseas expansion, or acquisition of less sanguine competitors. For many companies, it's the fuel for getting to Plan B. Adapting to a digital world? Dow Jones made the transition more easily than competitors like the *New York Times* because, in part, of their working capital model and their commitment to retain it.

But there's more to the links issue than may meet the eye. Astute readers may have noticed that Dow Jones's working capital model was implemented, in reality, by asking subscribers to pay up front. That's a revenue model issue, too, isn't it? Right you are. Costco's working capital model was driven largely by membership fees paid up front—a revenue model issue—that in turn enabled it to adopt a gross margin model with low, low prices and razor-thin gross margins. So why do we see these cases as working capital stories?

We've placed the Dow Jones and Costco cases in the working capital chapter because their working capital models lie at the heart of their long-running success. In their essence, working capital models are about the *timing* with which cash flows into and out of the business. In most industries, that means the timing with which customers pay, the timing with which suppliers are paid, and the timing or speed with which inventory (or piles of other current assets) can be turned over and over again.

So, as you think about how to get your venture or established company to break through to a better working capital model—to help you reach a better Plan B—the working capital questions you will ask, for the most part, are about timing issues like these. But because the timing issues are inherently linked to revenue model and operating issues, it's worth your while, as you think about analogs, antilogs, and leaps of faith in those arenas, to add timing to your questioning early in your dashboarding process. Changing the timing of cash flows can shake up an industry, as the Costco story indicates. And, as the Dow Jones story indicates, getting subscription money up front is another good way to go. Could your business offer subscriptions for what you or your competitors now sell in another way? That's what Netflix did to shake up the DVD rental industry. It's a working capital question, but one for your revenue model, too. In parallel fashion, could your business reduce the level of inventory it carries by introducing just-in-time supply chain processes as we saw in the Toyota model described in chapter 4? This is a working capital model question, but it's also tied to your gross margin model.

Getting Customers and Suppliers on Board

How might you convince your customers and suppliers to play ball in helping you reach the Holy Grail of negative working capital? The answer, as in most business dealings, is WIIFM—*What's in it for me?* Customers need a good reason to part with their money in advance. Do you offer early-bird discounts? (But please don't forget about the importance of a healthy gross margin model, if you do!) Do you offer other incentives for payment up front? Can you offer a subscription-based model, rather than pay-as-you-go?

WIIFM works the same way for suppliers, too. On their side of the transaction, you've got to find a persuasive argument why it is in their interest to give you better terms—be it lower prices or stretching your payables. Why do they need you as a customer, or as a bigger customer than you now are? Maybe it's the additional volume you'll give them in a critical product line they want to grow. Maybe there's a smaller supplier eager to win a larger share of your business who will give you better terms than the one you do business with now. However you do it, you'd better find an answer that's in their interest, too.

At the end of the day, as this chapter makes clear, getting to zero or negative working capital won't happen for those who confine their managerial attention to their company's income statement. Building a great working capital model is a crucial strategic issue. It's largely about your balance sheet, about finding inventive ways to manage the working capital structure of your business, about finding analogs that work.[37]

Your working capital analogs and antilogs are out there, including those in this chapter alone. Others might be just around the corner from where you live or work. Once you have found them and successfully adapted them to your own business setting, you'll be amazed at how much better you sleep. The danger of running out of cash may soon be behind you!

Can a Company Stretch Its Working Capital Model Too Far?

Stretching working capital, especially with suppliers, is like playing musical chairs. As long as the music keeps playing (the economy keeps rolling) everyone is happy. When the music stops at the customer end of the pipe, those at the back end—such as suppliers giving overly generous terms—can suffer, and perhaps go bankrupt. Losing key suppliers is probably not what you had in mind in asking for lengthy terms!

Where to Look to Understand an Analog's Working Capital Model

It's all on their balance sheet, with possible clues (like Costco's membership fee income) on the income statement. More precisely, as we noted at the beginning of this chapter, working capital is all about the current assets and current liabilities portions of the balance sheet. So start your search there.[38] If there are sizeable items therein—especially those that are unusually named, such as *deferred income* or *deferred revenue* or Dow Jones's *unearned subscriptions*—it's worth digging into them through your network to see what they really mean. That's where the hidden treasures often lie.

What's Next?

There is more on the balance sheet that has to be funded than working capital, of course. There is the rest of the investment that it takes to put a company in business or keep it there—printing presses for Dow Jones, retail stores for Costco, new product R&D for others, and much more. It is our hope that by now you've uncovered some analogs that point the way toward generating the cash you need from your gross margin or working capital models, rather than from investors, the more conventional route. After all, who wants to give up equity to investors if you can find the cash somewhere else? For many of you, though, this won't be the case, at least not entirely. So we now turn to the fifth and final element of your business model, your investment model.

John and Randy's Working Capital Checklist

Your working capital model will be constructed from a set of building blocks that are unique to your industry. If you are a manufacturer, your main building blocks will be accounts receivable, accounts payable, and inventory. If yours is a service business, there may not be inventory, but you might have something else. If you are an importer of kitchen gadgets—which miraculously dice, chop, and blend in an instant—to be sold on late-night TV, you'll have letters of credit for the merchandise that's en route from Asia, plus prepaid advertising, depending on the terms you can negotiate with your media suppliers. Thus, your first step, as we saw for your operating model, is to once more pull out the chart of accounts for your industry and see the categories on your balance sheet in the working capital sections, on both the assets and liabilities sides.

Once you've done that, you'll need to find analogs and antilogs—the cold, hard facts—that will begin to tell you the values for what you need to know. They are driven by the three key strategic questions we must ask as we build a working capital model:

✓ Considering your revenue model, when (how many days ahead of or behind delivering the goods or services) can you encourage your customers to pay? Can you get them to pay earlier? Why or why not?

✓ How quickly or slowly (measured in days from when the supplies are delivered or the work is performed) must you pay key suppliers and employees? What are the industry norms? Why might you be able to alter them?

✓ How much cash (measured in days) must you tie up in inventory or other prepaid items—current assets, in accounting lingo—before they are ready to be sold? What are the industry norms? Why might you be able to alter them?

Are there any leaps of faith you can identify, which if borne out in your next experiment, would enable you to dramatically differ, in working capital terms, from others in your industry? What are they, what are your hypotheses, and how will you test them?

CHAPTER 7

It Takes Money to Make Money

Your Investment Model

F OR JOHNNY, GETTING INTO THE LEMONADE BUSINESS was easy as pie. He had little need for up-front investment. He used the family's old card table for his lemonade stand. He made a sign out of some poster board left over from a science project. He borrowed his mom's extra pitcher. And, best of all, Johnny's mom had fronted him the cash for his initial supply of lemons and sugar.

For most of the people who launch new ventures, it takes some up-front cash to open shop. And getting that cash is rarely easy. Investors—whether the three Fs (family, friends, and fools), business angels, or seasoned venture capital professionals—worry about risk. Will the new venture make it in spite of the long odds? Oh, and they also want a return on their investment. So they want a stake in the business. The riskier the idea and the larger their investment, the larger the stake they require. Similarly, risk-averse corporate investment committees want spreadsheets and paperwork *ad nauseam* before they'll fork over the cash. Thus developing your investment model—to get the cash you need to get started—is a real challenge for most new ventures, whatever the setting.

In earlier chapters, we've seen how start-up companies like Google and Silverglide used one or more elements of their business models to move from a Plan A that was not economically viable to a Plan B that was. We've seen Toyota and Costco create business models that made life difficult for competitors across entire industries. Though some of the companies we've profiled were already in business, chances are good that many of you are still contemplating how best to get into business in the first place. That's where your investment model kicks in.

Investment Model Defined

As we noted in the introduction, your investment model is all about figuring out two things:

- First, how much cash you'll need to get into business, including—we hasten to add—a modest cushion of spare cash to make one or more transitions from Plan A to Plan B or Plan Z.

- Second, your investment model also aims to take your company through the rocky period until it can consistently generate enough cash to achieve break-even cash flow, so that you don't need to invest any more, except, perhaps, to grow the business, which, by then, has already been proved viable.

More crucially, for savvy entrepreneurs, the investment model is all about figuring out how to get started with as little investment as possible. Less investment means giving away less of the business to investors, if you need them at all. Less investment means less credibility lost when you, almost inevitably, declare that Plan A is not working—Sorry, dear investor!—and you're switching to Plan B. And less investment means fewer sleepless nights, if you've mortgaged your house to pursue your surefire entrepreneurial dream!

As should be clear from the bulleted points above, by *investment* we do not confine ourselves to what accounting lingo calls *assets*—tangible things like factories, equipment, and the like. We also include any money you must spend from the time you get started until the time the rest of your business model starts humming, generating—no longer burning—cash on a regular basis. Software development? Check. Pricey patent lawyers? Ditto. Acquiring customers, whether by advertising or a sales force? Investment, too, in our business model framework.

But there's a caveat here. Minimizing the need for investment applies principally to the *spending* side of the investment equation—figuring out how your business can get by on less capital. On the capital-*raising* side of the equation, the story is actually a bit different, since, as we've seen, your Plan A is not likely to work, right out of the box. There are leaps of faith you'll need to answer through your dashboards. And some of them won't yield the results you expect. As you iterate your way toward a more viable Plan B, you'll almost inevitably find that it will take you more money to get there than you will have imagined initially. So raising more capital than you think you will need is almost certainly a good idea. How much more? That's a function of your own attitude toward risk and reward, knowing that the more capital you raise, the more of your company you'll have to give up to investors. But be careful that your stash of extra capital does not let you stray from your focus on testing the hypotheses growing out of the leaps of faith that you've deemed most crucial to the validity—or not—of your Plan A. Otherwise you won't make real progress and you'll simply burn more cash. In short, raising too much investment capital can make you sloppy and undisciplined.

As you develop your investment model, you'll confront a few key questions. These come in two phases:

1. The prelaunch phase:
   - What are the hard assets—facilities, equipment, and so on— you'll need prelaunch? What will they cost to buy, rent, or lease?
   - What are the development activities that must be completed before you can launch? What will they cost?
   - What are the leaps of faith you must test prior to launch? What will it cost to test them?
   - Which of the above can you delay or find a way to do without, or do more cheaply or simply?

2. The postlaunch phase, until you hit cash flow breakeven:
   - What revenue and gross margin can you generate to contribute to your ongoing costs?
   - How lean an operating model can you run pre-breakeven?

3. And there's one more:

  – Which key leaps of faith, if proven, will signal stepwise
    reductions in risk? How much cash will it take to reach each
    of them, and how much of your funding can be postponed
    until later?

Taken together, these seven questions go to the heart of your investment model, a key objective of which is to reduce or eliminate the amount of cash it will take to get you to cash flow breakeven, if your gross margin and working capital models have not already accomplished that objective. Whether you find answers from analogs or antilogs, from quotations of real costs, or by dashboarding to test hypotheses that grow out of your leaps of faith, you'll need answers—numbers, please—to all of them!

Goal for Chapter 7: Raise Less Money . . . Seriously!

Our goal in this chapter, in part, is to get you out of the mind-set that money grows on trees. It doesn't. Raising money is almost always difficult, and most of the time the less money you need to raise up front, the better. The two companies we study built investment models that enabled them to generate surprising—even stunning—results on very modest investments.

- We begin by following the journey from Plan A to Plan B of Skype, with a business model that has the potential to disrupt the global telecom industry. The Luxembourg-based company offers long-distance calling for free—any time, anywhere, as long as both the caller and recipient have a PC—by combining the peer-to-peer software expertise its founders had developed in an earlier venture with Voice over Internet Protocol (VoIP) technology. Skype shows us that to start a new company, a big up-front investment isn't always necessary, especially if the founders have the expertise to spend their own time (not someone else's money) to design a compelling product before investment is needed.

- We then return to the skies and look at Europe's Go ("Go") airline, which, on its journey to a viable Plan B, found ways to compete head-to-head with the likes of Ryanair, whose story we recounted in chapter 5. The Go story offers some important lessons for starting ventures inside an established company and about investment models more generally.

In reading these cases, you will notice two themes. First, you will see that, ultimately, less investment really does spell higher returns for you, the entrepreneur. And that is probably one of your goals. You'll also obtain from these two cases a window into the trade-offs involved in taking capital from external investors.

Case 1: Skype Reinvents the Telecom Industry

Let's start with a short quiz about two recent start-ups in the telecom industry, both of which set out to exploit the power of the Internet and undercut existing pricing on long-distance telephone calling.

Question 1: During the thirteen months from its inception in August 2003 to September 2004, Skype signed up 7 million users. How many marketing dollars do you think Skype spent to attract these users?

☐ Zero

☐ $1–$1 million

☐ $1 million–$10 million

☐ More than $10 million

Question 2: Now, how much do you think New Jersey–based Vonage spent on marketing to attract the 1.4 million subscribers it had not one, but four years after its inception?

☐ Zero

☐ $1–$1 million

☐ $1 million–$10 million

☐ $246 million

Let's begin with the answer to question 2. In its first four years of existence, Vonage spent some $246 million on marketing alone. In that time, it attracted nearly 1.4 million users and posted an operating loss of $192.9 million.[1]

If you chose zero for question 1, you are correct. And contrary to what one might expect, the company that made less up-front investment was— dramatically!—the more successful of the two. In its first year of operation, Skype didn't spend a single penny on marketing. Yet it attracted 7 million users.[2] That's a big difference in marketing spent for lopsided results. Indeed, Skype and Vonage had very different investment models for starting their businesses—one required very little investment, the other quite a lot.

Investment? Who Needs It?

Is it possible to start a company with almost no initial investment? Just ask Niklas Zennström and Janus Friis. They've made a career out of it. Their biggest hit, Skype, was sold to eBay for $2.6 billion. Hmmm . . . little initial investment, leading to a $2.6 billion sale. That sounds like a pretty good ROI and an outstanding investment model!

Zennström and Friis met in 1991, while working on a European telecom project called Tele2. The two Scandinavians (Zennström is Swedish, Friis is Danish) were fascinated by peer-exchanged data, otherwise referred to as Peer-to-Peer or P2P. The concept behind P2P was that individuals could share information directly with one another over the Internet. As Zennström recalled, "We realized that P2P, with a distributed base, could be used for lots of applications, so we decided to create the technology and build the business from there."[3] His and Friis's first such venture, KaZaA, was founded on technology that gave users the ability to exchange files—music or otherwise—from one personal computer to another. The exchange didn't require an intermediary server or other hardware in the middle. They had the skills to develop the software. Hence, there was no up-front investment to start KaZaA.

Launched in 2000, KaZaA soon became the world's largest P2P file-sharing site. While highly successful at attracting users, KaZaA became famous, like Napster in the United States, for allowing users to illegally swap music. With the recording industry chasing KaZaA for copyright infringement, Zennström and Friis sold the company in early 2002 for a very modest $500,000. Small change, given their grand ambitions.

But the two entrepreneurs weren't finished with P2P. In fact, they had only just begun. They set out to find a use for their P2P technology that would not land them in jail. A legal Plan B, based on the illegal KaZaA analog!

Zennström knew what they wanted to accomplish: "The question we were asking was: how can we disrupt existing business models and create sustainable competitive advantage?" They decided to "do a KaZaA" on the long-distance telephone industry, allowing users to make calls over the Internet using P2P technology.[4] The two started developing Skype in the summer of 2002, finishing the first phase of their product by February 2003.

Skype's first beta version was made available to the public in August 2003. Zennström described the new venture as, ". . . a peer-to-peer telephony company which enables people worldwide to make free, unlimited, perfect-quality telephone calls over the Internet and to make calls to any other user who is using Skype as well."[5]

The duo's Plan B was revolutionary. Like KaZaA, Skype used P2P technology. And, like KaZaA, Skype required very little initial investment. The Skype software application allowed computers—when connected to the Internet—to talk to one another and to share voice data in almost the same way that KaZaA retrieved a file from another person's PC.[6] After downloading Skype to their computers, users needed only speakers and a microphone, as well as access to a high-speed Internet connection. Users could then make calls worldwide to anyone else that had Skype, absolutely free! By relying on its users' computers and broadband bandwidth, the company required no centralized servers and no dedicated network that telecom companies like AT&T and British Telecom had taken a century to build.

Zennström's and Friis's Plan B and Plan C

Skype's plan was to offer a free telephony service, allowing users to make calls from one Skype user to another—computer to computer, instead of using a telephone, Skype's key leap of faith—without charge. As we know from studying Google, free won't generate revenue. But, Zennström and Friis had good reason to make their initial service free. At the time Skype launched, it was founded on a closed Internet protocol, meaning it was not interoperable with other telephony services or technologies. That meant that Skype users could talk only with other Skype users. As a result, the only way Skype would be perceived as valuable to future users was if it had an enormous user base. What's the use of downloading Skype if the people you want to call haven't done so as well?

So, the goal was to attract as many people to use Skype as possible. The strategy for doing so was simple: making their calls totally free. Thai students studying in London, for example, would tell their families in Bangkok to download the Skype software and—poof!—long distance calls to and from their families back home became free!

Zennström explained, "The marginal cost to us of each call is zero because everything is peer-to-peer communication. We can provide free communications without losing money on it."[7] Behind the scenes, Zennström and Friis spent very little on infrastructure. What few operating costs Skype had were almost exclusively R&D and payroll, easily funded through the first several months from their KaZaA proceeds.[8] They let word of mouth from callers to intended recipients drive their marketing efforts. Their leap of faith was that they could get millions of users signed up for the free service, then worry about revenue. Google, an analog, had shown this to be possible. Plan C could come later, since getting into business cost so little. The good news was that in three short months, by November 2003, with 2.6 million users already on board, Skype's initial leap of faith was borne out.[9] Customers were signing up in droves.

Time for Plan C, and Some Investment!

Skype's first material need for investment would hit when SkypeOut, a service that would let subscribers make cut-rate calls from their Skype-enabled PC to a traditional phone, would be launched. At that point, Skype would have to invest in some telecommunications infrastructure. Since SkypeOut would interact with traditional phone users, Skype would have to purchase gateways and other hardware to convert its VoIP traffic to telephone signals. The company also needed to start paying connection and termination fees to the telephone companies. The goal of all this investment? Begin generating revenue.

All of these things would come at a cost. That investors would open their wallets for this change in their business model was another leap of faith. That November, with risk considerably lower because milestones had been met, Skype won $9 million of funding from Draper Fisher Jurvetson, a venture capital firm.[10] Other venture capital investors, including Bessemer Venture Partners and Mangrove Partners, chipped in. By January of 2004, the company had raised $19 million in venture funding, which, Zennström said, "should be enough for us to get to breakeven and be self-financing."[11]

With investment in hand, Plan C kicked into gear. Skype started offering its premium services, initially SkypeOut, for which users were charged
by the minute. SkypeIn was next, allowing Skype subscribers to receive
inbound calls from ordinary phones. Soon after these services launched,
Skype started offering voice mail, instant messaging, videoconferencing,
webcasts, and text messaging, each for a fee. By August 2005, some 2 million of Skype's 40 million users were taking advantage of one of its premium services.[12] Revenue generation had begun, at least among 5 percent
of Skype's customers. Plan C was working!

Let's compare Skype to Vonage, its American counterpart. By early 2005
Vonage had raised $408 million in financing (compared with Skype's $19
million) to support marketing and other costs in its American rollout.[13]
Vonage was not P2P, so Vonage needed network equipment, computers,
and all kinds of other fancy telecom gear before it could complete its first
call. And with the cost of all that gear, there was no way Vonage could offer
its calls for free, not nearly the compelling proposition that Skype offered.
Skype's early users had spread the word virally—free calls were a powerful
incentive—but Vonage had to buy its customers one at a time. So Vonage
spent massive amounts of money—more than half of its $533 million in
operating expenses in 2005—to acquire customers.[14] It's no wonder that
the Vonage investment model required so much money up front, unlike
that of Skype. "Typical customer acquisition cost in the phone industry
is several hundred dollars (per customer)," Zennström said. "We believe
in zero."[15]

"When we started Skype, our vision was to create a business that could
fundamentally transform the telecommunications industry and have a big
impact, by letting the whole world talk for free," Zennström said. "We
wanted to create a great, sustainable communication business."[16] Federal
Communications Commission chairman Michael Powell said, "I knew it was
over when I downloaded Skype . . . When inventors are distributing . . .
a program to talk to anybody else, and the quality is fantastic, and it's free, it's
over. The world will change now inevitably."[17]

With revenue starting to come in, Skype was on its way. By the end of
2004, with very little capital investment, Skype had generated $7 million
in revenue. In September of 2005, eBay purchased Skype for $2.6 billion
(plus $1.5 billion more if the company met certain milestones; though as
things turned out it did not). The two founders and their investors made

boatloads of money, as did their two hundred employees.[18] But did eBay? Its leap of faith was that Skype could transform its rapidly growing user base into a revenue and cash-flow-generating money machine.

In the first quarter of 2006, Skype brought in revenue of $79 million for eBay. By the first quarter of 2007, Skype had 196 million registered users. Only a small fraction of them, however, were placing calls of the revenue-generating variety—disappointing news for eBay, and the reason that Skype's founders and investors never collected the extra $1.5 billion that was contingent on performance. Still, thanks to their Spartan investment model, the original $2.6 billion in proceeds provided them and their investors with a very nice return! Was the Skype acquisition a good deal for eBay? By 2008, Skype was generating revenue at an annual rate of nearly $600 million and was expected to contribute $100 million of cash flow to eBay's coffers. "As five-year-old companies go, this is in the upper echelons of success," said Josh Silverman, Skype's president.[19] But rumors abound that eBay overpaid and that Skype is being dressed for sale. Whether a buyer will emerge, and at what price, remains to be seen.

Lessons from Skype

From the Skype story we've learned that a dash of ingenuity and the right technology can enable some kinds of businesses to get started on investment models of nil. It's almost always better, as an entrepreneur, to have proven some leaps of faith before raising major money, because doing so cuts your and your investors' risk. In turn, that means you get to keep more of your company's equity than you would if you need investors' capital for the earliest tests. If Zennström and Friis had raised venture capital to get started, they'd have kept far less of the proceeds of the sale to eBay, perhaps millions, not billions. Skype's is an investment model analog to remember.

A second key lesson from Skype is the manner in which the company was able to acquire customers largely cost-free. The nature of their business gave their earliest customers powerful incentives to get their friends and families to become active Skype members, too. If you can find a way in your proposed business to get the cost of customer acquisition down to little or nothing in the early days, that's among the powerful things you can do in building a viable investment model. But most customers won't spread the word on your behalf, in viral fashion, just because you'd like them to. They'll need powerful incentives, or they just won't do it. The power of "free" for Skype was vastly different from the Vonage pitch of much more modest savings on long-distance calls.

Skype's founders faced the challenge of starting from scratch, though they did have both the skills they needed and a nest egg from their sale of KaZaA to add to the pot. But for many executives in established companies, turning a good idea into a new product line produces a slightly different mix of challenges. Let's examine another investment model in just such a situation, the creation of Go, one of Ryanair's followers as a no-frills airline in Europe.

Case 2: Go Gets Going

Let's take another short quiz.

> *Question:* In 1997, how much did it cost to buy a brand new 737 airplane from Boeing?
>
> ☐ $5 million
> ☐ $10 million
> ☐ $25 million
> ☐ $50 million

If you guessed $50 million, you are pretty close. So how was it possible for Barbara Cassani to start budget airline Go (officially named Go Fly), with only £25 million (equivalent to about $40 million at the time) and make the company profitable within just three short years? The answer provides a good example of an impressive investment model in a corporate setting.

In 1987, not long after she finished her graduate work in international relations and embarked on her career, Cassani left Coopers & Lybrand to join British Airways (BA). Ten years and seven jobs later, Cassani was offered the chance to work on Project Hyacinth, BA's code name for a low-cost airline venture. BA, with pricing on its European routes under siege from Ryanair and others, thought it could play their game.

But the challenge didn't look easy. For one thing, BA expected at least an 18 percent return on its investment. And the concept of doing anything low-cost was completely foreign to BA's modus operandi and culture.

Project Hyacinth Gets Its Money and Gets Started

Cassani presented her Plan A proposal to the BA board in October 1997. The plan laid the framework for how a new airline could compete with the three existing, low-cost carriers in Europe. The premise was to keep start-up and operating costs to a minimum, offering competitive pricing (like the analog discount carriers already in business) but also good service, something that, in Cassani's view, the European no-frills carriers lacked (antilogs, in this respect), but Southwest Airlines (an analog) did much better.

Cassani and her team went to work on her plan. Finding an analog outside her industry, she modeled her proposed airline after the telephone banking company First Direct.[20] Cassani liked First Direct's customer-friendly business. She also liked First Direct's cost model. First Direct had no branch offices. Rather, the company relied exclusively on telephone banking. From Cassani's perspective, First Direct's agents provided exceptional service to customers 24 hours a day, 365 days a year. And First Direct didn't have to invest a lot of money in office space. She said, "This is what I wanted to do with my company . . . At the heart of what we are trying to do is make it really, really low price and then surprise people with the service being just that little bit nicer or our people being that bit friendlier."[21]

Cassani's team figured each flight would cost £5,000 for plane, pilots, crew, fuel, check-in, baggage handling, and maintenance. They believed sales and marketing costs would come to about £22 per passenger in the first few years. With these cost estimates, Cassani's leap of faith was that £25 million would suffice to bring the new airline to market and to breakeven in just three years. In November of that year, Cassani's wish was granted. She got approval from the board to proceed and was given a £25 million investment. She also received the independence she needed from BA for Go to be an autonomous subsidiary—able to make its own decisions with little input from BA's executives. Cassani said, "I requested complete independence to achieve the results and be judged by them."[22]

Building Go's Investment Model

Cassani and her team were thrifty, spending no more than necessary to get things done. The £25 million, Cassani knew, wouldn't last long. She rented office space from BA's pensions department, "then we begged and borrowed some bashed equipment and sorted a single telephone line. We were able to get the secondhand desks and chairs from another British Airways sub-sidiary, Air Miles, for almost nothing."[23] Cost containment was paramount: "Between cramped offices, secondhand furniture, no company cars, no free parking, outsourcing and general penny-pinching, we developed an endur-ing low-cost culture in Go."[24] Following Southwest's and Ryanair's analogs, Boeing 737 aircraft would comprise the entire fleet.[25]

Cassani had a target launch date of April 1998—just six months after having been handed the Hyacinth project and four short months after get-ting her funding. She was given three years to reach breakeven. The clock was ticking. Her biggest effort to limit her investment requirement was to lease aircraft rather than buy them outright. Initially, Go leased two used planes for just £235,000 per month. Copying easyJet, another low-cost air-line analog, check-in staff and engineering/maintenance services were out-sourced, saving recruitment, hiring, and training costs. She bought crew uniforms on the cheap for approximately £200 each (compared with the £2,000 spent by BA on its uniforms). And, the team bought a simple, low-cost system for reservations. BA's existing system was simply too costly.

Go Takes Off

In a matter of months, Cassani and her team had created a brand, chose routes, sold seats, found and secured planes, recruited and trained crew, received an Air Operator Certificate; all on a shoestring budget.

Go's inaugural flight, for Rome, departed on May 22, 1999, from London's Stansted airport, where Cassani had negotiated a good deal for landing rights. At that time, Go had ninety employees and two aircraft, and was offi-cially in last place in a race with three other European low-cost airlines: easy-Jet, Ryanair, and Debonair. Fast, but penurious, growth would be critical to success in this already highly competitive industry segment.

Cassani's team knew that they had to get the absolute most out of every penny spent. There had to be extraordinary efficiency and utilization on every capital and operating expense they made. As Cassani pointed out, "In no-frills airlines, costs don't increase directly in line with revenue. Full or empty, the cost of operating a plane stays about the same."[26] But all this attention to budget became a balancing act. Go wanted to differentiate itself from its competition by being low cost but high quality: "The trick was figuring out how to have good service without undermining the low-cost structure."[27]

By the end of its first year, Go had brought in £31 million in sales—well below what Cassani had forecasted. And its costs were too high. Plan A was not working. The company lost nearly £7 million in the three months of April, May, and June 1999.[28] Go had routes from Stansted to six destinations—Rome, Milan, Copenhagen, Lisbon, Bologna, and Edinburgh, with direct, no-frills competition on Rome and Edinburgh.[29] There was only one way out of the red and into the black, in Cassani's view: grow some more, and fly to new and less-competitive destinations. She needed a Plan B.

Cassani and her team made a decision to no longer grow as a "me-too" company, constantly mimicking the other low-fare carriers. Slightly better service to the commonly served destinations wasn't enough. Go had to do something different.

Go's Plan B Reaches Altitude

While it was still focused on low-cost travelers, Go decided to fly where no other low-cost European carrier had gone before. Operation Summer Sun launched in 1999, adding routes to underused airports serving some of Spain's most popular coastal vacation spots, such as Alicante, Ibiza, and Palma. The company then became the first low-cost carrier to fly into Prague, and in the winter added flights to ski destinations such as Lyon and Zurich. Cassani wrote, "We had found a new market for low-cost travel that hadn't been tapped."[30]

The new plan seemed to work. After two years of existence, Go had six hundred employees and £100 million in sales.[31] By September 2000, Go had achieved five straight months of profits, thanks to sun-seeking Brits. The company had posted a loss of £21.8 million in fiscal 1999–2000, but it was on the road to profitability at last, provided traffic held up during the coming slower winter months.[32]

Then, with almost no warning, BA got cold feet. It decided to put Go up for sale. On November 6, 2000, BA made a public announcement, "Following the successful establishment of Go as a leading no-frills airline in Europe, British Airways intends to realize the value created and offer the subsidiary for sale."[33]

Outside Investors Jump In

Instead of letting another low-cost carrier purchase the airline, Cassani led a management buyout (MBO) of Go. She and eighteen other top execs invested their own money. Aided by cash from 3i, a London-based private equity firm, they acquired Go for £110 million. In June 2001, BA's chief executive, Rod Eddington, said in a statement, "The deal represents an excellent return on our initial £25 million investment in the airline three years ago."[34] From Cassani's perspective the MBO was a win. She now had the chance to prove her chic but cheap model could work.

As promised, Go quickly reached full-year profitability. For the year ending March 31, 2001, Go posted pretax profits of £4 million on £159.7 million in revenue. Traffic was up 46 percent over the previous year.[35] In the summer of 2001, Go really took off, earning £10 million in profits in July and August alone.[36] Even in the aftermath of the terrorist incidents in New York on September 11, Go proved its staying power. Despite higher insurance rates and fewer passengers, Go made it through the fall of 2001 unscathed, selling 83 percent of its seats.[37] With its low fares and good service, Go received one accolade after another, winning *Business Traveler* magazine's top low-cost airline award and best low-cost airline in Britain from the U.K.'s *Daily Telegraph*. To Cassani and her team, the future looked bright.

Then, in December 2001, came a surprise. EasyJet, Go's U.K.-based nemesis, approached 3i with an interest in buying Go. The proposed offer was too good for 3i to pass up, equating to a 280 percent return on investment—nearly three times its money—in less than one year.[38] The transaction was done quickly, over the protests of some of Go's owner-managers, who thought there was still plenty of runway ahead as an independent airline. By the spring of 2002, the deal was completed. Go was sold to easyJet for £384 million, making easyJet Europe's biggest low-cost airline at the time and putting sizeable chunks of change into 3i's and Cassani's teams' pockets. But the fun of running a fast-growing independent venture was over.

Lessons from Go

The Go story provides a useful reminder that some of the most instructive analogs—First Direct, in Go's case—don't have to come from your own industry. And analogs from outside your industry are less likely to have been noticed and copied by your competitors. Everyone in the airline industry already knew about Southwest and Ryanair. But First Direct's low-cost but friendly service model was something quite different, an inspiration for Barbara Cassani and her team and a key ingredient in Go's ability to attract and retain its early customers.

We've seen that even in an established company, if you can beg, borrow, or steal what you need, so much the better. Lease, don't buy, at least at the outset, because it saves precious cash. If you can outsource instead of building from scratch, that may get you far enough down the runway to prove whether your plans—or planes—will fly. You can probably revisit such decisions later, after breakeven is achieved. And outsourcing usually saves time, too, getting you into business quicker.

Another lesson Cassani learned about starting a venture inside an established company was to move her operation out of BA's mainstream, so she and her team could do things differently. In an established company, it's hard to build an inherently different business model from the one already in use. Setting up an office that is away from the glare of the corporate floodlights can be very helpful.

Finally, Cassani's team knew that a viable investment model must not only minimize or offload the costs of getting started. It also had to minimize early operating losses until breakeven was reached. All too often, entrepreneurs or those starting ventures inside big companies assume that profits will ensue almost from day one. It's a fantasy, we're sorry to say. You must include in your thinking about your investment model the losses you will incur until you reach cash flow breakeven, your burn rate, as venture capital investors call it. And as any experienced entrepreneur or investor will tell you, it will probably take twice as long, and three times as much money, as you expect!

Lessons Learned About Investment Models

We said at the beginning of this chapter that a key goal of any investment model is to find a way to get the business started and to cash flow breakeven with as little investment as possible, while including some cash cushion for iterating to Plan B. There are exceptions to this rule, such as where network effects are central to the strategy, as for Skype; where economies of scale make it necessary to "get big fast," as we'll see in the Amazon case in chapter 8; and where a competitive footrace must be won. In such cases, raising more capital may be in order. But generally, whether it's your money or others', leaner is usually better. So, since

money doesn't grow on trees, what are the lessons for building your investment model?

- Counterintuitively, when it comes to raising capital, less can
  be more.

- There are trade-offs involved in taking institutional venture capital
  that it's wise to understand before pursuing that route.

Less Capital, or Later Capital, Can Be Better

Most of the time, identifying your leaps of faith and testing hypotheses to
prove or refute them is best done on less cash invested, wherever possible,
rather than more. You may view disconfirming results of your hypothesis
tests as good progress. But not all your investors are likely to agree! If you've
burned a lot of their money on hypothesis testing, they may not be happy.

Thus, for entrepreneurs, asking for £25 million up front, as Cassani did,
is usually a bad idea. Why? All the risks lie ahead of you, and your
investors will want to be compensated for those risks through a larger
stake in your company. Staging your investment so that more capital
comes in after key leaps of faith are tested and milestones met will probably leave you and your team with a larger share of the company than if you
ask for too much cash too early. Perhaps more important, if Plan A does
not work and you must move on to Plan B, you'll have a better chance of
raising more capital if you've not already burned too much of it. Who
wants to give money to someone who goes through capital like it's water?

So identify your analogs and antilogs, develop your leaps of faith and a
plan to test the hypotheses that grow out of them. Then raise just enough
funding to get through enough tests so that risk drops significantly, after
which you can raise more capital on much better terms. Knowing the size
of the stash you'll need to cover hypothesis tests that don't pan out isn't
easy, of course. It's an approach that's not for the faint of heart, but it will
help you remain frugal and keep your eye on the ball.

The Trade-offs Involved in Taking Venture Capital

As John tells his students, "The day you take a dollar or pound or rupee
from most venture capital investors is the day you have agreed to sell your
business." Why? Investors, perhaps unlike you, aren't in it for the ride.
They are in it for the liquidity, most commonly achieved by selling your

(and their) company, as happened in both of the cases in this chapter. They sold Skype to eBay and Go to easyJet. The little-known secret is that nowadays the vast majority of venture capital exits are the sale of the company to another, larger company. Initial public offerings happen—think Amazon or Google—but not very commonly.

So, if you have a start-up in mind and you are developing your investment model, think carefully about what your entrepreneurial dream holds for your future. Do you want to run your company for a long time, at the risk of undercapitalizing it, or do you want to accelerate it with venture capital at the risk of harvesting it with a sale, and, like Skype's Niklas Zennström and Janus Friis, do it all over again?

As Randy points out to his students and to the companies that his fund invests in, the best venture capitalists add significant value through their networks and their experience, alongside their capital. They also reduce risk by having learned how to build companies from scratch. It's their everyday job. They've seen numerous analogs and antilogs and they've known some of them intimately. What they offer you is a smaller slice of what may become, with their capital and assistance, a much larger pie. These are real pluses. But because it's their money, what comes along with their capital is their significant participation in your company's destiny, for better or worse, and in your role therein. And if you and they don't agree? Well, their money bought them a seat at the table and they are entitled to their say.

If you need lots of capital to prove or refute your leaps of faith or to cover the investment required, venture capital investors are about the only sources from which you can raise it. So if you build an investment model that requires venture capital, do so thoughtfully and deliberately, not just because venture capital is the "cool" thing to do.

Q&A with John and Randy

By now we hope we have convinced you to think carefully about building your investment model and how much cash you really need—or don't need. But there are probably a number of questions about how to really build it still swirling in your head. Among them may be these:

- It's easy to say you should try to get by on less up-front investment. But how can you really do it?

- How should you decide which sort of investor—3Fs, angels, or VCs—is right for your venture?

- How open should you be with prospective investors about your pitfalls so far in getting to Plan B?

- What if you're in a large company? Do the lessons of this chapter still apply?"

Getting By on Less Cash

As you build your investment model, don't let your first draft be your last. Think twice—and then twice more—about the cash you'll need to get started and to get to break-even cash flow. Then consider how you can put a bold red line through each of the items. Can you borrow it? Lease it? Delay it? Outsource it for less cash up front, even if it costs a bit more? Or even get somebody else to pay for it? Can you turn fixed costs (which increase your risk of running out of cash) into variable costs, even though doing so will cut profit margins, at least in the short term? Doing these things to trim your need for cash can give you a longer runway for identifying leaps of faith and testing hypotheses and can transform your risk and your overall business model. Drawing those red lines and then implementing the steps they imply—finding lessors or outsourced suppliers, for example—can let you get started on building your business, rather than spending your precious time beating a trail to investors' doorsteps with little more to show than your still-unproven idea and a slide presentation.

What Sort of Investor Is Right?

Once you are on to an investment model that will enable you to test some key leaps of faith and maybe get a first customer on less money than you had ever thought possible, choose the right sources for your initial funds. Banks? Forget it, unless you care to max out your personal credit cards or mortgage your house, neither of which is likely to make your mom or your spouse very happy. Banks are a waste of time at this point, because they'll usually only lend against collateral or proven cash flow. Your nascent business has neither.

What about seasoned business angels or venture capitalists? There's a time and place for their money and expertise, but, unless you have relationships with VCs or angels, testing your initial leaps of faith is probably better done with money from two of the three Fs, family and friends. Why? They love you! Tell them up front that Plan A almost certainly won't work, and that they'll probably lose the entire grubstake you've asked for. Then, if Plan A fails, you and they won't feel quite so bad. Keep them informed of your dashboard results, and whatever the outcome, they'll still love you. And maybe, if you are lucky or smart, their modest amount of cash will get you to Plan B.

Once you have iterated your way toward a better business model, though, you may decide that, with some key milestones met and risk correspondingly reduced, professional investors—whether angels or VCs—can provide useful business-building skills and cash to boot, all of which can help you build a successful business for the long term.

How Open Should I Be About My Journey to Plan B?

Ideas, as the saying goes, are a dime a dozen. An idea that has been at least partially proven, with the concept shown workable and a few customers on board, is a whole different animal. Simply put, the farther along you are, the lower the risk.

With a bit of experience filling your sails, investors' worries shift from proving the concept or demonstrating marketability to whether or not you and your team can execute. So talking prospective investors through your dashboarding journey to date—and the next steps in your plan—is a good idea. They'll probably appreciate that you understand the risks and that you're willing to take prudent leaps of faith and test the hypotheses that grow out of them.

What If I'm in a Big Company?

In our experience, the principles in this chapter—minimizing the capital you need, staging its commitment, using analogs from outside your industry, and so on—hold for ventures inside large companies as they do for raw start-ups. The same logic applies.

What's Next?

We have now seen how each of the five elements of your business model can form the bedrock of a Plan A or Plan B that will work, and may, if you're sagacious and a little lucky, wreak havoc with your competitors.

Really, though, as you probably have noticed, it takes more than just one of the five elements to create a winning business model that will stand the test of time. For each of the examples we've seen so far, there were other business model elements that also came into play, though perhaps less prominently or fundamentally than the ones we focused on. Thus, in chapter 8, we bring the business model elements together by examining companies whose business models, by design, were truly multidimensional.

John and Randy's Investment Model Checklist

Building your investment model looks easy on the face of it. Just add up the costs of everything you'll need to get started, and ask for the money! Nothing, really, could be further from the truth. There are two key phases in your investment model, and each has questions you'll need to answer with evidence.

The prelaunch phase

✓ What are the hard assets—facilities, equipment, and so on—you'll need prelaunch? What will they cost to buy, rent, or lease?

✓ What are the development activities that must be completed before you can launch? What will they cost?

✓ What are the leaps of faith you can test prior to launch? What will it cost to test them?

Now think twice, and twice more: which of the above can you delay or find a way to do without, or do more primitively or simply? Fancy can wait.

The postlaunch phase, until you hit cash flow breakeven

✓ What revenue and gross margin can you generate to contribute to your ongoing costs?

✓ How lean an operating model can you run pre-breakeven?

Finally, every leap of faith tested, every milestone met, reduces risk. The later you can wait to raise each round of money, the better the terms on which you can raise it. Thus:

✓ Which key leaps of faith, if proven, will signal stepwise reductions in risk? How much cash—see above—will it take to reach each of them, and how much of your funding can be postponed until later?

CHAPTER 8

Can You Balance a One-Legged Stool?

Multidimensional Business Models

WE HAVE GONE EASY on you in the previous five chapters. Taking the five elements of the business model one step at a time, we've had the luxury of examining each element under a microscope. We've seen little-known newcomers like Silverglide and Shanda, well-known start-ups like eBay and Costco, and long-established companies like Toyota and Dow Jones employ one of these elements as a foundation for their success.

Business is never so straightforward. Metaphorically speaking, what each of these companies built was not a one-legged stool. Their business models were, in reality, multilegged. One leg—the key business model element on which our earlier analyses focused—was made of solid steel, providing rigid, unwavering support. But the other business model elements, to which we gave little attention, were also in place. They provided balance and stability, perhaps even elegance and grace.

What's more, companies are successful when the five elements of their business models work together, like the different instrumental parts—strings, brass, reeds, percussion, and so on—in a Mozart symphony. Toyota's gross margins were impressive, but wouldn't have meant anything had the company not had a revenue model that made customers want to drive Toyotas and an operating model that was as efficient as its gross margin model was lucrative. Go's investment model worked for two main reasons: (1) because Barbara Cassani and her team soon found their way to Plan B, a better revenue model serving sunny Spanish resorts; and (2) because her focus on costs of all kinds, not just investment, made Go's gross margin and operating models work efficiently, too.

Goal for Chapter 8: Pull your Business Model Thinking Together to Build Economic Viability and Sustainable Competitive Advantage

In this chapter, we examine three highly entrepreneurial companies whose success rested on a combination of the business model elements in chapters 3 through 7, where no single element stood out. Instead, their farsighted founders wove an intricate combination of two or more elements into difficult-to-imitate patterns that made them economically viable and gave them rapid growth and sustainable competitive advantage in three of the most hotly competitive industries on the planet today: apparel retailing, wireless telephony, and Internet retailing. Each of these stories shares three common themes:

- The business model grew out of a customer-focused strategy. The key benefit to be offered to customers—the customer promise—was crystal clear at the outset and remained so.

- The founder created a thoughtful combination of two or more business model elements—a strategy for the business—that was fundamentally different from current industry practices, the industry's existing Plan A.

- The strategy had favorable implications for generating and sustaining positive cash flow thereby enabling the founder to rapidly grow the business, too.

As such, the examples vividly illustrate a key contention we hold: that creating one's business model—considering one element at a time and all of them together—is a fundamentally strategic activity. The strategy, as expressed in the five business model elements, is what drives cash flow, profitability, and growth, as ultimately reflected in the financial statements, whether planned or actual. Thus, in our view, the financial statements, rather than being a driver or goal of the business creation process, become simply the *by-product* of clear and disciplined strategic thinking. Analogs, antilogs, the leaps of faith that follow from them, and the well thought out dashboards that measure the outcomes of the hypothesis tests are what make this process happen. And the business model that results—a revenue model, gross margin model, and all the rest—is the output of the process.

We will now view three cases through our business model lens, to show how and why their multidimensional business models worked successfully:

- Fast-growing Spanish retailer Zara exemplifies the balanced approach to its business model, bringing success from the outset with its initial Plan A.

- Amazon.com, now much more than a bookseller, has woven its business model together into a more efficient operation as it iterates toward its Plan Z.

- Celtel International, the hugely successful mobile telecom operator serving sub-Saharan Africa, built a strong multidimensional business model that operated beautifully from day one.

We'll also see how each of these companies, like Southwest in the airline industry, broke industry rules to create a disruptive Plan B, a new business model for its industry (apparel retailing, online retailing, and mobile telephony, respectively) that has stood the test of time and that, in Zara's case, defies imitation, even today.

Case 1: Zara Invents Fast Fashion

In 2008, Inditex, the Spanish-based retailer, operated more than one thousand Zara stores and nearly three thousand others in over seventy countries. Its flagship chain, Zara, sold women's, men's, and children's clothing and accessories. Daniel Piette, the fashion director of the French luxury goods group LVMH, described Zara as "possibly the most innovative and devastating retailer in the world."[1] Chic: yes. Profitable: yes. High-priced: no.

Zara's is a story of how a carefully crafted combination of sourcing, merchandising, and distribution strategies created a unique new pattern of revenue, gross margin, and working capital models that enabled Zara to grow like wildfire and take its young fashionista customers by storm.

Early in his life, Amancio Ortega worked in a small retail shop in his hometown of La Coruña, Spain. In the early 1960s he started designing and producing garments on his kitchen table, opening his own store in 1963.[2] His goal was to make and sell garments—housecoats in particular—for "cheaper than anyone else."[3] Twelve years later, espousing the same mission, Ortega opened the first Zara store, offering fashionable clothing at affordable prices. Throughout the 1970s and 1980s Ortega opened Zara stores across Spain. International expansion followed, throughout Europe, the Americas, the Middle East, and Asia in the 1990s. In its public offering in May 2001, Inditex, Zara's parent company, raised $2 billion for 26 percent of the company. By fiscal year 2006, Inditex passed the €5 billion mark in sales and was highly profitable.[4] How did Zara do it? Let's explore its strategy in light of its gross margin model first, in contrast to that of another apparel retailer, Gap.

Zara's Fast Fashion Strategy Boosts Gross Margins

To get a sense of just how dramatic Zara's entrance into the retail market was, consider fashion retailer Gap (founded in 1969). If you have never been to a Gap store, let us describe what you would see. Usually you'd find yourself in a fairly spacious store chock full of clothing for men, women, and sometimes kids. Typically, the back quarter of the store would be reserved for sale racks, and it would seem as though literally 25 percent of the clothing was marked down.

In contrast to its Gap antilog, markdown merchandise will rarely be found at Zara. How does Zara avoid marking down its merchandise? First, it prices its apparel affordably from day one, not at some higher price that will then go on sale. However, what is "affordable" varies by country and city. If Parisian customers are willing to pay higher prices than those in Barcelona, Zara sets its pricing accordingly.

Second, and more importantly, Ortega's fast fashion strategy gets the credit. His company's strategy revolves around four processes, all tailored for speed: design, production, distribution, and sales. These processes run so smoothly that it takes Zara as little as two weeks for a new item of clothing to go from design to the store (as much as twelve times faster than its competition).[5] Inditex CEO José Maria Castellano says, "We can create a new fashion line in days. Our competitors manufacture most of their collections in advance. But that involves guessing what customers will want six or nine months down the line. Our model minimizes the risk of being saddled with lots of unsold stock, and it maximizes full prices because very little gets remaindered."[6] Adds Zara's Carmen Melon, "We only send our stores what they need. There is no stock that doesn't move; we have no extra inventory."[7]

From the start, as part of its strategy, Zara designed its own fashions, often copying a designer garment that, say, Britney Spears or another celebrity had just worn. It treated each new style as a leap of faith, starting with a small production run, rather than placing a bold bet, and testing this small quantity of merchandise in the marketplace. The small runs that Zara created reduced its exposure to fashion faux pas and kept "margin-stripping markdowns to a minimum," said Kris Miller, a New York-based retail analyst with Bain & Co.[8] If the merchandise sold well, as hypothesized, Zara produced more, but not so much more that it would have an overabundance—just enough to sell through the items quickly. If an item didn't do well immediately, the company halted production. "It is our way of minimizing fashion risk," Castellano said.[9] As a result of its limited production runs, Zara rarely had to mark down its goods. In fact, Zara held but two sales each year.

There was one more piece in the Zara tapestry that completed the pattern. While it bought some staples in the Far East—for instance, black T-shirts, which are unlikely to ever go out of style—Zara didn't use low-cost countries, such as China or Bangladesh, to produce its fast fashion production runs. Doing so would have made it impossible to get new styles—some eleven thousand each year[10]—to stores quickly. Instead, the company contracted the assembly of most of its goods to companies in neighboring Spanish and Portuguese towns. By producing its merchandise in Europe, Zara spent about 15 percent more on labor than its rivals did by manufacturing in low-cost labor markets.[11] But the slightly higher manufacturing cost was more than offset by other benefits. Mike Shearwood, managing director of Zara UK, explained why: "The extra margin is superior because there is no wastage, no markdowns, and no problem of getting a collection wrong."[12]

Zara's Revenue Model Lures Shoppers to Return for More

Fast fashion had implications for Zara's revenue model, too. It meant that some items disappeared within a week of entering a store. For Zara shoppers, this created a feeling of scarcity, as the shopper knew that the item may not be in the store the next time they shopped. "They've built up an excitement around snapping up new clothes before they go," according to Bain's Miller. Scarcity made shoppers more apt to buy an item when they saw it for the first time and it made them more likely to go back to the store often to see what was new. And, for fashionistas who would die if they saw someone else wearing the same outfit, the chances of that happening were considerably reduced.

Zara's Working Capital Model

Manufacturing close to its principal European market and turning inventories quickly was good for Zara's working capital model too. The processes of the Spanish and Portuguese suppliers Zara used were tightly integrated with Zara's systems.[13] This meant that, in return for predictable high-volume business with Zara, these suppliers gave it favorable sixty-day terms. With customers buying their clothes with cash or credit cards, Zara had its customers' cash in hand in less than a week. Fast-turning inventory paired with quick customer cash and slow pay for its merchandise: an attractive working capital model, indeed!

Fast Fashion Versus Slow Fashion

Let's return to Gap to see what all of this means in a competitive sense. Buying most of its apparel in Asia, Gap buyers placed bold bets on which fashions would sell in the upcoming season, still months away. Bell-bottoms or straight legs? Short skirts or shorter? Fuchsia blouses or tangerine? Leaps of faith, all! These big bets were difficult to test, too. Further, Gap was required to pay some of its vendors in advance, before its inbound merchandise was shipped. It used letters of credit to ensure payment to these vendors, tying up cash. In 2006 Gap showed $55 million in "restricted cash" on its balance sheet, representing the letters of credit it needed to pay its suppliers.[14] And once the garments arrived in the United States or Europe in container-sized lots, some sat in Gap warehouses from which store inventories were then replenished. What a difference! Compared with Zara, Gap had more precious cash tied up in letters of credit. More Gap merchandise was sitting in inventory. As a result, Gap suffered far more exposure to the vicissitudes of always-fickle fashion trends. No wonder the back quarter of a Gap store always seems to be on sale!

Ortega's fast fashion strategy and Zara's results speak for themselves. In 2006, Zara parent Inditex became Europe's largest clothing retailer, over-taking Swedish fashion retailer H&M.[15] Gap, whose performance had steadily slipped since 1999, was left in the dust. John Thorbeck of Supply Change, an Oregon consulting firm, puts it succinctly: "Zara has proven that speed and flexibility matter more than pure price. They've turned the old way of doing business on its head."[16]

Growing fast and profitably when times are good is one thing. Perhaps a more stringent test of a robust business model is how fast-growing companies perform when times get tough. As the global credit crunch hammered many retailers' performance in late 2008, Inditex continued to out-perform its competitors. For its year ended January 2009, Zara's revenue was up again, to €10.4 billion ($14 billion), up from €9.4 billion in 2007–2008, though earnings were flat at €1.25 billion. Gap, on the other hand, reported an eight percent decline in its full-year 2008–2009 revenue, to $14.5 billion. While many of its competitors resorted to deep discounting to keep the cash registers ringing, Inditex chose not to. "We prefer to stick to our commercial policy even in the current environment," reported Marcos Lopez, Inditex director of capital markets. "The key driver in our stores is the right fashion. Price is important, but it comes second."[17] And a superb business model sure doesn't hurt!

Lessons from Zara's Strategy and Business Model

Why has Zara's fast fashion strategy worked so well, and caused headaches for its competitors? Ortega's strategy favorably impacted at least three of the five elements of Zara's business model:

- *Revenue model:* The customers wanted the latest fashions, and Zara was best positioned to deliver what was hot: "Buy it today, because it won't be here next week. Oh, and come back next week to see what new things we'll have in store." And it was able to make better fashion judgments in season, rather than in advance. Zara had the latest fashions that its trendy customers wanted to buy.

- *Gross margin model:* Initially, Zara's cost of goods sold (COGS) was slightly higher than the Asia-reliant competition, as the company's fashion assortment was produced in more expensive local European countries. However Zara made up the difference by yielding better overall gross margins, owing to far fewer markdowns than its competitors.

- *Working capital model:* With customer's cash in the till, fast-turning inventory, and generous payment terms from tightly integrated suppliers, Zara was in an excellent position to grow its business on its customers' and suppliers' cash.

Zara competes very successfully in one of the most brutally competitive industries in the world—apparel retailing—and has extended its model to other fashion categories like home furnishings and decor. Amancio Ortega's business model was so ingeniously designed from the beginning that he did not have to iterate much—if at all—to get to a business model, what we now know as fast fashion, that was a disruptive breakthrough for his industry, making life difficult for Gap and others. Best of all for Zara, the model is complex enough that only a few others have been able to imitate it successfully, thereby putting in place Zara's foundation for sustainable competitive advantage for more than two decades. In our view, Ortega, a true visionary and retailing pioneer, is to apparel retailing as Southwest's Herb Kelleher is to airlines.

We now move from high street fashion to the cash-drenched, mid-1990s in the United States. Thanks to the dot-com boom, just about anyone could raise millions in venture capital with a business plan scrawled on a cocktail napkin, or so it seemed. There, at the same time that Zara was choosing next month's fashions, a hedge fund analyst named Jeff Bezos had a very different idea. On a cross-country trip with his new wife—complete with a just-married sign on the back of the car—Bezos put together a plan for an online bookseller, Amazon.

Case 2: Amazon: A Dot-Com Business Model That Worked (Eventually!)

Arguably, Amazon made it through its first nine years of red ink because its investment model—raising boatloads of money from private, then public, shareholders; then the corporate bond markets, too—was fortuitously timed during the frenzied and exuberant days of the dot-com heyday. All this cash gave Bezos the runway to identify and examine new leaps of faith, one after another, and gave him the wherewithal to continue to invest in the business following the dot-com bust. The story we want to tell here, however, isn't the story of Amazon's early rise and Bezos' restless brilliance. It's the considerably later story—and less-known tale—that interests us. It took Amazon nearly a decade to finally piece together a business model— its Plan Z—that delivered positive cash flow, thereby assuring its long-term survival and impact. That its early success in raising so much cash gave Amazon the staying power to figure things out is undeniable. Without all that cash, Amazon might well have bitten the dust along with many of its dot-com counterparts. But the step-by-step story of how Bezos and his team iterated beyond the red ink is packed with lessons that apply to companies of all kinds, not just dot-com wonders.

Amazon.com launched as a bookselling Web site in 1995. We fast forward to 1999. By focusing his company on the three things customers wanted from an online retailer—the best selection, the lowest prices, and the cheapest and most convenient delivery—Bezos had led Amazon to astonishing growth.[18] His initial "Get Big Fast" (GBF) strategy had worked, in a sense. Revenue for 1999 was $1.6 billion. Not half bad for a four-year-old company. The product assortment had grown beyond books to consumer electronics, music, toys, tools—practically any consumer product you could think of. To support its growth, Amazon's distribution center space had grown from 300,000 square feet to more than 3 million, thanks to five new automated warehouses built in 1999, at price tags of $60 million each.[19]

But Amazon was also burning cash at an alarming rate. Reported losses had mounted to $720 million. In business model terms, Amazon's gross margin model and its operating model were simply out of sync. Despite the soaring sales curve generated by its ever-expanding GBF revenue model, there wasn't enough gross margin to cover the operating costs— warehouses, staff, information technology, and the like. And cash was tied up in a doubling of inventory from twenty-one to forty-nine days in order to head off the poor service complaints that other dot-commers were hearing from customers. But it created a serious problem for Amazon's bottom line and cash flow.

In 2000 Amazon reported losses of $1.4 billion by its year-end. Under the GBF strategy, while revenues were growing, the company had not managed its skyrocketing expenses very well (recall Patagonia founder Yvon Chouinard's costly wake-up call from chapter 4). There was no formal budget at all.[20] The question often repeated by the business press, "Will Amazon.com ever make money?" grew from a whisper to a full-throated roar.[21] Amazon's stock price suffered, putting into question its ability to raise more cash in the way it had before.

Amazon Tightens Its Belt and Starts Iterating Its Operating Model

Bezos looked outside Amazon to get serious about managing costs and working capital, as well as revenue growth. Bezos brought in Jeff Wilke from AlliedSignal to be Amazon's vice president of operations. Wilke sang a new tune: "Our operational performance this year will be evaluated on the bottom line. If it doesn't show up on the bottom line, we're not working on the right stuff."[22]

In Wilke's view, Amazon's key challenge for 2000 was to learn: "We have a large distribution center network that we built mostly last year, with a huge amount of information technology and nice automation in the right places. Now, we put people into it for the first time, and . . . people who are just learning how this thing works during the holidays are ramping up to a level that the company—in fact, no one—has ever seen. That creates an enormous opportunity to learn."[23]

Over the next year, by automating everything possible, a huge leap of faith, the company improved efficiency.[24] The devil was in the operational details. "Your order spends several hours in our process," said Wilke. In his view, every time a person could touch or influence an order, that touch point introduced the possibility of a mistake. Making mistakes and checking to catch them was inherently inefficient. "So if we can get picking to be 100 percent perfect, we'll never have to go back later in the process and send that bucket of goods all the way to be repicked."[25] Achieving perfect picking saved time, saved money, and made Amazon people more efficient.

In Wilke's view, a key part of the challenge was to improve Amazon's supply chain. By cutting in half the time it took Amazon to get a toy, a book, a DVD, or any other product, Amazon lowered its inventory. Less inventory meant fewer people to handle it, thus lower operating costs. It meant further growth could be accommodated without adding additional distribution capacity, spreading existing operating costs over a wider revenue base.

As its supply chain improved, its internal processes got smoother, and the Amazon people learned how to operate in an automated environment, Amazon's operating model would get better.

Amazon Shaves Dozens of Days from Its Working Capital Model

Wilke's medicine worked magic with Amazon's working capital model, too, enabling inventory to turn much faster, from forty-nine days of inventory in 1999 to seventeen days in 2001.[26] CFO Warren Jenson joined the party, working on the trade terms with Amazon's suppliers. He was able to extend Amazon's accounts payables days from twenty in 1999 to fifty-two in 2001.[27] The result of all these changes was that Amazon's working capital picture shifted radically. As Jenson put it, "We're driving toward negative working capital as fast as we can, because it is an advantage to our business model."[28]

What's more, as Amazon improved its operations and working capital, it was able to improve its service to customers. In reporting the company's 2001 fourth quarter results, Jenson said, "Our improvements in productivity allowed us to lower book prices and now allow us to offer free shipping" on some orders.[29]

Amazon Iterates Its Revenue Model and Gross Margins Soar

Meantime, other Amazon executives were exploring ways to get out of the red. By taking a giant step back, Bezos and his team realized that they had something to sell that generated far better margins than books, DVDs, or lawn furniture. In fact, they were sitting on an enormous asset that could help other companies do business online. At its roots, Amazon was an extraordinary e-commerce platform; a platform that other companies might pay for to support their own e-commerce. Yet another iteration, and another leap of faith. Bezos explained, "We've been talking about ourselves as a 'platform.' It's a foundation or a workbench from which you can do a lot of things. In our case, it consists of customers, technology, e-commerce expertise, distribution centers, and brand."[30]

Amazon iterated its revenue model from a straight e-tailer to an online service provider, selling platform solutions as well as merchandise. First, the company started accommodating third parties such as used-book sellers, allowing them to sell their own goods on Amazon's site. Amazon collected commissions on sales generated by these third parties. We've already seen how attractive eBay's gross margin model was, and here Amazon was essentially copying the eBay analog, but in a business-to-business setting.

Next, in its first large-platform deal, Amazon provided an e-commerce backbone for the biggest American toy retailer, Toys "R" Us, taking over responsibility for all of Toys "R" Us's e-commerce activities. A large deal with Target, the large U.S.-based discount chain, soon followed. Amazon provided Target with a similar backbone to Toys "R" Us.[31] In return, Target gave Amazon a small cut of its online sales. In addition to its operating and working capital models, Amazon's gross margin model, as the eBay analog predicted, was starting to look better, too, as COGS on these online platform deals was, like eBay's, very modest.

Mark Stabingas, Amazon's vice president of worldwide business development and services sales, articulated the subtle but crucial change in Amazon's strategy. "We're thinking about ourselves as a technology company and a technology platform. The universe of opportunity is larger than if we just want to think about ourselves as a retail business."[32] By selling its platform, Amazon was no longer reliant on individual customers who spent a few hundred dollars a year on goods. Its new customers—corporations seeking online retailing expertise—were willing to spend millions for a proven e-commerce platform. And, there were far fewer costs associated with selling a platform. Amazon didn't have to worry about inventories or warehouses or book publishers or shipping, though in some cases it agreed to do those things too. Amazon spokesman Bill Curry said, "It's important to acknowledge who has what expertise. We have the expertise in online sales, fulfillment, and customer service. We can get to profitability sooner by playing off those skills."[33]

A *BusinessWeek* article summarized Amazon's improving prospects: "With gross margins of 60 percent and higher—more than double Amazon's total gross margins—these (technology services) deals will deliver the cash that could finally push the company into the black. Even more important, such margin-rich revenues address Amazon's perpetual profitability challenge. In 2001, technology-service deals will total about $200 million. That's only 7 percent of Amazon's $3 billion annual revenues, but the business accounts for 18 percent of its gross margins."[34]

As *BusinessWeek* had predicted, by the end of 2001, things were starting to look up. The company's revenue was still growing, from $2.7 billion in

2000 to $3.1 billion in 2001. It had cut its losses in half. Operating expenses were starting to drop as a percentage of sales. And, due to its new services business, gross margins were finally starting to improve. Amazon had its first profitable quarter in the forth quarter of 2001. The combination of a still-strong revenue model, improved operational efficiency, and the new services business paid off.

In 2003, Amazon had its first fully profitable year, with $35 million in profits on revenue of $5.3 billion. In 2004, the company earned $588 million of net income on revenue of $6.9 billion. Perhaps best of all, Amazon's days of working capital were minus twenty-four, freeing up nearly half a billion dollars of spare cash it could use for other things, like new systems development to support new technology services deals. Soon after, Amazon boosted its working capital model again by adding AmazonPrime, a $79 membership service (recall cash-up-front analogs Dow Jones and Costco from chapter 6) allowing members to access free two-day shipping, as well as overnight shipping for a paltry $3.99, among other perks.[35] By 2007, Amazon accounted for 6 percent of the $136 billion in U.S. online sales, up from 5.1 percent in 2006. And its free cash flow had risen by 140 percent. Says Citigroup Internet analyst Mark Mahany, "That's pretty dramatic."[36]

Lessons from Amazon's Relentless Iteration

In three short years, from 2000 to 2003, Amazon evolved iteratively from a dot-com high-flyer that was burning cash to a well-run, highly efficient provider of online retailing and other services, with positive cash flow and its long-elusive profitability finally in hand. What was it that enabled Amazon to turn the corner?

- *Operating model:* For one, its GBF strategy enabled it to reach sufficient scale that it was worthwhile to automate virtually all of its processes. Automating, in turn, enabled Amazon to improve on its already superb reputation for great customer service while cutting its operating costs at the same time. Too often, companies gain efficiency at the expense of good customer service. With the customer-centric Bezos at Amazon's helm, that simply was not going to happen.

- *Revenue and gross margin models:* Second, Amazon realized that its scale and its skills had given it something other companies needed—the ability to do business online without incurring years of potentially loss-making learning. Amazon had already learned, and was able to peddle its learning, as high-margin services, to others. By 2008 third-party shipments accounted for a third of its unit sales.

What Amazon has really done, though, is what this book is all about. In that sense, Amazon is our poster child. In the words of *Fortune* magazine's Josh Quittner, Amazon's "rise into *Fortune 500*-dom actually has little to do with innovation and more to do with iteration. If anything, Amazon demonstrates how a cutting-edge Internet company—of all things—can succeed slowly. The trick is taking a million tiny steps—and learning quickly from your missteps."[37]

Bezos freely admits that great lessons are born from leaps of faith: "A lot of decisions around consumers are like that. When you do the math, it's not clear what will happen."[38] We couldn't agree more. Identify your analogs, antilogs, and some leaps of faith. Develop and test hypotheses with a dashboard. And determine the effect of your strategic decisions on the five elements of your business model. If Jeff Bezos can iterate to success, so can you.

But beware the temptation to follow Amazon's "Get Big Fast" strategy. Such a strategy can be effective, provided that a company can raise boatloads of cash and can get big enough, fast enough, to reach economies of scale. But those are two very daunting conditions, so we don't recommend the Amazon model as an analog for just any business. There are hundreds, if not thousands, of failed dot-com companies whose powerful antilogs argue against the GBF approach. In fact, had Amazon not raised so much cash when it could, it would have been exposed to the vagaries of the capital market in the dot-com bust, and who knows where it would be today?

Of course, a lucky few of you will have the pleasure of striking the right balance on your first attempt. Our next case is such an example: In nine short years, Celtel International put cell phones into the hands of 27 million consumers in the farthest corners of the most impoverished continent on the planet, Africa. Celtel's founders and investors earned billions in the process. Unimaginable, perhaps, but true. Let's examine the Celtel story.

Case 3: Celtel International: Where Others Saw Poverty, Mo Ibrahim Saw Opportunity

At the turn of the twenty-first century, there were 800 million people in Africa, some 600 million of them in sub-Saharan Africa. Africa was home to thirty-four of the fifty poorest countries on Earth,[39] where per capita GDP ranged from $180 to $5,000 per year, a far cry from the industrialized nations of North America, Western Europe, and Japan, whose GDPs ranged from $24,000 to $36,000.[40]

With such poverty, it was not surprising that the telecom infrastructure was inadequate. In most of sub-Saharan Africa, less than 1 percent of the population had access to traditional land-based telephone lines, compared to more than sixty-four landlines per one hundred people in the United States.[41] With the exception of South Africa, cellular telephony had barely entered the sub-Saharan marketplace. And a nearby telephone was not all that sub-Saharan Africans lacked. Few citizens of countries like Malawi, Uganda, and Nigeria had bank accounts, credit cards, or mailing addresses. The roads were terrible, often washing away in the monsoon seasons. Governments were unable or unwilling to deliver or maintain these basics, and they were plagued with high levels of corruption, to boot.

In light of that, Africa appeared to be a great place to start a new business, right? Not! Most of us would turn our heads from what looks like a high-risk, low-reward opportunity. But not Dr. Mohamed ("Mo") Ibrahim. Ibrahim, a native of Sudan, saw Africa as ripe for mobile telecom expansion. It was a daunting leap of faith, perhaps. But his experience with the mobile telephone industry in Europe combined with his interest in and connection to Africa propelled him to make a move that would ultimately change the landscape—and potentially the economic situation—of sub-Saharan Africa.

Ibrahim grew up in Egypt and studied to become an engineer in the United Kingdom. He spent the early years of his career in the telecom industry with British Telecom (BT). He left BT in 1989 to set up Mobile Systems International (MSI), his own telecommunication consulting company, helping the growing cellular industry design their networks.[42]

In the late 1990s, his company shifted gears, moving from telecom consulting to mobile telephony operations focused on the sub-Saharan

African marketplace. Ibrahim recalled what it was like. "Mobile communications was like the Wild West in the 1990s. Everybody was fighting over licenses. But no one wanted to go into Africa. There was fear. There was ignorance. There were worries. Some of it was understandable," he recounted.[43] But his view differed: "I realized just how negative the image was of this region of the world. Since I'm African by origin myself, I was obviously well aware of the daily difficulties faced by people in Africa. But I felt that my contacts greatly overexaggerated the risks, that there was an enormous gap between their perceptions and the reality."[44]

Opportunity, Yes—but Can Celtel's Revenue Model Attract Subscribers?

Ibrahim saw enormous potential in the African market. His leap of faith was that there had to be a way to provide cellular telephony to this population in a profitable way. He set out to do just that. The first question Ibrahim and his team had to answer was about his revenue model. "How can I get this population to give up some of their very meager disposable income?"[45] He found an interesting analog. In Kenya, working men found a way to purchase a beer at the end of each work week. They afforded themselves this luxury without regard for their income. Ibrahim thought, "If someone is willing to pay for a beer at the end of the week, then an individual with similar wages would likely be willing to shell out a small amount of money to communicate by telephone."[46]

Ibrahim set out to capitalize on the beer-money phenomenon, making telephony as accessible and inexpensive as a bottle of Tusker lager. Rather than offering the fixed-rate monthly call plans common in most of the world, all antilogs, Ibrahim opted for a prepaid, pay-as-you-go strategy. His leap of faith was that customers would buy, along with a simple but adequate low-priced handset (another antilog here, as handsets in the West were frequently subsidized and provided for "free" with a monthly calling plan and fixed-term contract), prepaid scratch cards good for minutes of usage, whatever they could afford at the end of the week. When the minutes were gone and they had earned some more money, they would buy another scratch card.

Let's put Celtel's revenue model story aside for a moment to consider the company's operating model. After all, its operating model was heavily dependent on a cellular system that Celtel would have to build from scratch.

Celtel's Operating Model

Besides being customer-friendly, the prepaid, no-subsidized-handset, no long-term contract strategy had wider implications. It cut the costs of the operating model, as no expensive billing system was needed and there would be no telephone bills to mail—not that the postal systems in sub-Saharan Africa worked, anyway! And it meant that even customers who had little to spend would be profitable, unlike those in the West, for whom the cost of subsidized handsets had raised the bar to reach profitability.

To further strengthen his operating model—in the same way that analogs Southwest Airlines, Ryanair, and Go had decided to fly all their routes with Boeing 737 aircraft—Ibrahim decided to use a single wireless technology, GSM (Global System for Mobile), the one used throughout Europe. Doing so would ensure interoperability among customers and countries and kept operating costs down.

But difficult challenges remained. Licenses to operate cellular systems were granted by governments, which expected cash in return. And subscribers couldn't place calls until the cellular network—cell towers, switches, a network operating center, and so on—was in place. Ibrahim's investment model would have to raise cash to buy the licenses and put the wireless system in place. Thus, there were two huge leaps of faith. First, could sufficient investment capital be raised to start and scale an infrastructure-heavy business in such an unlikely market? Second, would African consumers part with enough of their beer money to make the business model work?

Celtel's Investment Model

At the time of Ibrahim's entrée into Africa, many sub-Saharan governments were beginning to open up their telephony markets, offering licenses to operators at far lower prices than licenses in more developed countries. Jonathan Newman, an executive at another African cellular operator, said, "Governments realized that because returns here are lower, the business model just doesn't stack up if they charge big license fees."[47] Ibrahim convinced Western-funded backers to invest in his company to take advantage of these deals, notwithstanding the risks.

With investment cash in hand, MSI started grabbing as many licenses as it could.[48] In 1998, Ibrahim and his team purchased licenses to operate in Zambia, Congo-Brazzaville, and Sierra Leone. By 2000, they had added

Malawi, Gabon, Chad, the Democratic Republic of Congo, Burkina Faso, Niger, and Uganda. Kamiel Koot, the company's CFO, summarized, "We are doing now what Vodafone was doing in the early 1990s, no different, picking up licenses, building businesses greenfield."[49] In 2004, the company rebranded itself Celtel, and acquired a license to operate in Kenya, east Africa's largest economy. By 2006 the company had licenses in more than a dozen countries, adding Tanzania, Nigeria, and Madagascar to its sub-Saharan portfolio.

Some of the risk that Celtel undertook by acquiring so many licenses so quickly, long before the beer money hypothesis had even been tested, was mitigated by the value of the assets that these licenses—the right to do business in each country—represented. This asset-based analog is a classic, developed originally by the nineteenth-century railroad barons, and copied in other industries as well, including cable and satellite television. Private developers and redevelopers of airports in India are doing exactly the same thing today: building new airports for the right to the revenues they will generate in the future—everything from passenger and gate fees to duty-free shopping.

The Beer Money Model Pans Out

"What about the beer money?", you ask. "Would African customers living on a few dollars a day spend their hard-earned cash on cell phone calls?" Starved for a way to communicate with one another, the African population jumped at Celtel's offerings.

Marten Pieters, Celtel's CEO, recalls, "What people often don't realize is that in Africa there is hardly any alternative to mobile telephony apart from traveling, which can be dangerous. So even for those with lower incomes, mobile telephony can be a very cost-effective solution."[50] Just like the men in Kenya who afforded themselves a beer, sub-Saharans proved willing to pay for the ability to communicate. Pieters continued, "People are willing to spend more of their disposable income on mobiles than in other countries because they do not have access to many other services."[51]

As surprising as it may seem, Celtel's African customers were just as hungry for mobile phones as their European counterparts. They were spending their beer money and then some.[52] In 2002, the average monthly revenue per user (ARPU) for Celtel's sub-Saharan customers was around $300 per year, similar (perhaps shockingly) to European levels.[53] As Celtel started expanding into less urban areas with even poorer populations, its ARPU did decline. In 2005, ARPU was down to $21 per month, around $250 per year.[54] But while ARPU declined over the years, the number of subscribers increased, enough to offset the smaller payment per user. Pieters said, "We don't subsidize handsets, and operate a pay-as-you-go model. A new customer of ours, more or less from day one, covers his marginal cost and very quickly becomes profitable. That's why we can live with lower ARPUs."[55]

Celtel's Working Capital Model

The Celtel strategy, with prepaid scratch cards and no subsidized handsets, had even more power. Let's look more carefully at Celtel's working capital model. While Celtel was generating strong revenue and posting profits, the company was also driving a very healthy balance sheet. In 2003, for example, 95 percent of Celtel's customers used prepaid methods.[56] As a result, Celtel's deferred revenue (revenue it collected from customers prior to services rendered) totaled $40 million. At the same time, the company's accounts payable to its suppliers for new towers and switches to grow its network totaled $33 million. And Celtel held virtually no inventories—it was a service business. Celtel had more than $70 million of its customers' and suppliers' cash to invest into growing the business!

Further, Celtel's gross margin model was inherently attractive. Once the network was in place, the cost of placing a subscriber's call—Celtel's cost of goods sold—was essentially zero. Moving electrons from Nairobi to Dar es Salaam cost virtually nothing.

Though raising capital to buy the licenses had not been easy, once the initial cell-phone systems were in place, the rest of the business model took over, helping to fuel incredible growth. By 2007, just nine years after entering the mobile marketplace in Africa, Celtel counted more than 27 million customers in fourteen countries, and had reported 2006 revenue of $2.5 billion.[57] The company had been profitable since 2003. In 2005 Celtel was acquired for $3.4 billion by MTC, a fast-growing Kuwaiti operator serving the Middle East and other emerging markets. Ibrahim earned close to $1 billion, and many of his employees—hundreds of them, including many Africans—became millionaires. And with only a 5 percent penetration rate in its markets, Celtel had plenty of room to grow its business even more.[58]

Lessons from Celtel's Balanced Approach

Celtel crafted a business model that worked pretty much as planned, right from the outset. What were the legs to Celtel's multilegged stool?

- *Revenue model:* With its customer-friendly pre-paid scratch cards and no long-term contracts, Celtel made it easy for its always cash-strapped customers to buy airtime when they needed it. And paying cash for the phone to get started was an expense that an extended family, or even a community, could share.

- *Gross margin model:* Celtel's inherently attractive gross margin model—with negligible COGS entailed in transmitting its cus-tomers' calls—was a huge benefit. Attractive gross margin models like Celtel's are one of the hallmarks of most service businesses.

- *Operating model:* Without a pricey billing system, nor bills to mail, and with its single GSM technology, Celtel's operating model was very efficient.

- *Working capital model:* The prepaid strategy and generous supplier terms provided a continuously renewable supply of working capital from customers and suppliers for growing the business.

With these four elements—the revenue, gross margin, operating, and working capital models—set to work so well together, it's no wonder that Ibrahim was able to convince investors that the huge sums for acquiring licenses and installing the initial networks would be sums well spent. Once each country was up and running and the electrons started flowing, the system would be a cash machine. Thus, with four legs supporting it, the stool looked stable and well balanced, in investors' eyes. The fifth leg of the stool—the investment model—looked far less risky and made the stool virtually untippable.

Lessons Learned About Multidimensional Models

Business models—like stools—are not built one leg at a time. And the analogs and antilogs that underlie the companies featured in this chapter did not have to come from within the industry to prove effective. We've found three common themes underlying each of the featured models:

- Each company delivered, at the heart of its revenue model, something that was crystal clear and that customers valued.

- Each company's business model was fundamentally different from what prevailed in its industry at the time.

- The five elements of the business models did not stand alone; the implications of one element for the company's economic viability were meaningful for another element, and all were interlinked in such a manner that made the business viable from a cash flow perspective and easy to grow.

Let's briefly address each of these points in a bit more detail.

A Clear Customer Promise That Customers Value

Each of our examples began with a customer promise, something the business would stand for, in customer terms, that customers valued. For Zara, it was customer delight, the very latest fashion apparel at affordable prices. Amazon promised its consumers an online, one-stop shopping experience that was incredibly customer focused. It offered its business customers the benefit of Amazon's finely tuned e-tailing know-how and infrastructure to resolve the pain they were experiencing in taking their bricks-and-mortar businesses online. Celtel, too, resolved customer pain, offering sub-Saharan Africans widespread and affordable telecommunication, where essentially none had existed before, and where real time communication other than face-to-face had been nigh on impossible. But making customer promises is easy. Delivering on them, in a way that generates cash so the business is cash flow viable and can grow, is the hard part. And that's why thinking strategically about your business model, whether before or after you get started in business, is so important.

Doing Things Differently

None of the examples in this chapter represents "business as usual" in its industry. There were antilogs aplenty. Zara rewrote the rules of slow fashion retailing that were based on long lead times from low-cost Asian factories to distant Western markets, and created its fast fashion model. Amazon, once it got serious about managing cash flow, got serious about getting to negative working capital—working capital nirvana, as we noted in chapter 6—and about rooting out inefficiency. It became the provider of choice for others—from Toys "R" Us to Target to mom-and-pop sellers of all kinds—who wanted to sell things online. It was, by then, a far cry from its online bookseller roots and the rest of its competitors. Celtel boldly asked its impoverished customers to pay for their phones—no subsidies up front—and used a prepaid pay-as-you-go revenue model in contrast to the prevailing European practice of subsidized handsets, monthly calling plans, and lengthy customer contracts.

The Five Business Model Elements Work Together to Create Cash for Growth

Too often aspiring entrepreneurs and managers in established firms confine their focus to only one part of their company's business model. The sales force worries about the revenue model, or if they are incentivized on gross margin, about the gross margin model as well. The procurement team focuses on the gross margin and operating models, by keeping costs down, whether for COGS or operations. And so on. But, ultimately, if everyone thinks about the business in business model terms, decisions are made differently.

Zara's Amancio Ortega saw the big picture of how his fast fashion strategy had favorable implications for the various elements of his company's business model and for his ability to grow Zara quickly. Jim Wilke, Amazon's operations guru, understood how his efforts would improve his company's working capital model, not just its operating model. Others on the Amazon team saw how Amazon's growing capabilities could be leveraged into higher-margin services revenue. Celtel's Mo Ibrahim saw that if he could just raise enough capital to get his cellular systems in place, the rest of the business model would take over, enabling his business to grow exponentially. None of these patterns was simple. As a result, they probably looked strange—even untenable—to others in their industries. As a result, they went largely uncopied and thereby provided lasting sources of competitive advantage and rapid growth.

Q&A with John and Randy

Now that we've brought the business model elements together, you may be wondering where you should start in thinking about your own business model, whether it's for a start-up you are contemplating or a new and better Plan B that might take your existing company to new heights—or even disrupt your industry. This question is important, so we've devoted part of chapter 9 to an organizing framework and a process that help you get started on your journey to a new and better business model. As you might imagine from having stayed with us this far, that process begins with analogs and antilogs, out of which grow leaps of faith and hypotheses to test to prove or refute them, all driven by a dashboarding process that evolves over time.

But before we move on to our final chapter, we'd like to answer the question about *where* to get started. We tackle it by addressing it in terms of cash and cash flow, and point out two explicit connections among the five business model elements we'd like you to make.

- Your revenue model, gross margin model, and operating model directly affect your working capital model.

- In turn, these four models directly affect your investment model.

Let's take these two issues one at a time.

The Implications of Your Revenue, Gross Margin, and Operating Models for Your Working Capital Model: Timing Is Key

By now it should be clear that the timing with which you ask your customers to pay for whatever it is that you sell them lies at the heart of your working capital model. So, as you think about what you will sell, to whom, why and how much or how many they will buy, and on what basis (your key revenue model questions from chapter 3) the question of *when* they will pay—compared to when you will deliver what they buy—is an all-important question that needs to be at the forefront of your thinking. The *timing* is crucial, in working capital terms, if you wish to create or grow your company using your customers' cash. Thus, as you develop your revenue model, don't forget to think about it in working capital terms.

Second, your gross margin model is crucial. It should ensure that the cash that your revenue model generates is not all consumed by COGS. It should also leave enough cash flow on the table to cover what your operating model—and perhaps your investment model, too—require, while also feeding your working capital model. If your gross margin model doesn't work, getting paid up front won't do you much good. Equally important, though, is the timing with which your COGS will be paid for. As we have seen from Amazon in this chapter and Costco in chapter 6, growing your company using your suppliers' cash is a good way to go.

Third, the timing with which you pay the operating expenses in your operating model is every bit as important as the timing of your supplier payments for COGS and the timing of your customer cash. Don't overlook timing considerations when you plan your operating model and their implications for the days of working capital you'll have at your disposal.

The relationships we've just described are illustrated in figure 8-1.

The Implications of Your Revenue, Gross Margin, Operating, and Working Capital Models for Your Investment Model

As we've seen in the Celtel story, a favorable working capital model—in tandem with thoughtful decisions about your revenue, gross margin, and operating models—can take lots of pressure off your investment model. In some

FIGURE 8-1

Implications of the business model elements on one another

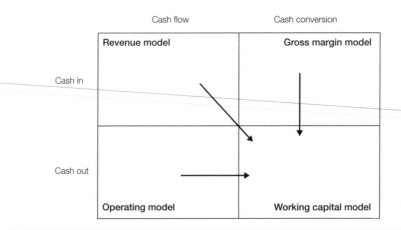

FIGURE 8-2

Driving your investment model with the rest of your business model

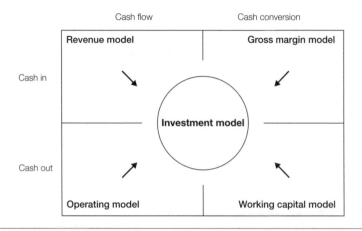

cases, it can sharply reduce the investment you'll need, or even eliminate it entirely. The relationship we've just described is illustrated in figure 8-2. If you can get by without investment, at least for some time until you've met some milestones and reduced risk, any capital you eventually raise will come on much better terms.

What's Next?

In chapters 1 and 2, we covered the *process* of getting to a better business model in our chapters on analogs, antilogs, leaps of faith, and dashboards. In chapters 3 to 8, we fleshed out the *content* of your successful business model organized by the five elements in our business model framework. It's time to weave it all together.

In chapter 9, our final chapter, we explore the reasons that many new ventures never reach their own Plan Bs. We address the three sources of cash for starting or growing your business—investors are but one—that this book has uncovered. We address some final questions you may still have. We direct some attention to your entrepreneurial dream. And, most important of all, we get you started on putting the lessons of this book to work, using a business model grid that, together with your dashboards, will give you a more structured learning path—a path we hope leads you to a successful Plan B or Plan Z!

John and Randy's Multidimensional Business Model Checklist

Business models are not built in stovepipe fashion, one element at a time. In order to build a business model that works, you'll need to consider all of the five elements as a package, and determine how each influences the others.

Thus, with your future cash flow in mind, as you develop your business model elements consider these questions, all with evidence to answer them—from your analogs, antilogs, and the hypothesis tests that seek to prove your leaps of faith:

- ✓ As you consider your revenue model, consider the timing with which revenue will come in. How will your revenue model decisions affect your working capital model?

- ✓ As you consider your gross margin model, consider the timing of your COGS payments, as well as the adequacy of your gross margin. How much cash will your gross margin model leave on the table and how will your gross margin model affect your working capital model?

- ✓ As you consider your operating model, consider the timing of your various expense payments. How will your operating model affect your working capital model?

- ✓ As you consider the working capital model that grows out of your revenue, gross margin, and operating models, consider the extent to which it can fund the investment you require. How will your working capital model affect your investment model?

CHAPTER 9

Getting Started on Discovering *Your* Plan B

A S YOU KNOW BY NOW, this is not a book about "business planning." It's a book about, in a sense, "business discovering." *Getting to Plan B* is about a process of *discovering*, over time, a fluid pattern among the five business model elements that, working together, will make the economics work, so you don't run out of money along the way.

Like learning, discovery rarely occurs in a single eureka moment, though there may well be a few such moments along the way. Discovery takes discipline, patience, and the right tools for the job. What tools?

- Some analogs and antilogs from which you will learn

- A few leaps of faith together with hypotheses to prove or refute them

- A sequence of dashboards to guide your journey and mark the need for midcourse corrections

- And a mind-set that embraces the five business model elements as a framework for organizing what you discover

As for any journey into the unknown, planning is absolutely essential, not least because your port of departure is your Plan A. You need a stake in the ground, a starting point—an entrepreneurial dream, perhaps, that captures the essence of your Plan A—from which to embark on your journey to Plan B and its better business model that will actually work. But useful as your stake in the ground is, we are reminded of the words of General Dwight D. Eisenhower, on the merits and limitations of planning for the

D-day landings: "Plans are useless, but planning is indispensable."[1] We don't believe that your Plan A is useless, actually. But it's probably off target in more ways than one, as many of the examples in this book attest.

Essential though planning is, it is not sufficient in entrepreneurial settings, whether for raw start-ups or for new ventures hatched within established companies. It's nearly impossible to plan reliably for an unknown future, especially when the planning concerns an innovative new venture, like many of those we've seen in this book, or a radical, new-to-the-world product. Worse, too much planning, conducted in too much detail, can distract you from the most crucial tasks at hand—testing your most important leaps of faith. Too much planning can blind you to a more attractive opportunity whose name is Plan B or, like PayPal's Max Levchin, Plan G. What, then, are the implications of this book and the process it articulates for the time-honored culture and practice of business planning? This is the first of a handful of remaining issues that we address in this closing chapter:

- We share some lessons we've learned about many of the business plans we've seen and why so many of them simply don't deliver.

- We examine how best to get started on putting the lessons of this book to work on your business.

- We explore the lessons learned about the three best sources of the cash you will need to embark on or continue your journey.

- We answer a few final questions about getting on with your journey toward Plan B.

- And we explore the crucial importance of your entrepreneurial dream.

Most Business Plans Don't Deliver

That's an audacious statement, perhaps. But unfortunately, it's true. Let's consider the business planning culture that pervades all things entrepreneurial today. There are dozens of best-selling books on business planning; Web sites, too; plus software packages, business planning consultants, university courses, and more. So, amid all this good advice, why do most business plans fail to deliver? Why do so many plans, with their fancy graphics and impassioned cover letters attached, go unanswered, straight into the trash? In short, why do most business plans attract few customers, generate little revenue, and raise no money?

To begin to answer these questions, let's consider what a typical business plan seeks to do. It articulates in a hopefully convincing way, in words, numbers, graphs with hockey-stick projections, and so on, why the idea—the lovingly articulated Plan A, though it's never called that—will work, and how much money everyone will make when it does. Whether it's been prepared to raise venture capital or to win the support of the corporate investment committee, the message is nearly always the same.

What the evidence—the cold, hard facts—tells us, however, is that most often what ultimately works, if anything works at all, is not the Plan A that was so persuasively articulated in the original plan. Instead, it's Plan B. Or, as we have seen in this book, the plan that finds traction has a letter even farther down the alphabetical queue.

Some Common Threads of Clueless Business Plans

Why don't most business plans deliver? Over the years, the business plans we have seen share some common—and unfortunate—traits. First, far too many business plans are written in the first burst of enthusiasm without a shred of real evidence to support their assertions. Simply put, most business plans are written too soon. Analogs, antilogs, tested hypotheses? Few or none. A telltale sign makes it easy to spot this problem. Sentences that begin with the phrase "We believe . . ." are dead giveaways. What the phrase "We believe . . ." most often means, in actuality, is "We haven't a shred of real evidence about this, because we've been too busy writing this business plan to actually gather any evidence, but we hope that . . ." The unfortunate consequence is that most plans lack any tangible evidence in support of the most of the assertions they make. Assumptions, sometimes. Evidence, rarely. Most are built, like a house of cards, on unproven foundations.

Second, rarely is there anything like a plan to discover and learn. The plans assume that most everything is already known up front—not the case, as the company histories that comprise this book have shown. Third, and related to the second point, the rampant uncertainty about what lies ahead goes entirely unacknowledged. As General Douglas MacArthur is reputed to have once said, "No plan ever survives its first encounter with the enemy."

The process we've articulated in this book exists to counter such disastrous practices—to enable you to anticipate and move beyond a failing Plan A. It is a process designed for learning and discovering, rather than for pitching and selling. It addresses the harsh reality that most of the time we know much less than we think we know about our proposed new ventures.

Putting This Book's Lessons to Work

If you've read this far, you now know the answer to what you should do next, no matter what the stage of your venture or idea or the shape it's now in. And you already know what the building blocks are:

- An identified customer pain and a solution that you believe resolves it, or an opportunity to offer consumer delight where it is absent today

- Next, some relevant analogs and antilogs, building on what others have done before

- Which lead to some as-yet-untested leaps of faith, clearly prioritized, so you know which to prove—or refute—first

- Which lead to a set of hypotheses to test them

- A dashboard to focus your and your people's attention on what's most important right now and to provide the signals for your midcourse corrections

- All comprehensively organized, in just the right sequence, to inform and create the five elements of your business model

So how do you put these building blocks to work? Figure I-1, the business model grid with which we organized this book way back in the introduction and repeat here for your convenience, is your organizing framework (see figure 9-1). Your dashboards are your guide for your discovery journey

Your task to begin putting flesh on the bones of your entrepreneurial dream, without writing a business plan just yet, is to fill in at least one or

FIGURE 9-1

The business model grid

Your current idea and the customer pain that it resolves or the consumer delight it offers:

Business model element	Relevant analogs and the numbers they give you	Relevant antilogs	Leaps of faith around which you will build your current dashboard	Hypotheses that will prove or refute your leaps of faith
Revenue model	A1		C1	D1
Gross margin model				
Operating model				
Working capital model				
Investment model	A5			D5

more of the cells in each row of the grid. For your revenue model, for example, you might have an analog or two that can tell you with some confidence just how, from whom, and at what cost your revenue will be generated. If so, that's the detail—a short paragraph to yourself, including numbers, please—that you need for cell A1. Perhaps your analogs and some antilogs lead to a leap of faith that you'll need to examine experimentally about how your revenue model will play out. If so, that is another paragraph to yourself for cell C1, with your hypothesized answer—again, most of the time with numbers, please—to that leap of faith in cell D1. A draft of the dashboard you will use to guide your experimental path and signal any necessary midcourse corrections in developing your revenue model is next (see figure 9-2, repeated here from figure 2-1). With these steps completed, you'll have jump-started your critical thinking about your revenue model.

Next, working a row at a time, repeat the process for your gross margin model, your operating model, your working capital model, and your investment model. Then, prioritize your set of paragraphs and dashboards, not necessarily in the sequence shown in the business model grid. Which are the most crucial to examine first? Which can wait until earlier answers

FIGURE 9-2

A prototype dashboard for discovering *your* better business model

Hypotheses	Metrics	Actual period 1	Actual period 2	Actual period 3	Insights obtained, course corrections needed
Leap of faith 1:					
Hypothesis H1:					
Hypothesis H2:					
Leap of faith 2:					
Hypothesis H3:					
Hypothesis H4:					

are in hand? When you are done, for the first time around, what will you have? You'll have three things:

- A series of short paragraphs to yourself that, collectively, describe your Plan A in considerably more detail than the one-liner at the top of the business model grid

- Some dashboards to both set your planned route toward a possible, but as yet unknown, Plan B and to course-correct as your venture evolves

- All of which, taken together, comprise, in effect, the strategy you initially envision, viewed though a business model lens

More importantly, you'll have a learning plan, rather than a business plan, that will enable you to either discover that your Plan A is viable, if you are both lucky and shrewd, as we saw with eBay and Celtel, or lead you to a more viable Plan B—or Plan Z.

Planning these learning tasks takes work, but it doesn't take much paper. No more than a page for each row—each element of your business model—plus some dashboards attached. Take the time necessary to refine your thoughts and make them clear and concise. As the old quip goes, "If I had more time, I would have written a shorter letter."

As you know by now, the process will be iterative. Where your path will lead, no one knows, least of all you! As you think though the rows of the business model grid, you will find yourself iterating from one row to another and back again because, as we saw in chapter 8, the elements don't stand alone. A few weeks or months from now, some cells in your business model grid will have changed based on what you have learned from your journey. As you also now know, pretty much everything has been done before. It's just that no one has put the pieces—your analogs and antilogs and leaps of faith—together in the precise way that you plan to do. You'll be standing on the shoulders of giants—those who have gone before you and learned, perhaps even succeeded, as well as others who have been slain.

Three Sources of Cash

"Ah," you're thinking, "When are John and Randy going to tell me how to raise the cash I am so fervently seeking?" Actually, we already have! Though money still doesn't grow on trees, what we've said is that there are three great sources of cash—not just investors—to fund both your discovery journey and your business as it evolves:

- *Chapter 4's gross margin nirvana:* Assuming your revenue model also works, if you can find a way to generate gross margins that approach 100 percent, like eBay, or even Patagonia's more modest but very attractive levels, those margins will go a long way to funding your business. What high-margin goods or services can you sell today or tomorrow to fund the initial stages of your discovery journey?

- *Chapter 6's negative working capital:* If you can develop a working capital model that gives you the customer's cash up front, as we saw with Dow Jones and Costco, you may not need very much investment, perhaps none at all. What customers can you think of that will find your offering so compelling, that they—like Aggregate Knowledge's beta sites that we saw in chapter 2—will pay you now to start your journey with them? Or what suppliers can you find to bankroll the initial stages of your journey with generous terms for their vendor finance?

- *Chapter 7's investment model:* Not every business will be able to fund the initial stages of its journey from patient suppliers or a high-margin customer that offers cash up front. This is where your investment model comes into play. The lessons of Skype and Go that we saw in chapter 7 are two inspiring analogs of how to get by with less cash, and the lessons at the end of that chapter explore the various ways of raising the rest of the capital you need.

Some Final Questions Answered

Lest we end this book with any known stones still unturned, let's wrap up with a few final questions—some of which we touched on briefly at the start of the book—with answers to help you on your way.

On my journey to Plan B, do I need a contingency plan up front? There's a temptation to think that, since Plan A probably won't work, you should have Plan B in your hip pocket, ready to pull out at a moment's notice. Don't do it. A contingency plan would probably be just as flawed as your Plan A, so you'd have to go through the same steps for it as you will in going from your preferred Plan A to a completely unknown Plan B. Your time and talent are scarce commodities, so we suggest that you not even think about Plan B until your dashboarding process takes you there. Focus on your dashboards and your hypothesis tests, and Plan B or Plan Z will reveal itself soon enough. There's little point in speculating, when you'll have real evidence in due course.

I'm still not sure where to look for my analogs and antilogs. Where should I start? First, read, or watch the business news. Your local, national, and international business news will constantly replenish your source of analogs and antilogs. Business news takes on a new kind of curiosity when you realize that it is a daily source of great analog and antilog stories.

Consider companies that might be your competitors, but dig into other industries, too, for insights that your own industry may be overlooking. That's what Barbara Cassani did as she and Go brought a different kind of customer service ethic to Europe's no-frills airline industry.

Dive into your social network for some insights. Get out from behind your broadband connection and start talking to people who have done something like what you propose to do. Ask them about analogs and antilogs. What companies, in your proposed industry or others, should you emulate, for which elements in your business model? From what companies should you differ, at all costs?

And, not least, as we noted in chapter 1, there are dozens of great analogs and antilogs between the covers of this book. From Africa to China to India to Europe to North America. From numerous raw start-ups, to corporate spinouts like Go, to great work in large organizations like Toyota and Dow Jones. But these are only a start, just enough to whet your appetite.

When do I need my first dashboard? Yesterday! Your real learning doesn't begin until you are dashboarding. Once you have identified your life-or-death leaps of faith and a set of hypotheses to examine them, you can put your first dashboard to work. It will focus your attention and correct your path when you find you are off course. It will challenge your ideas with real-world evidence. It will give you some insights you lack today. Then, with concrete knowledge about your venture growing day by day, you'll be putting the pieces in place for what will be, before long, an evidence-based business plan that carries less risk. If you do this well, you'll encourage the likes of our colleagues to take your business plan—and more importantly, you!—seriously.

What if I'm in a big company, where the impediments to change are high, where reluctance to take risk reigns from on high? Reread the story of Go, and the lessons that Barbara Cassani learned about getting a venture that was truly different up and running inside a large and conservative company. Reread the stories of Apple's onslaught on the music industry and of Toyota's relentless focus on creating the best gross margin model in its industry. One of these analogs may be the ticket to getting your top management—maybe that's you!—to find a way forward.

Follow our process and start gathering some experimental evidence to support your Plan A. Dashboarding is crucial at this stage! If some early, real-world tests can convince the people around you that you've got a viable business model in the works, you may get more support than you expect.

When does the analog-antilog-leap of faith-dashboard process end? We're glad you asked. It doesn't. Stopping this process is the beginning of complacency, just what your competitors ordered for you. The process of asking questions, building on the learning of others, and seeking real, in-the-marketplace answers will keep your organization nimble. Remember that Aggregate Knowledge (chapter 2) had a real breakthrough regarding its customers' behavior long after its Plan A was humming. Had its dash-board not signaled the need for a midcourse correction, Paul Martino would never have taken the time to understand the change in behavior and get to Plan B. Aggregate Knowledge avoided a potentially fatal mistake by dashboarding!

If you read about the companies we've profiled in this book a year or two from now, we're sure you'll find that most of them are, in at least some parts of their businesses, on to a new and different Plan B or Plan Z. They don't rest. Neither should you.

What if my venture is nonprofit, or even a government entity? What if I'm not in California or London? As you'll have seen in the company histories in the last eight chapters, the principles and tools in this book do not restrict themselves to any one kind of venture or any single setting. We've examined companies large and small, old and new. Start-ups and restarts. Nonprofits and for-profits. In developed economies and emerging ones. The principles and tools herein provide a solid foundation for gen-erating positive cash flow, every start-up's dream, in any kind of venture, anywhere. Ignore them at your peril.

Dreaming *Your* Entrepreneurial Dream

In chapter 1, we introduced you to Fred Swaniker, who along with a Stan-ford MBA classmate created the African Leadership Academy. One of Swaniker's inspirations—for becoming an entrepreneur, not just starting the ALA—was born when he attended an intimate breakfast with Carlos Ghosn, the CEO of Nissan and Renault. You'll recall he said, "I realized that if an ordinary person could lead such a successful global organization, so could I. It gave me the gall to think big."

The men and women featured in this book are ordinary folk, too. They combined their own skills and mind-sets with their business or philan-thropic ambitions. They kept open minds as they iterated toward stronger business models. They created some of the world's most exciting products and services, enriching your life and ours. You can, too.

So think back to the big ideas and noble goals that many of the founders of the companies profiled in this book pursued from the outset. Mo Ibrahim set out to bring accessible and affordable telecommunication to sub-Saharan Africa, where virtually none had existed before. The Google guys set out to organize the world's information and make it immediately accessible to anyone who needed it, anywhere, any time. Mari Kuraishi and Dennis Whittle of GlobalGiving wanted to efficiently funnel charitable contributions directly to the people in the developing world, allowing GlobalGiving to put donations to work efficiently and immediately. As best-selling author Jim Collins says, "When you've built an institution with values and a purpose beyond just making money—when you've built a culture that makes a distinctive contribution while delivering exceptional results—why would you surrender to the forces of mediocrity and succumb to irrelevance?"[2]

After you've massaged your confidence, we suggest you think big. As Danny Rimer, general partner at Index Ventures in London, notes, "The Skype deal with eBay probably has had repercussions in terms of entrepreneurialism, not only in Britain but across Europe. It's had the effect of providing confidence to entrepreneurs to really go after big opportunities."[3] What's your big opportunity?[4] Your entrepreneurial dream?[5] Put your dream to paper. If you don't have an idea just yet, you can always start by making a list of things that bug you—a buglist, we call it. You'll be surprised how many things stand to be improved! As renowned venture capital investor John Doerr points out, "Great business opportunities emerge from solving big problems."[6]

In short, we hope you, too, will make a difference, if you can, in whatever way is meaningful to you; and meaningful to the society—or the small corner thereof—in which you live and work. Perhaps it will be your next venture that will inspire future generations of entrepreneurs to follow in your shoes.

So there you have it. A process for answering the single, simple, life-or-death question about your entrepreneurial dream: How can I break through to a better business model that will actually work? By using a set of tools to help you take off the rose-colored glasses and embark on your own unique learning journey, with your eyes and ears open, your antennae all the way up. Please write home with your travelogue, so we can help make your business an inspiration and an analog for others! We wish you Godspeed. Have an exhilarating ride!

NOTES

Introduction

1. The Max Levchin story reported here is based on an interview in Jessica Livingston, *Founders at Work* (Berkeley, CA: Apress, 2007), 1–16.

2. Ibid., 2.

3. Ibid., 3.

4. The Kauffman Foundation, *2008 State New Economy Index*, November 2008, 3.

5. Global Entrepreneurship Monitor, *2008 Executive Report*, http://www.gemconsortium.org/article.aspx?id=76.

6. Albert L. Page, "Assessing New Product Development Practices and Performance: Establishing Crucial Norms," *Journal of Product Innovation Management* 10, no. 4 (1993): 273–290.

7. Livingston, *Founders at Work*, 3.

8. Ibid., 6.

9. Kevin Allison, "Founders Take Aim at a Bigger Target," *Financial Times*, February 20, 2008.

10. *Revenue* is the word accountants use for the money that comes in from the customers who buy what you sell. For a manufacturing company, that's money you receive for the widgets you sell. For a service business, such as haircutting, for example, it's the cash you get for your haircuts. For a radio station or a Web portal, it's what your advertisers or subscribers pay to place their ads.

11. *Gross margin* is accounting lingo for the difference between the revenue you get when you sell something and what that something costs to produce (cost of goods sold, in accounting parlance)—excluding your other costs like keeping the lights on and the doors open.

12. *Operating costs* are the rest of the costs you incur from month to month; everything but the cost of what you sell.

13. *Working capital* is cash you must tie up while you wait for customers to buy and pay for what they buy. It might be inventory on your shelves. It might be the paper invoice you hold while you wait for them to pay what they owe you for what they have bought. On the flip side, it's cash you hold—cash due to a supplier, perhaps, in thirty or sixty days, which you can use as long as you hold it.

14. *Investment*, in the sense in which we will use this word, is the amount of money you have to invest initially until such time as the money customers give you—your revenue on an ongoing basis—is enough to cover your ongoing costs.

Chapter 1

1. Georges Polti, "36 Dramatic Situations," http://changingminds.org/disciplines/storytelling/plots/polti_situations/polti_situations.htm.

2. Apple, "Form 10-K," filed with the U.S. Security and Exchange Commission, December 29, 2006, 113.

3. Katherine Mangu-Ward, "iWorld: Why the iPod Personalizes Everything," *Reason*, March 2007, http://www.reason.com/news/show/118519.html.

4. Benny Evangelista, "Walkman vs. iPod: Sony Takes Aim at Apple with New Music Players," *San Francisco Chronicle*, July 5, 2004, http://www.sfgate.com/cgi-bin/article.cgi?f=/c/a/2004/07/05/BUG267F5521.DTL.

5. Jupiter Media Metrix, "Global Napster Usage Plummets, but New File-Sharing Alternatives Gaining Ground," July 20, 2001, retrieved from http://www.comscore.com/press/release.asp?id=249.

6. Leander Kahney, "Straight Dope on the iPod's Birth," *Wired.com*, October 17, 2006, http://www.wired.com/gadgets/mac/commentary/cultofmac/2006/10/71956.

7. Apple, "Form 10-K."

8. Jane Black, "Where 'Think Different' Is Taking Apple," *BusinessWeek,* August 5, 2003, http://www.businessweek.com/technology/content/aug2003/tc2003085_3215_tc112.htm.

9. Ibid.

10. Apple Launching New Music Store Service," AP Online, April 28, 2003, retrieved from Factiva.com.

11. Black, "Where 'Think Different' Is Taking Apple."

12. Craig Buchanan, "The Death of DRM," February 6, 2007, http://craigb6.blogspot.com/.

13. Robert X. Cringely, "Broadcast Denied," March 29, 2007, http://www.pbs.org/cringely/pulpit/2007/pulpit_20070329_001882.html.

14. Randall Stross, "How the iPod Ran Circles Around the Walkman," *New York Times,* March 13, 2005, http://www.nytimes.com/2005/03/13/business/worldbusiness/13digi.html?ei=5090&en=b90493bfe6c9e003&ex=1268370000&adxnnl=1&partner=rssuserland&adxnnlx=1185478183-g5IoYOlk+ziBVFhrK/K3iw&pagewanted=print&position=.

15. Apple, "Form 10-K."

16. Andrew Edgecliffe-Johnson, "Apple Brings in Variable Pricing on iTunes," *Financial Times,* January 6, 2009.

17. http://earthtrends.wri.org/pdf_library/country_profiles/pop_cou_356.pdf.

18. Central Intelligence Agency, "The World Factbook: India," https://www.cia.gov/library/publications/the-world-factbook/print/in.html.

19. *Kiranas* are small, neighborhood shops that comprise the backbone of traditional Indian retailing. They offer their customers numerous services, including convenient locations, free delivery (on the family bicycle), and, sometimes, credit. Gaurav Sabnis, "Kirana Will Still Rule," *Indian Economy Blog,* November 29, 2006, http://indianeconomy.org/2006/11/29/kirana-will-still-rule/.

20. Interview with Kishore Biyani by Suzanne Stoller, August 2007.

21. Surajeet Das Gupta, "Meet India's King of Retail," *Business Standard*, January 15, 2005, http://www.rediff.com/money/2005/jan/15spec2.htm.

22. Biyani interview.

23. Ibid.

24. Das Gupta, "Meet India's King of Retail."

25. Rajiv Banerjee, "New Marketing Tip: Shelf Management," *Economic Times,* December 14, 2005, retrieved from Factiva.com.

26. Marks & Spencer, http://www.marksandspencer.com/gp/node/n/46001031/026-1521226-5581208?ie=UTF8&mnSBrand=core.

27. "Now What's in Store?" *Business Standard*, December 1, 1998, retrieved from Factiva.com.

28. Das Gupta, "Meet India's King of Retail."

29. Eric Bellman, "Chaos Theory: In India, a Retailer Finds Key to Success Is Clutter," *Wall Street Journal*, August 8, 2007, http://online.wsj.com/article/SB118651168871890705.html?mod=hpp_us_pageone.

30. Ibid.

31. http://www.pantaloon.com/companyinfo.asp.

32. "Retailing: The coming boom," *Business India Intelligence*, July 11, 2007, retrieved from the Factiva Database.

33. All quotations and data for this section on the African Leadership Academy are taken from interviews by Debra Dunn with Fred Swaniker and Chris Bradford in December 2007 and January 2008.

34. African Leadership Academy, http://www.africanleadershipacademy.org/site/about/students/.

Chapter 2

1. All quotations and data regarding GlobalGiving are taken from interviews conducted by Debra Dunn with Dennis Whittle in December 2007 and January 2008.

2. We thank GlobalGiving for allowing us to share its dashboards with our readers. They have been edited for clarity.

3. "GlobalGiving Fact Sheet," http://www.globalgiving.com/aboutus/media/backgrounder. html.

4. The Aggregate Knowledge case history was developed through a series of interviews by Suzanne Stoller with Aggregate Knowledge founders Paul Martino and Christopher Law in July 2007.

5. "Personify Raises $20 Million in New Funding," *Business Wire*, April 18, 2001.

6. We are grateful to Aggregate Knowledge for sharing its real-life dashboards with us, portions of which are shown in this chapter. Key data have been eliminated to ensure confidentiality.

7. "Aggregate Knowledge Unveils the Internet's First Discovery Service," *PR Newswire*, January 30, 2007, retrieved from Factiva.com.

Chapter 3

1. For an overview of the Maslow hierarchy of needs, see Frank G. Goble, *The Third Force; the Psychology of Abraham Maslow* (New York: Grossman, 1970), chapter 4.

2. Peter Drucker, *Innovation and Entrepreneurship: Practice and Principles* (New York: Harper & Row, 1985).

3. Financial information from Google, 2007 10-K statement, http://investor.google.com/documents/2007_google_annual_report.html.

4. Google Inc., "Amendment No. 7 to Form S-1 Registration Statement," filed August 13, 2004, http://www.sec.gov/Archives/edgar/data/1288776/000119312504139655/ds1a.htm.

5. David A. Vise, *The Google Story* (New York: Bartem Dell, 2005), 38.

6. Google, S-1 and 10-K statements.

7. Google Inc., "Amendment No. 7."

8. Google S-1 and 10-K statements.

9. Vise, *The Google Story*.

10. Google S-1 and 10-K statements.

11. The best resource, in our view, to assist you in developing your company's vision—its core purpose, core values, and the future you envision—is Jim Collins and Jerry Porras, "Building Your Company's Vision," *Harvard Business Review*, September 1996, 65–77.

12. John Mullins, "Silverglide Surgical Technologies (A)," Case no. CS04-004 (London: London Business School, 2005), 4.

13. Ibid., 5.

14. Ibid.

15. Ibid.

16. Bruce Einhorn, "China's Net Gamers. Ready to Rumble," *BusinessWeek*, February 25, 2005, http://www.businessweek.com/technology/content/feb2005/tc20050225_9968_tc119.htm.

17. Ibid.

18. Shanda Entertainment 2004 Annual Report, p. 5, http://www.snda.com/en/investor/download/SNDA%20AR%20Narrative%202004.pdf.

19. Emma Brockes, "China Fact: 'If I Was a Lowly Official They Would Be Proud,'" *Guardian*, November 8, 2004.

20. Paul Hyman, "MMOG Publishers Conjure Up New Business Models," *Hollywood Reporter*, December 14, 2005, http://www.hollywoodreporter.com/hr/search/article_display.jsp?vnu_content_id=1001698964.

21. Brian Bremner, "China Gaming: Shanda's Back in the Action," *Business Week*, February 14, 2006.

22. Mure Dickie, "Shanda Losses Reveal Extent of Its Challenge," *Financial Times*, March 1, 2006, http://www.ft.com/cms/s/0/76390336-a8c9-11da-aeeb-0000779e2340.html?nclick_check=1.

23. Ibid.

24. Hyman, "MMOG Publishers Conjure Up New Business Models."

25. Ibid.

26. "Online Firm Eyes Tie-in Products," *Shanghai Daily*, July 2, 2004, retrieved from Factiva.com.

27. Dickie, "Shanda Losses Reveal Extent of Its Challenge."

28. Bremner, "China Gaming: Shanda's Back in the Action."

29. Dickie, "Shanda Losses Reveal Extent of Its Challenge."

30. Bremner, "China Gaming: Shanda's Back in the Action."

31. "Internet Game Giant Gets Bounce in Earnings," *Shanghai Daily*, February 14, 2007, retrieved from Factiva.com.

32. Shanda, press release, http://ir.snda.com/phoenix.zhtml?c=178252&p=irol-newsArticle&ID=1112093&highlight=.

33. Shanda press release announcing launch of Shanda Literature: http://www.snda.com/en/news/news.jsp?id=555.

34. John Doerr, personal conversation with Randy Komisar, November 2008.

Chapter 4

1. Adam Cohen, *The Perfect Store: Inside eBay* (Boston: Little, Brown, and Co., 2002), 20.

2. Ibid., 24.

3. Ibid., 25.

4. Adam Cohen, "eBay's Bid to Conquer All," *Time*. January 28, 2001, http://www.time.com/time/magazine/article/0,9171,97068,00.html.

5. Cohen, *The Perfect Store*, 44.

6. Ibid., 144.

7. Ibid., 278.

8. Ibid., 246.

9. eBay 10-K, February 2, 2007, http://investor.ebay.com/annuals.cfm.

10. Russ Banham, "Sittin' on the Dock of eBay" *CFO*, December 22, 2000, http://www.cfo.com/article.cfm/3002060/c_3046573?f=magazine_coverstory.

11. Jeffrey K. Liker, *The Toyota Way: 14 Management Principles from the World's Greatest Manufacturer* (New York: McGraw-Hill, 2004), 17.

12. Ibid., 15.

13. Ibid., 25.

14. Alex Taylor III, "Why Toyota Keeps Getting Better and Better And Better," *Fortune,* November 19, 1990, http://money.cnn.com/magazines/fortune/fortune_archive/1990/11/19/74363/index.htm.

15. Ibid.

16. *The Economist* comments that for Japan's car manufacturers the main profits are in exports, 15 July 1984.

17. Quoted in James R. Healey, "Toyota Wheels Lexus into Upscale Market," *USA Today,* December 8, 1988.

18. Ibid.

19. Liker, *The Toyota Way*, 4.

20. Taylor III, "Why Toyota Keeps Getting Better and Better And Better."

21. Retrieved from: http://quicktake.morningstar.com/StockNet/Income10.aspx?Country=USA&Symbol=TM&stocktab=finance; http://www.corporateinformation.com/corpinfo2.asp?cusip=C39290080; and http://finance.yahoo.com/q/co?s=TM on May 2, 2007.

22. Norihiko Shirouzu and John Murphy, "A Scion Drives Toyota Back to Basics," *Wall Street Journal*, February 24, 2009.

23. Amanda Griscom Little, "Don't Get Mad, Get Chouinard," *Grist,* October 22, 2004, http://www.grist.org/cgi-bin/printthis.pl?uri=/news/maindish/2004/10/22/little-chouinard/index.html, accessed July 2007.

24. Susan Casey, "Patagonia: Blueprint for Green Business," *Fortune,* May 29, 2007, http://money.cnn.com/magazines/fortune/fortune_archive/2007/04/02/8403423/index.htm.

25. Ibid.

26. Yvon Chouinard, "Let My People Go Surfing," *Outside Magazine,* October 2005, http://outside.away.com/outside/features/200510/Chouinard-chouinard-1.html.

27. Little, "Don't Get Mad, Get Chouinard."

28. Chouinard, "Let My People Go Surfing."

29. Little, "Don't Get Mad, Get Chouinard," 1.

30. Casey, "Patagonia: Blueprint for Green Business."

31. Chouinard, "Let My People Go Surfing."

32. Casey, "Patagonia: Blueprint for Green Business."

33. Ibid.

34. Chouinard, "Let My People Go Surfing."

35. Susan Ives, "A Conversation with Ivon Chouinard," Trust for Public Land, September 2007, http://www.tpl.org/tier3_cd.cfm?content_item_id=5307&folder_id=1545.

36. Casey, "Patagonia: Blueprint for Green Business."

37. Susan Lisovicz, Gayla Hope, "Yvon Chouinard Profile," *CNNfn Business Unusual,* July 25, 2001, retrieved from Factiva.com.

38. Casey, "Patagonia: Blueprint for Green Business."

39. Alexandra Alter, "Young Entrepreneurs Create Virtual Summer Jobs," *Wall Street Journal,* European Edition, May 21, 2008.

40. Ibid.

Chapter 5

1. Quentin Fottrell, "The Rise and Rise of Ryanair," *Sunday Business Post,* June 6, 2004, http://archives.tcm.ie/businesspost/2004/06/06/story57027153.asp.

2. Daniel McGinn, "Is This Any Way to Run an Airline?" *Newsweek,* September 28, 2004, www.msnbc.msn.com/id/6098255/print/1/displaymode/1098/.

3. Dan Milmo and Ian Griffiths, "Keep It Simple—and Don't Mention the Add-Ons," *Guardian,* October 6, 2006, http://www.guardian.co.uk/airlines/story/0,,1888934,00.html.

4. Kerry Capell, "Ryanair Rising," *BusinessWeek,* June 2, 2003, http://www.businessweek.com/magazine/content/03_22/b3835074_mz014.htm.

5. "Ryanair Model Validated," *Aviation Week and Space Technology*, July 10, 2000.

6. "Ryanair Chooses 737-800, Citing Lower Costs, Attractive Prices," *Aviation Daily,* January 25, 2002.

7. Capell, "Ryanair Rising."

8. Yves Clarisse, "EU Ruling on Ryanair Could Hurt Low-Cost Airlines," *Reuters News,* September 19, 2003, retrieved from Factiva.com.

9. Ibid.

10. "Ryanair Model Validated."

11. Kerry Capell, "Wal-Mart with Wings," *BusinessWeek,* November 6, 2006. http://www.businessweek.com/magazine/content/06_48/b4011064.htm?campaign_id=rss_magzn.

12. Capell, "Ryanair Rising."

13. Milmo and Griffiths, "Keep It Simple."

14. Matthew Maier, "A Radical Fix for Airlines," *CNN Money,* March 31, 2006.

15. Ryanair Annual Report & Financial Statements 2006. Retrieved from: http://www.ryanair.com/site/about/invest/docs/2006/060901annualreport.pdf.

16. Capell, "Wal-Mart with Wings."

17. "Ryanair Mulls Charge for Toilets," BBC News Web site, http://news.bbc.co.uk/1/hi/business/7914542.stm, accessed February 27, 2009.

18. Quentin Fottrell, "Ryanair net drops 10%," *Wall Street Journal*, European Edition, June 4, 2008.

19. 2007 performance data sourced from http://www.marketwatch.com/tools/quotes/financials.asp.

20. Kevin Done, "Runway Success," *Financial Times Boldness in Business,* March 20, 2009, 18–21.

21. Capell, "Ryanair Rising,"

22. Maier, "A Radical Fix for Airlines."

23. Roger Baird, "Ryanair to Rough 10% of Fleet in Cost-Cut Drive," *City A.M.*, June 4, 2008, 5.

24. Anusha Bradley, "Five Airlines Will Survive Oil Price Spike—Michael O'Leary," *City A.M.*, June 4, 2008, 1.

25. http://www.oberoihotels.com/Oberoi_Awards.aspx.

26. Retrieved from: http://www.zoomsystems.com/pages/1a_history.html.

27. Bary Alyssa Johnson, "Zoom Systems Offers iPod Vending Machines," *PC Magazine*, October 25, 2005, http://www.pcmag.com/print_article2/0,1217,a=163423,00.asp.

28. Ibid.

29. Ibid.

30. Ibid.

31. "Zoom Systems Expands at Major Airports," *PR Newswire U.S.*, September 1, 2005, retrieved from Factiva.com.

32. Ibid.

33. "Motorola Looks to 'Reinvent' Mobile Retail Experience with On-Demand Solution," *Wireless News*, September 24, 2006, retrieved from Factiva.com.

34. Dan Waldman, "Sony Accesses a New Retail Channel," *KidScreen*, August 1, 2006, retrieved from Factiva.com.

35. "Zoom Systems Expands at Major Airports."

36. "Electronics *and* Appliance Stores: Profitability, Operating, Balance Sheet, and Financial Ratios National Averages for all U.S. Corporations," retrieved from: http://www.bizstats.com/corporate-statistics.htm.

37. Ibid.

38. Johnson, "Zoom Systems Offers iPod Vending Machines."

39. Kristi Arellano, "Chips, a Soda and an iPod?" *Denver Post*, February 15, 2006, retrieved from Factiva.com.

40. Bindu Nair, Michael P. Niemira, "Unlocking the Power and Perspective of ICSC's Data Goldmine," *Research Review* 13, no. 1 (2006): 32.

41. John Eckberg, "Getting Gizmos Hits the e-Spot," *Cincinnati.com*, December 16, 2008, http://news.cincinnati.com/article/20081216/BIZ01/812160326.

42. Christina Sosa, "San Francisco's Zoom Systems widens horizon for high-ticket vending machines," *Bakersfield Californian*, July 24, 2004, retrieved from Factiva.com.

43. Research and development figures were retrieved from http://marketwatch.com/tools/quotes/financials.asp/.

44. www.rmahq.org, www.bizstats.com.

45. www.companieshouse.gov.uk.

Chapter 6

1. Shawn Tully, "Raiding a Company's Hidden Cash," *Fortune*, August 22, 1994, http://money.cnn.com/magazines/fortune/fortune_archive/1994/08/22/79649/index.htm.

2. Dow Jones, "Form 10-K," filed with the U.S. Security and Exchange Commission, 1997.

3. For the details of how to calculate "days" from a set of financial statements, see John W. Mullins and Neil C. Churchill, "Managing Cash: What a Difference the Days Make," *Business Horizons*, November–December 2004, 79–82.

4. Cash-days calculated from performance data reported by Morningstar.

5. The story of *DowVision*'s creation is from Wallys W. Conhaim, "Dow Jones: a Business Information Powerhouse Migrates toward the Web," Dow Jones and Company, Inc., May 15, 1997, retrieved from Factiva.com.

6. Dow Jones, May 31, 2007, http://www.dowjones.com/Products_Services/Electronic Publishing/DJFinInfoServices.htm.

7. "Dow Jones & Company Closes $528 Million Market-Watch Acquisition," press release, January 24, 2005, http://www.dowjones.com/Pressroom/PressReleases/Other/US/2005/0124_ US_DowJones_6580.htm.

8. Dow Jones Company History, http://www.dowjones.com/TheCompany/History/History.htm.

9. "Dow Jones Agrees to Sell Six Local Newspapers for $282.5 Million," press release, October 27, 2006, http://www.dowjones.com/Pressroom/PressReleases/Financial/2006/1027_FIN_ 6440.htm.

10. Cash-days calculated from performance data reported by Morningstar.

11. Eric Dash, "Mexican Billionaire Invests in Times Company," *New York Times,* January 20, 2009, http://www.nytimes.com/2009/01/20/business/media/20times.html?_r=1&scp=2&sq= Carlos%20Slim&st=cse.

12. John Helyar, "The Only Company Wal-Mart Fears," *Fortune,* November 24, 2003, http://money.cnn.com/magazines/fortune/fortune_archive/2003/11/24/353755/index.htm.

13. Les Gilbert, "Warehouse Club Clout Grows," *HFD-The Weekly Home Furnishings Newspaper,* May 22, 1989.

14. Matthew Boyle, "Why Costco Is So Addictive," *Fortune,* October 25, 2006, http://money.cnn.com/magazines/fortune/fortune_archive/2006/10/30/8391725/index.htm.

15. Shelly Branch, "Inside the Cult of Costco," *Fortune,* September 6, 1999, http://money. cnn.com/magazines/fortune/fortune_archive/1999/09/06/265289/index.htm.

16. Calculated from performance data reported by Morningstar.

17. Costco 2006 10-K, 6.

18. Cash-days calculated from performance data reported by Morningstar.

19. Branch, "Inside the Cult of Costco."

20. Carol Tice, "Merchandising Masters," *Puget Sound Business Journal,* June 25, 2003, http://seattle.bizjournals.com/seattle/stories/2003/07/28/focus1.html?t=printable.

21. Boyle, "Why Costco Is So Addictive."

22. Ibid.

23. Branch, "Inside the Cult of Costco."

24. Boyle, "Why Costco Is So Addictive."

25. Helyar, "The Only Company Wal-Mart Fears."

26. Ibid.

27. Boyle, "Why Costco Is So Addictive."

28. Ibid.

29. Helyar, "The Only Company Wal-Mart Fears."

30. Cash-days calculated from performance data reported by Morningstar.

31. Boyle, "Why Costco Is So Addictive."

32. Jon Gertner, "Costco Nation," *Money,* October 1, 2003, http://money.cnn.com/ magazines/moneymag/moneymag_archive/2003/10/01/350563/index.htm.

33. Boyle, "Why Costco Is So Addictive."

34. Tully, "Raiding a Company's Hidden Cash."

35. John Plender, Martin Simons, and Henry Tricks, "Cash Benefit," *Financial Times,* December 7, 2005, 19.

36. For an approach to determining how fast your company can grow from its own internally generated cash, and for improving its cash-generative ability, see Neil C. Churchill and John W. Mullins, "How Fast Can Your Company Afford to Grow?," *Harvard Business Review,* May 2001, 135–143.

37. For a systematic way to find hidden cash on your balance sheet, see John W. Mullins and Neil C. Churchill, "Managing Cash: What a Difference the Days Make," *Business Horizons,* November–December 2004, 79–82.

38. Several kinds of different working capital models are dissected in Churchill and Mullins, "How Fast Can Your Company Afford to Grow?"

Chapter 7

1. Vonage, Form S-1, filed with the U.S. Security and Exchange Commission, February 8, 2006.

2. "Call for Nothing" [profile of Niklas Zennström], *New Media Age*, August 19, 2004, retrieved from Factiva.com.

3. Ibid.

4. Ibid.

5. Liz Claman, "Skype—Founder and CEO Interview," CNBC/Dow Jones Business Video, February 6, 2004, retrieved from Factiva.com.

6. Peter J. Howe, "Free Calls? So What's Not to Like?," *Boston Globe*, November 14, 2003.

7. John Gapper, "How to Make a Million Connections," *Financial Times*, July 7, 2005, http://www.ft.com/cms/s/2/e82cb1f8-ef0c-11d9-8b10-00000e2511c8.html.

8. Evan Hansen, "Skype Goes for the Gold," CNET News.com, March 17, 2005, http://news.cnet.com/Skype-goes-for-the-gold/2100-7352_3-5621463.html?tag=txt.16.

9. Howe, "Free Calls?"

10. Chris Oakes, "Something Out of Nothing: New Venture for KaZaA Founder," *International Herald Tribune*, January 26, 2004, http://www.iht.com/articles/2004/01/26/skype_ed3_.php.

11. Gapper, "How to Make a Million Connections."

12. Kambiz Foroohar, "Skype's Online Calling Rings Through Industry," *Seattle Times,* August 1, 2005, http://seattletimes.nwsource.com/html/businesstechnology/2002413722_btskype01.html.

13. Tim Richardson, "Vonage Rings up $200M Investment," *The Register*, May 9, 2005, http://www.theregister.co.uk/2005/05/09/vonage_fund/.

14. Vonage, *Annual Report 2006*, 68.

15. Hansen, "Skype Goes for the Gold,"

16. Andy Reinhardt, "Skype's 'Aha!' Experience," *BusinessWeek*, http://www.businessweek.com/technology/content/sep2005/tc20050919_2468.htm.

17. Ben Charny, "Can Skype Live up to the Net Phone Hype?" *CNET News*, September 27, 2004, http://news.cnet.com/Can-Skype-live-up-to-the-Net-phone-hype/2100-7352_3-5383876.html.

18. Erica Davis, "Skype Backers Win Big in eBay Acquisition," *Venture Wire*, September 13, 2005, http://www.dfj.com/cgi-bin/artman/publish/printer_159.shtml.

19. Adam Lashinsky, "Is Skype On Sale at eBay?"*Fortune European Edition*, October 27, 2008, 32.

20. Barbara Cassani and Kenny Kemp, *Go: An Airline Adventure* (London: Time Warner Books, 2003), 38.

21. Ron Clark, "Budget Airline Chief Earns Her Wings," *The Herald* (U.K.), September 4, 2000, retrieved from Factiva.com.

22. Ibid.

23. Cassini and Kemp, *Go*, 42.

24. Ibid., 119.

25. Ibid., 44.

26. Ibid., 163.

27. Ibid., 83.

28. Ibid., 175.

29. Michael Harrison, "Go Fuels Low-Cost Air Travel War with Expansion Plan," *The Independent*, October 1, 1998, http://www.independent.co.uk/news/business/go-fuels-lowcost-air-travel-war-with-expansion-plan-1175469.html.

30. Cassani and Kemp, *Go*, 180.

31. Ibid., 211.

32. Daniel Morrissey, "BA Sells Go for up to £110 Million to 3i," *Reuters News,* June 14, 2001.

33. Cassani and Kemp, *Go*, 215.

34. Morrissey, "BA Sells Go for up to £110 Million to 3i."

35. Ibid.

36. Cassani and Kemp, *Go*, 259.

37. Ibid., 274.

38. Ibid., 288.

Chapter 8

1. Leslie Crawford, "allzarage," *Globe and Mail* (Toronto), March 30, 2001, retrieved from Factiva.com.

2. Ibid.

3. Barbara Barker, "Inside the Inditex Empire," *Women's Wear Daily*, July 30, 2002.

4. Inditex, *Annual Report Fiscal Year 2006*, http://www.inditex.com/en/shareholders_ and_investors/investor_relations/annual_reports.

5. "Zara Clothing Retail Model Based on Lean Inventories and Market Flexibility Could Change the Future of Manufacturing," *PR Newswire*, September 9, 2001, http://www. prnewswire.se/cgi-bin/stories.pl?ACCT=104&STORY=/www/story/09-09-2001/00015 68743&EDATE=.

6. Crawford, "allzarage."

7. Barker, "Inside the Inditex Empire."

8. Rachel Tiplady, "Zara: Taking the Lead in Fast-Fashion," *BusinessWeek*, April 4, 2006, http://www.businessweek.com/globalbiz/content/apr2006/gb20060404_167078.htm.

9. Crawford, "allzarage."

10. Brian Dunn, "Inside The Zara Business Model," *Daily News Record*, March 20, 2006, retrieved from Factiva.com.

11. "Zara Clothing Retail Model Based on Lean Inventories and Market Flexibility Could Change the Future of Manufacturing."

12. Kristina Smith, "Spaniard in the Works," *Property Week*, November 17, 2000, http:// www.propertyweek.com/story.asp?storyCode=3001238.

13. Inditex, *Annual Report Fiscal Year 2005*, 18, http://www.inditex.com/en/shareholders_ and_investors/investor_relations/annual_reports.

14. Gap, Form 10-K, April 2, 2007, http://www.gapinc.com/public/Investors/inv_fin_sec_ filings.htm.

15. "Inditex Has Cash Surprise in Store," *Birmingham Post*, June 14, 2007, retrieved from Factiva.com.

16. "Zara Clothing Retail Model Based on Lean Inventories and Market Flexibility Could Change the Future of Manufacturing."

17. Cecilie Rohwedder, "Zara Grows as Retail Rivals Struggle," *WSJ Online*, March 25, 2009, retrieved from Factiva.com.

18. Josh Quittner, "How Jeff Bezos Rules the Retail Space," *Fortune* European Edition, May 5, 2008, 109–114.

19. "Jeff Bezos: There's No 'Shift in the Model,'" *BusinessWeek*, February 21, 2000, http://www.businessweek.com/2000/00_08/b3669094.htm; and Quittner, "How Jeff Bezos Rules the Retail Space."

20. Katrina Brooker, "Beautiful Dreamer," *Investor's Guide 2001*, December 18, 2000, retrieved from Factiva.com.

21. "Jeff Bezos: There's No 'Shift in the Model.'"

22. Ibid.

23. Ibid.

24. Russ Banham, "Amazon Finally Clicks," *CFO Europe*, April 2004, http://www.cfoeurope. com/displayStory.cfm/2569740.

25. "Jeff Bezos: There's No 'Shift in the Model.'"

26. See Zara Spreadsheet, worksheet "Amazon".

27. Ibid.

28. Ross Snel, "Amazon.com Says on Track for Pro Forma Profit," *Dow Jones News Service*, April 25, 2001, retrieved from Factiva.com.

29. Warren Jenson, chief financial officer for Amazon in 2001, is quoted in *Amazon's 2001 Fourth Quarter Financial Results*, January 22, 2002, http://phx.corporate-ir.net/phoenix.zhtml?c=97664&p=irol-reportsOther.

30. "Jeff Bezos: 'There's No 'Shift in the Model.'"

31. Russ Banham, "Amazon Finally Clicks."

32. Elana Varon, "Amazon.com, Software Vendor," *CIO*, October 15, 2003, http://www.cio.com/article/29855/E_Commerce_Strategy_Amazon.com_Software_Vendor.

33. Jane Black, "The Shape of a Profitable Amazon," *BusinessWeek*, November 20, 2001, http://www.businessweek.com/bwdaily/dnflash/nov2001/nf20011120_7174.htm.

34. Ibid.

35. Announced in *Amazon's 2004 Fourth Quarter Financial Results*, February 2, 2005, http://phx.corporate-ir.net/phoenix.zhtml?c=97664&p=irol-reportsOther.

36. Quittner, "How Jeff Bezos Rules the Retail Space."

37. Ibid.

38. Ibid.

39. Victor W. A. Mbarika and Irene Mbarika, "Africa Calling: Burgeoning Wireless Networks Connect Africans to the World and Each Other," *IEEE Spectrum*, May 1, 2006, http://www.spectrum.ieee.org/may06/3426.

40. Wieland, "Celtel's Scramble for Africa."

41. Mbarika and Mbarika, "Africa Calling."

42. Mark Turner, "A World Waiting for Wireless," *Financial Times*, August 21, 2001, retrieved from Factiva.com.

43. Jason Nissé, "Mohamed Ibrahim: Mobile Chief Who Did More to Unite Africa Than Any Politician," *The Independent*, December 11, 2005, http://www.independent.co.uk/news/people/profiles/mohamed-ibrahim-mobile-chief-who-did-more-to-unite-africa-than-any-politician-518912.html.

44. "African Mobile Growth Surges Ahead," *allAfrica*, May 5, 2004, retrieved from Factiva.com.

45. Personal communication from Celtel cofounder Terry Rhodes to John Mullins, October 2007.

46. Ibid.

47. Rebecca Harrison, "Booming Cell Phone Sector Rare Africa Success Story," *Reuters News*, June 28, 2005, retrieved from Factiva.com.

48. Emily Hayes, "UK Group Wins New African Licence and Scans Continent for More," *Mobile Communications International*, November 12, 1998, retrieved from Factiva.com.

49. Eric Onstad, "MSI Cellular Shines in Africa amid Telecoms Malaise," *Reuters News*, September 27, 2002, retrieved from Factiva.com.

50. Wieland, "Celtel's Scramble for Africa."

51. Robert Budden, "Celtel Predicts African Boom," *Financial Times*, September 7, 2004, http://www.ft.com/.

52. Onstad, "MSI Cellular Shines."

53. Julian Mattocks, "Celtel Revenues Jump 42% to $446 Million," February 23, 2004, http://www.celtel.com/mobile/en/news/press-release13/index.html.

54. Lesley Stones, "Big Capital Drive Pays for Celtel as Profit Doubles," *allAfrica*, March 7, 2005, retrieved from Factiva.com.

55. Wieland, "Celtel's Scramble for Africa."

56. Mike Hibberd, "Africa Growing Up Fast," *Mobile Communications International*, July 1, 2005, retrieved from Factiva.com.

57. "African Mobile Growth Surges Ahead."

58. Stones, "Big Capital Drive Pays for Celtel as Profit Doubles."

Chapter 9

1. Quoted in Richard M. Nixon, *Six Crises* (Garden City, NY: Doubleday, 1962).

2. Jim Collins, "The Secret of Enduring Greatness," *Fortune*, May 5, 2008, 40.

3. Paul Durman, "Return of the Dotcom Kids," *Sunday Times* (London), November 13, 2005, Section 3.

4. For more on assessing the opportunity you have in mind, there's a terrific book, *The New Business Road Test*, which you may want to read. We know it's terrific because John Mullins' name is on the cover! See John W. Mullins, *The New Business Road Test: What Entrepreneurs and Executives Should Do Before Writing a Business Plan*, 2nd edition (Harlow, England, and New York: Prentice Hall/Financial Times, 2006).

5. For more on dreaming big dreams, there's another wonderful book, *The Monk and the Riddle,* which you may want to read. We know it's wonderful because Randy Komisar's name is on the cover! See Randy Komisar with Kent Lineback, *The Monk and The Riddle: The Education of a Silicon Valley Entrepreneur* (Boston: Harvard Business School Press, 2000).

6. Personal conversation with Randy Komisar, January 2009.

ACKNOWLEDGMENTS

From John: As is the case for every significant piece of output I've ever been involved with, the book you have in your hands is the product of many people's work, not simply our own. The research journey that led to this book began in the classroom, with my talented London Business School students. They continue to amaze me with their motivation and passion for starting new ventures. Their business models really will work, and just might disrupt their industries along the way. They have taught and given me more than I can ever hope to repay.

A Chris Ingram Research Fellowship—thanks, Chris and thanks, London Business School—allowed me to carve several weeks out of my teaching schedule in October and November of 2006. My good friend and thought leader in technology entrepreneurship, Tom Byers at Stanford University, kindly gave me a desk at Stanford and was generous in sharing his rolodex, too. Thanks, Tom.

I am indebted to a long list of people in London, California, and elsewhere who were generous with their time and their insights—our ideas are stronger for it. But special thanks go to the many entrepreneurs and investors who helped me along my journey toward a better way of thinking about business models: Steve Blank, Adam Burdess, Tom Claflin, Jerry Engel, Sean Foote, Connie Gaglio, Richard Gourlay, Rob Johnson, Peter Kent, Mike Lyons, Audrey MacLean, Terry Opdendyk, Tony and Lee Pantuso, Laura Parkin, Gary Schoenfeld, Tina Seelig, Mike Tennefoss, and Peter Wendell. My London Business School colleagues were similarly generous, while also being helpfully candid when my still-nascent ideas veered off track. John Bates, Jeremy Dent, Gerry George, Keith Willey, as well as Stanford professors George Foster and Irv Grousbeck, thanks to you all; any errors that remain are mine.

Gathering and distilling ideas is one thing. Putting ideas on paper in a way that others can grasp them—with examples of real companies to bring them to life—is no trivial task. Fortunately, the wonderful Suzanne Stoller, whose research provided a solid foundation for my earlier book, was changing jobs at just the right time. She was kind enough to stretch her interlude to work with Randy and me on this project. Our hats are off to you, Suzanne! This book exists because of Suzanne's hard work and her insights into the lives of the nearly twenty companies featured in these pages, aided by additional research assistance from Felicia Collins.

Getting our ideas from proposal into print was the next of our challenges. Don Lamm and Christy Fletcher helped us clarify our thinking and get publishers interested. Our HBSP editor Jacqueline Murphy shared our belief that the ideas in this book would provide value to readers, and she pushed and cajoled us when pushing or cajoling were needed. Connie Hale added some timely suggestions as the book started to take shape. Finally Mica Bevington took our still-rough draft manuscript, sharpened its logic, wove its multifaceted collection of ideas and perspectives together, and made the prose sing. Thanks to you all!

I thank my parents, Jack and Alice Mullins. They imbued in me a love of learning and of numbers and writing, too. Last but not least, I thank Donna, my wife of nearly thirty-six years and my longtime traveling companion, for our fantastic daughters Kristina and Heather, and for her patience, her love, and her wonderful company on all of my journeys, intellectual and otherwise. Donna has been with me every step of the way—celebrating the delicious "aha!" moments, and seeing beyond the frustrating dead ends. As always, she helped me to reach the ideas that now comprise this book.

—John Mullins
London, February 2009

From Randy: As with everything I have ever accomplished, I am very indebted to friends and family for all their help and support.

John Mullins conceived of this book and generously invited me to partner with him. It has been a creative adventure and a great pleasure. John deserves more of the credit than I. Suzanne Stoller did the hard work of adding flesh to our early skeleton. Mica Bevington nipped and tucked until it was a book worth reading.

My wonderful wife Debra Dunn, an acclaimed thought leader, teacher, and mentor of social ventures, encouraged us to include stories illustrating the successful application of our ideas to the for-benefit sector. She generously crafted those cases for the book.

The entrepreneurs I admire so much shared their wisdom and experience without hesitation—Chris Bradford, Jim Fruchterman, Mari Kuraishi, Paul Martino, Umesh Mishra, Mark Moore, Chris Law, John Love, Primit Parikh, Mike Ramsay, Fred Swaniker, and Dennis Whittle. Regrettably not all of them are explicitly singled out but each of them contributed greatly to the concepts, messages, and insights in this book.

My remarkable partners at Kleiner Perkins Caufield & Byers gave me the time, space, and encouragement to write again. Tom Byers, my friend and partner in teaching entrepreneurship at Stanford University, gets the credit for the introduction to John that set this work in motion. And my career-long mentor, Bill Campbell, keeps reminding me why we do this hard work.

—Randy Komisar
Menlo Park, February 2009

INDEX

Accor and cutting costs, 127
accounts payable, 137
accounts receivable, 134, 146
Advanced Micro Devices, 51
advertisers, 72
advertising networks, 60
Aer Lingus, 116
Africa, 26–28
African Leadership Academy (ALA), 214
   analogs and antilogs, 27–29
   business and government leaders, 29
   defining parameters, 27–29
   difficult decisions, 30–31
   faculty and administrative staff, 29–30
   financial model, 29, 30
   leaps of faith, 15, 29–30, 31
   lessons from, 31
   Plan A, 30
   Plan B, 30–31
   raising capital, 29
   small-scale trial, 29–30
   students, 29–30, 31
   tomorrow's leaders for Africa, 26–31
Aggregate Knowledge (AK), 42, 61, 211, 214
   acceleration mode, 58
   analogs and antilogs, 53–54
   B2B (business-to-business) customers, 54
   customers, 58
   dashboards, 54–55, 58–61, 63
   fundamental questions, 62
   go-to-market strategy, 56
   growth, 58
   leaps of faith, 54–57, 59–60
   lessons from, 60–61
   market potential, 56
   objectives, 56–57
   online discovery, 52–61
   Overstock.com and, 58
   paying customers, 56
   personalized advertising message, 60
   Plan A, 60
   Plan B, 57–60
   process flow, 59
   product area progress, 59
   product-management process, 59
   prospective customers, 56
   quantifiable metrics, 56
   revenue model, 54
   scalability, 58
   search engine, 54
   technology, 55
Air France/KLM, 119
airlines, 92, 168
Air Miles, 169
AlliedSignal, 188
AltaVista, 68
Amazon.com
   AmazonPrime, 191
   automating, 191
   as bookselling Web site, 187
   burning cash, 187
   business model, 181, 187
   cash flow, 191
   customer service, 191
   delivery, 187
   distribution center, 187
   dot-com business model, 186–193
   e-commerce platform, 189
   economies of scale, 172
   efficiency, 188
   GBF (Get Big Fast) strategy, 187, 191–192
   gross margin model, 187, 191–192
   gross margins, 96, 189–191
   growth, 187
   initial public offerings, 174
   inventory, 188
   investment model, 186–187
   leaps of faith, 187
   lessons from iterations, 191
   negative working capital, 200
   online sales, 191
   operating model, 187–189, 191
   Plan Z, 181, 187
   platform solutions, 189
   prices, 187
   profitability, 190–191
   raising cash, 187
   resolving pain, 199
   revenue, 187
   revenue model, 189–192
   service to customers, 189
   supply chain, 188–189

Amazon.com (*continued*)
  Target and, 190
  as technology company and technology
    platform, 190
  Toys "R" Us and, 190
  used-book sellers, 189
  working capital, 191
  working capital model, 189
AmazonPrime, 191
American and European boarding
  schools, 27
American Standard and negative working
  capital, 151
analogs, 6, 8, 14, 208
  advertisers, 72
  advertising networks, 60
  African Leadership Academy, 27–29
  Aggregate Knowledge, 53–54
  answering questions about, 45
  antilogs and, 83–84
  Apple, 16–18, 20
  cost of goods sold, 109
  critically examining, 15, 33
  different industries and, 34, 171–172
  easyJet, 169
  eBay, 44
  emerging economics, 26
  Ephiphany, Inc., 54
  evidence, 83–84
  finding, 34
  First Direct, 168, 171–172
  Go airline, 195
  Google, 54
  gross margin models, 110–111
  Heifer International, 48
  identifying, 10, 173
  information about, 6–7
  insights, 32, 84–85
  Kiva, 51
  limits, 38
  mixing and matching, 16, 32–33
  Napster, 19
  newspapers and magazines, 34
  not appropriate, 26
  operating costs, 114–115
  panning out, 85
  Pantaloon, 22–23
  Personify Inc., 53
  products that will sell, 79–80
  quantifying expectations, 129
  relevant, 15
  right or wrong, 34
  Ryanair, 114–115, 169, 195
  social networks, 34
  Southwest Airlines, 117, 169, 195

  stopping process of, 213–214
  themes, 10–11
  unique twist, 16
  variety of roles, 15–16, 32
  where to look for, 212–213
antilogs, 6–8, 14, 208, ix
  African Leadership Academy, 27–29
  Aggregate Knowledge, 53–54
  analogs and, 83–84
  answering questions about, 45
  Apple, 16–18, 20
  cost of goods sold, 109
  critically examining, 15, 33
  different industries and, 34
  emerging economics, 26
  failed dot-com companies, 192
  finding, 34
  Gap, 182
  growth-for-growth's-sake pattern, 103
  Heifer International, 48, 51
  identifying, 10, 173
  inefficient, 127
  information about, 6–7
  insights, 32, 84–85
  limits, 38
  mixing and matching, 16, 32–33
  moving forward with, 35
  newspapers and magazines, 34
  operating costs, 114–115
  Pantaloon, 22–23
  pay-for-music sites, 18
  Personify Inc., 53
  quantifying expectations, 129
  relevant, 15
  right or wrong, 34
  social networks, 34
  stopping process of, 213–214
  storage and user-interface problems, 18
  themes, 10–11
  variety of roles, 15–16, 32
  vending machines, 123
  Walmart store layout, 24
  Web analytics companies, 60
  where to look for, 212–213
Apple Computer, 213, xii
  analogs, 16–18, 20, 110
  antilogs, 16–18, 20
  computing experience, 16
  consumer electronics, 15, 21
  digital music Plan B, 21
  iPhone, 21
  iPod, 16, 19, 21
  iTunes Jukebox, 19
  iTunes Store, 19–20
  leaps of faith, 18–20, 21

lessons from, 20–21
MP3 player, 19
music, 16, 18, 19–20
personal computers, 16–21
"razor and razor blades model" and, 20
record companies, 19
stealing great ideas, 20
vocal evangelists, 16
ARPU (average monthly revenue per user), 196–197
Artega, Amancio, 182
Ashoka, 48–49, 51
asset-based analog, 196
assets, 158
assumptions, 15
   as fact, 38
   initial, 41
ATMs (automatic teller machines), 125
AuctionWeb, 95–96
Automobile, 100

Bain & Co., 183
balance sheet, 134–135, 154–155
banking, 125
banks, 175
banner ads, 72
Barron, Clarence, 141
Barron's, 141, 143
Barron's Online, 143
Bayani, Ronalee, 29
Benchmark Capital, 96
Bengier, Gary, 97
Bergstresser, Charles Milford, 140
Berkshire Hathaway, 148
Bernstein, Leonard, 14
Bessemer Venture Partners, 164
Bezos, Jeff, 187–193
Big Bazaar, 22–24
big companies and impediments
   to change, 213
biggest risks, 42–43
big ideas, 215
Bill Gates software analog, 79–80
Biyani, Kishore
   designing stores, 25
   hypermarkets, 22–23
   leap of faith, 26
   locating stores, 25
   market demands, 24
   merchandising products, 25
   operating retail stores, 25
   refashioning stores for Indian
      markets, 41
   testing hypotheses, 25–26

BJ's, 145
BMW, 100
Body Shop, 2
Bonderman, David, 119
Bradford, Chris, 26–31
Brin, Sergey, 2, 69–74
British Airways (BA), 116
   aircraft in the air, 118
   Project Hyacinth, 167–168
   selling Go airlines, 170
British Telecom (BT), 193
Brotman, Jeffrey, 146
Brower, David, 106
bug list, 83
building blocks, 208
business angels, 175–176
businesses
   data overload, 41
   incorrect assumptions, 41
   pay-as-you-go, 154
   qualitative issues, 43
   quantitative measures, 43
   revenue, 65
   source of cash, 66
   subscription-based model, 154
business model grid, 208–209, 211
business models
   airlines, 92
   Amazon, 186–193
   better, 62
   copying or adapting, 128
   customer-focused strategy, 180
   economic viability, 180–181
   elements working together,
      3, 92, 180
   evidence-based, 64
   grid, 10–11
   gross margin model, 9
   investment model, 9
   key elements, 9, 66
   multidimensional, 179
   operating model, 9
   pattern of economic activity, 4–5
   Plan B, 10
   revenue model, 9
   running out of cash, 3
   strategy, 180
   sustainable competitive advantage,
      180–181
   tough times and, 185
   uniqueness, 127–128
   working, 4–5
   working capital linking other elements,
      152–154
   working capital model, 9

business plans
  common threads, 207–208
  dashboards and, 63–64
  detailed, 63–64
  discovery and learning, 207
  not delivering results, 206–208
  Plan A, 207
  refining, 33
  what lies ahead, 207–208
  without real evidence, 207
Business Traveler, 171
BusinessWeek, 190
Byrne, Patrick, 58

Calvert Foundation, 45
Calvert Web site, 48
capital, raising, 159
Car and Driver, 100
CareerJournal.com, 144
cash, 131, 134–135
  accounts payable, 137
  customers' money, 140–145
  fixed assets and, 138
  funding growth, 149
  getting by on less, 175
  growth and, 200
  on hand, 135–136
  increasing importance of, 139–140
  inventory, 137
  new ventures, 3
  raising less, 160–161
  running out of, 3, 9
  sales, 137
  someone else's, 136
  sources of, 211
cash balance, 135
cash flow, 86, 130
  changing timing, 153
  generating and sustaining positive, 180
  investment model, 202
  operating model, 202
  timing, 131, 139
  understanding, 91–92
Cassani, Barbara, 167–172, 212, 213
Castellaño, Jose Maria, 182–183
cellular systems, 195
Celtel International, 192
  African market, 194
  ARPU (average monthly revenue per user),
    196–197
  asset-based analog, 196
  attracting subscribers, 194
  balance sheet, 197
  beer money model, 194, 196–197

  cost of goods sold, 198
  deferred revenue, 197
  gross margin model, 197, 198
  growth, 197
  GSM (Global System for Mobile), 195
  investment model, 195–196
  leaps of faith, 194
  lessons from balanced approach, 198
  licenses, 195–196
  MTC, acquisition by, 197
  multidimensional business model, 181
  operating model, 194–195, 198
  poverty and opportunity, 193–198
  prepaid pay-as-you-go revenue model,
    194, 200
  profits, 197
  resolving pain, 199
  revenue, 197
  revenue model, 194, 198
  Western-funded backers, 195
  wireless system, 195
  working capital, 198
  working capital model, 197, 198
charitable contributions, 46
chart of accounts, 114, 126, 130
Chen Tianqiao, 79–84
Chouinard, Yvon, 93, 102–106, 188
Chouinard Equipment, 103
classical operating models, 125
climbing equipment, 103
CNN Money, 71
cost of goods sold
  airlines, 92
  analogs and antilogs, 109
  approaching zero, 97
  cost of materials, 110
  defining, 91
  driving down, 109
  eBay, 97
  excluding other costs, 91
  expenses related to product, 90
  finding necessary evidence, 109–110
  gross margin models, 106
  labor, 110
  manufacturing, 99
  OnSale, 96
  percentage of sales, 92
  rules and conventions, 91
  timing for paying, 202
  what's included and what's not, 92
  Zara, 185–186
Collins, Jim, 215
companies
  cost of goods sold, 94
  customers' behavior, 53

initial investments, 162–163
unsuccessful ventures, 6
values, 74
venture capital, 174
competitive advantage, 127
  Costco, 145
  sustainable, 180–181
  working capital model, 145
computers, 162
Condé Nast Traveler, 121
consumer delight, 78, 83, 208
consumer electronics, 21
consumers, wanting very best, 126
content
  framework to organize, 9
  process and, 10–11
Continental Airlines, 116
contingency plan, 212
Coopers & Lybrand, 167
Costco, 179, 211
  accounts receivable, 146
  bargains, 148–149
  basic items, 148
  cash flows, 153
  competitive advantage, 145
  customer cash, 149
  entrepreneurs, 152
  fast-changing goods, 149
  gross margins, 147–148
  immediate cash, 146
  impact of, 149
  inventory, 150
  launch of, 146
  lessons from, 150
  limited items, 148
  lower prices, 147
  members, 149
  membership fee, 146, 150, 153
  negative working capital, 150, 151
  packaging in volume, 147
  Plan B, 145–150
  pre-tax profit, 150
  Price Club, 145–146
  pricing, 147
  profit margins, 147, 150, 153
  profits, 146
  rapid growth, 150
  retailing industry and, 149–150
  revenue, 150
  targeting small businesses and upscale families, 148
  trading up and trading down concept, 148
  value, 150
  warehouses, 148

working capital, 146–147
  working capital model, 139, 149
cost of materials, 110
costs, 69
critical unknowns, 15
crucial beliefs, 15
crucial issues, 8
cryptography software, 4
Crystal Dynamics, xii
current assets and liabilities, 136
Curry, Bill, 190
custom dashboards, 41
customer cash, 144
customer delight, 6, 67
customer feedback, 75
customer-focused strategy, 180
customer pain, 208
customer promise, 199
customers, 66
  defining, 65
  negative working capital and, 154
  paying before product or service is produced, 140–145
  revenue models, 67–68
  targeting, 84
  what he wants and will buy, 3
  and WIIFM, 154
Customers' Afternoon Letter, 140
customer services and negative working capital, 152

Daily Telegraph, 171
dashboarding
  asking right questions, 38
  business planning and, 63–64
  hard lessons of failure, 40
  lessons learned, 61–62
  next steps, 62
  Plan B, 39–41
  quality of questions, 62
  what to do with data, 62
dashboards, 7–8, 35, 159, 208
  Aggregate Knowledge, 61, 63
  assumptions, 38
  business model, 209–210
  custom, 41
  defining, 38–42
  developing, 10
  Development Space, 46
  emphasis on numbers, 61, 62
  evidence-based business model, 64
  evolution, 60–61
  evolving business, 43
  formal, 63

dashboards (*continued*)
  getting answers, 61
  GlobalGiving, 61, 63
  granular, 55
  iterating with, 42–43
  key indicators, 8, 41
  laser-like focus, 61
  leaps of faith, 8, 63
  modifying, 43
  Plan B, 209
  prototype, 40, 61
  qualitative issues, 46, 62
  quantitative hypotheses, 62
  reasons to use, 41–42
  record-keeping, 42
  reflecting nature of business, 41
  signaling for corrections, 85
  specific objectives, 61
  stopping process of, 213–214
  strategically thinking, 8
  testing hypotheses, 8
  themes informed by, 10–11
  usefulness, 60
  when to create, 213
data, what to do with, 62
data overload, 41
data-starved entrepreneurs, 38
data underload, 41
Debonair, 169
decision making, 14
deferred income, 155
deferred revenue, 155
Dell and cutting costs, 127
Delta Airlines, 116
design process, 182–183
detailed business plan, 63–64
developing world, 51
Development Marketplace, 43–44
Development Space
  dashboards, 46
  donors, 46, 48
  dot-com bubble, 48
  foundation for, 49
  funding drought, 48
  Hewlett-Packard and, 49
  name change, 49
  Plan B, 48–51
  projects, 46
  responses to, 46
  start-up dashboard, 47
  Web site, 46
Diamond Media Systems, 18
digital music, 17
discovery engine, 52
Disney analog, 81

disruptive operating models, 125
distribution process, 182–183
Doerr, John, 215
doing things differently, 199–200
Donglei, Zhou, 81
donors, 46, 48, 51–52
"don't be evil," 71, 74
dot-com bubble, 48
Dow, Charles Henry, 140
Dow Jones & Company, 179, 211, 213
  Barron's, 141, 143
  Barron's Online, 143
  CareerJournal.com, 144
  cash flows, 153
  customer cash, 141
  Customers' Afternoon Letter, 140
  digital world, 153
  Dow Jones Financial Information
    Services, 142
  Dow Jones Industrial Average, 140
  Dow Jones Online News, 143–144
  Dowvision, 142
  electronic publishing and services,
    141–142
  entrepreneurs, 152
  Factiva, 142
  identifying content, 144
  individuals and small companies, 142
  large enterprises, 142
  leaps of faith, 141
  lessons from, 144
  MarketWatch.com, 142–143
  negative working capital, 144, 151
  net income, 144
  News Corporation and, 144
  NewsPlus, 142
  OpinionJournal.com, 144
  Plan A, 143
  Plan B, 141, 143
  print media, 140
  The Publications Library, 142
  RealEstate Journal.com, 144
  revenue model, 153
  selling community newspapers, 143
  subscription-free services, 144
  transition to digital age, 144
  unearned subscriptions, 155
  using customers' money, 140–145
  Wall Street Journal, 140–141, 143
  Wall Street Journal Interactive Edition, 142
  working capital model, 139,
    141–144, 153
  WSJ.com, 143
Dow Jones Financial Information
    Services, 142

Dow Jones Industrial Average, 140
Dow Jones Online News, 143–144
Dowvision, 142
Draper Fisher Jurvetson, 164
dreaming entrepreneurial dream, 214–215
Drucker, Peter, 65

EasyJet, 169, 171
eBay, 179, 211
    analogs, 44
    AuctionWeb, 94–96
    cost of goods sold, 94, 97
    eBay Motors, 97
    economic activity, 97
    generating revenue, 97
    gross margin, 96, 97, 151
    gross margin model, 93, 94–98
    growth, 96
    lessons learned from, 97–98
    PayPal, 4
    Plan A, 97
    public stock, 96
    purchasing Skype, 165–166
    revenue, 97
eBay Motors, 97
economic development, 2
economic fundamentals, 9
economic progress, 127
economic viability, 180–181
Eddington, Rod, 171
effective models, 82
Eisenhower, Dwight D., 205–206
emerging economies and analogs and
        antilogs, 26
entrepreneurial dreams, 2–3, 214–215
entrepreneurs
    assumptions as fact, 38
    data-starved, 38
    data underload, 41
    incorrect assumptions, 41
    leaps of faith, 166
    money up front, 173
    as risk manager, 78
    virtual-goods, 107–108
    what to do when Plan A fails, 2
Entrepreneurship Summer School, vii, xi
Epiphany Inc., 54
erroneous assumptions, 62
established companies, 172
evidence, grounding revenue model in,
        83–84
evidence-based business model, 64
Excite, 69
expected revenue, 130

expenses, 92
experimenting, 7
EZ Station, 81

Facebook, 74
Factiva, 142, 143
failed dot-com companies, 192
failure, hard lessons of, 40
fast fashion, 181–186
    versus slow fashion, 184–185
fast-growing companies, 2
Federal Communications Commission, 165
financial statements, 180–181
Financial Times, 142
First Direct, 168, 171–172
fixed assets, 138
fixed costs, 129
    turning into variable costs, 175
flexibility, 42
flimsies, 140
Food and Drug Administration (FDA), 75
Food Bazaar, 23
Ford, 102
formal dashboards, 63
Fortune 500, 150
Fortune magazine, 192
founders of companies, 215
framework to organize content, 9
free calls, 165
Friis, Janus, 162, 174
fundamental questions, 62

Gap, 182, 184–185
General Electric and negative working
        capital, 151
General Motors, 99, 101–102
Get Big Fast (GBF) strategy, 192
Ghosn, Carlos, 28, 214
global development and donors, 46, 48
global development projects, 45
GlobalGiving, 42, 215
    business model, 52
    dashboards, 50, 61, 63
    Development Space becoming, 48–51
    donations, 52
    donors, 51
    financial model, 49
    foundation board, 49
    fundamental questions, 62
    key strategies, 52
    leaps of faith, 52
    legal compliance, 49
    lessons from, 52

GlobalGiving (*continued*)
philanthropic support, 49, 52
Plan B working, 51
project legitimacy, 51
revenues, 52
small projects, 52
sponsor network, 48–49, 51
tracking and analyzing traffic and user
behavior, 49
Go airline, 160, 161, 212
analogs, 195
breakeven, 168–169
capital expenses, 169
cost containment, 169
EasyJet purchasing, 171
European low-cost airlines, 169
inaugural flight, 169
initial routes, 170
investment model, 167–172, 180
leasing aircraft, 169
lessons from, 171–172
low cost but high quality, 169
management buyout of, 170–171
mimicking low-fare carriers, 170
operating expenses, 169
Operation Summer Sun, 170
outsourcing services, 169
Plan A, 170
Plan B, 170
profitability, 170, 171
shoestring budget, 169
small investment in, 168–169
underused airports, 170
ventures inside established company, 161
Google, 2, 10, 215
automating process for advertisers, 72
banner ads, 72
core purpose, 74
cost-per-click model, 72
costs, 69
customer pain, 73
don't be evil, 71, 74
evil advertising, 70–72
finding better customer, 70
finding things on the Web, 54
home pages, 72
initial public offerings, 174
innovation, 74
leaps of faith, 70, 72
lessons from, 73
licensing, 70, 85
organizing and delivering information, 69
PageRank algorithm, 69
paid listings, 72
partnership-based revenue model, 73

paying advertisers, 54
paying customers, 69–70
Plan A, 68–74
Plan B, 2, 70
Plan C, 70–72
profitability, 72
relevance, 69
relevant marketing messaging, 54
revenue, 74
revenue model, 67, 68–74, 85
search technology and advertisers, 73
staying ahead of the pack, 73
technology and reach, 54
users, 69
venture capital firms, 70
Google News, 74
Google.org, 74
go-to-market strategy, 56
government entity, 214
Gozzi, Carlo, 14
granular dashboards, 55
gross margin models, 9, 86
Amazon.com, 187, 191–192
analogs, 110–111
business model grid, 209
cash flow, 130
Celtel International, 197, 198
checklist, 111–112
cost of goods sold, 90–92, 106
competitive advantages, 90
crucial, 202
eBay, 93, 94–98
lessons learned about, 106–108
managing margin mix, 90
operating expenses, 130
Patagonia, 93–94, 102–106
prices, 90, 106
profit, 130
providing delight, 109
resolving customer pain, 109
Toyota, 93, 98–102
value-based pricing, 107
Zara, 185–186
gross margins, 89
Amazon.com, 96, 189–191
approaching 100 percent, 211
AuctionWeb, 96
breathing room, 93–94
calculating, 91, 92
cost of goods sold, 90–92
covering operating expenses, 91
defining, 90–93
earning fatter, 101–102
eBay, 96, 97
efficient processes, 109

evaluating, 135
General Motors, 101
generating, 89–90, 109
higher percentage, 91
improving, 99
insufficient, 90
Kmart, 148
OnSale, 96
Patagonia, 106
rate, 91
Target, 148
Toyota Motor Company, 99, 101, 179
trimming, 109
Zara, 182
gross profit. *See* gross margins
growth-for-growth's-sake pattern, 103
GSM (Global System for Mobile), 195
guiding and tracking journey, 7–8

H&M, 185
Hammerstein, 14
Hartsfield-Jackson Atlanta International
    Airport, 122
Heifer International, 45, 48
Henley, Don, 19
Hewlett-Packard (HP), 49, 51
Home Valley, 79, 85
HotBot, 69
Hotmail, 74
Hughes, Brian, 123–124
hypotheses
    recording results of tests, 42
    testing, 85

Ibrahim, Mohamed ("Mo"), 193, 200, 215
ideas, 6
    evolving to compelling, 13
    not starting from scratch, 14–16
identifying leaps of faith, 173
incentives for payment up front, 154
income statements
    focusing time and energy on, 135
    working capital model, 155
Index Ventures, 215
India, 21–22
Inditex
    Europe's largest clothing retailer, 185
    new fashion lines, 182–183
    out-performing competitors, 185
    public offering, 182
    Zara stores, 181
industries
    competitive advantage, 127

eliminating operating expenses, 126
inefficient antilogs, 127
overcapacity, 152
totally new, 17
working capital requirements, 152
inefficient antilogs, 127
Infoseek, 68
initial assumptions, 41
initial public offerings, 174
innovative businesses, 33
international development projects, 48
Internet
    peer-exchanged data, 162
    philanthropic contributions, 45
    P2P technology, 163
    search engines, 68–69
    searching for things on, 54
inventory, 133–134, 137, 189
investment models, 9, 86, 212
    Amazon, 186–187
    business model grid, 209
    capital, 173
    capital-raising side, 159
    cash, 158, 175
    cash flow, 172, 202
    cash to start business, 158
    Celtel International, 195–196
    checklist, 177–178
    defining, 158–160
    developing, 157
    Go airlines, 167–172, 180
    leaps of faith, 160
    lessons learned about, 172–174
    licenses, 195–196
    little investment as possible, 158
    minimizing early operating
      losses, 172
    minimizing or offloading costs of getting
      started, 172
    network effects, 172
    postlaunch phase, 159
    prelaunch phase, 159
    raising capital, 159
    revenue, gross margin, operating,
      and working capital models,
      202–203
    right type of investor, 175–176
    Skype, 161–167
    spending side, 159
    venture capital trade-offs, 173–174
    wireless systems, 195
investments
    assets, 158
    competitive footrace, 172
    earning return on, 138

investors, 66
  banks, 175
  business angels, 175–176
  dashboarding and, 176
  liquidity, 173–174
  right type of, 175–176
  risk, 157
  venture capitalists, 175–176
iPhone, 21, 33
iPods, 16, 19, 20–21, 83
ISP (Internet service provider), 95
iterating and dashboards, 42–43
iTunes Jukebox, 19
iTunes Store, 19–20

Jackson, Peg, 124
jidoka (built-in quality), 99
Jobs, Steve, 16, 19–21, 33–34, 110
Jones, Edward Davis, 140
Jones, Tim, 119
Joswiak, Greg, 18

kaizen (constant improvement), 100
kanban (just-in-time system), 99
KaZaA, 162
Kelleher, Herb, 116, 128
key indicators, 8
Khaemba, Christopher, 31
Kiplinger Letter, 140
Kiva, 51
Kmart, 148–149
Koot, Kamiel, 196
Kuraishi, Mari, 44–46, 49, 215

labor and cost of goods sold, 110
L'Amoreaux, Claudine, 107
Landes, Faye, 96
leaps of faith, 7, 15, 63, 159, 208
  African Leadership Academy, 29–30
  Apple, 18–21
  AuctionWeb, 95
  breaking even, 168
  Celtel International, 194
  Dow Jones, 141
  erroneous assumptions, 62
  Gap, 184
  global development projects, 45
  Google, 70, 72
  identifying, 10, 15, 33, 62, 64, 85, 173
  innovation process, 35
  insights, 32
  investment model, 160

  lessons from, 192
  metrics, 39
  Pantaloon, 24
  Patagonia, 105
  Price Club, 145
  proving or refuting, 8, 32, 166
  quality questions, 62
  before raising money, 166
  revenue models, 84
  right or wrong, 34
  Shanda Interactive Entertainment, 79, 80
  Silverglide Surgical Technologies, 75, 76
  Skype, 163, 164
  stopping process of, 213–214
  style, 183
  systematically recording, 39
  testing hypotheses, 8, 38–39, 173
  themes, 10–11
  varied roles, 32
  ZoomSystems, 123–124
learning from experiences of others, 14
learning plan, 210–211
legal Plan B, 162
Legend of Mir II, 80
Levchin, Max, 1, 4–5, 7, 206
Lexus, 100–101
liabilities, 135, 140
licenses for cellular systems, 195
Linden Lab, 107
Lonergan, Liam, 116
long-distance telephone industry, 163
Lopez, Marcos, 185
Los Angeles Times, 142
Lufthansa, 119

MacArthur, Douglas, 207–208
Macy's, 22
Magellan, 68
The Magnificent Seven, 14
Mahany, Mark, 191
Mall, Damodar, 23
Mandel, Stephen, Jr., 145
Mandela, Nelson, 26
Mangrove Partners, 164
manufacturing and cost of goods sold, 99
Manz Wear Pvt. Ltd., 21
MarketWatch.com, 142–143
Marks & Spencer, 22–23, 25
Martino, Paul, 52–53, 55, 214
Maslow's hierarchy of needs, 65
massively multiplayer online role-playing
    games (MMORPGS), 79–80
materials and costs, 110
mechanization productivity gains, 126

Melon, Carmen, 183
Mercedes-Benz, 100, 101
methodical iteration, 42
metrics, 7
Microsoft economic activity, 97
milestones, 173
Miller, Kris, 183, 184
mobile telephony cost-effective solution, 196
Molière, 14
Morita, Akio, 17
Morningstar, Kevin, 75
Motorola and ZoomSystems, 124
MP3 player, 18, 19
MSI (Mobile Systems International), 193
muda (eliminating waste), 99
multidimensional business models, 179
    checklist, 204
    lessons learned about, 198–201
multilegged business models, 179
Munger, Charlie, 148
Murdoch, Rupert, 144
music industry, 16–18
MusicNet, 18
MySpace, 74

Napster, 16–17, 19
negative working capital, 137, 138, 211–212
    Amazon, 200
    American Standard, 151
    benefits, 139–140, 151–152
    business growth, 152
    business model, 153
    Costco, 150, 151
    customers and suppliers, 154
    customer services, 152
    Dow Jones, 144, 151
    dramatic changes, 144
    General Electric, 151
    as Holy Grail, 151
    periodicals publishers, 140
    Tesco, 151
    Whirlpool, 151
Neo Carta Ventures, 124
Netflix, 153
net income, evaluating, 135
net profit, 91
Newman, Jonathan, 195
News Corporation purchasing
    Dow Jones, 144
NewsPlus, 142
new ventures, 3, 157
New York Times, 140, 142, 144
New York Times Online, 144
Nissan, 28, 100, 214

noble goals, 215
Nokia, 107
nonprofits, 214
The North Face, 51
Nutter, Eric, 151

Oberoi Cecil, 121
Oberoi Hotels
    adding luxurious amenities, 121
    adding value, 127
    best hotel chain, 121
    lessons from, 122
    Oberoi Cecil, 121
    operating costs, 115
    operating model, 120–122, 128
    trained staff, 121
Ohno, Taiichi, 99
O'Leary, Michael, 117–120, 128
Omidyar, Pierre, 94–97
1% for the Planet, 105
online classified service, 53
OnSale, 96
operating and timing issues, 153
operating costs
    analogs and antilogs, 114–115
    bankrupting company, 114
    comparing to retail stores, 124–125
    competitors, 120
    defining, 113–114
    evaluating, 135
    fixed, 129
    increased, 114
    planning for, 129–130
    reduced or eliminated, 114
    rethinking, 114–115
    variable, 129–130
operating expenses, 91, 92, 126, 130
operating models, 9, 86, 113
    Amazon.com, 187, 191
    amenities, 121
    business model grid, 209
    cash flow, 202
    Celtel International, 194–195, 198
    chart of accounts, 114
    classical, 125
    competitive advantage, 127
    copying or adapting, 128
    customer experiences, 122
    disruptive, 125
    filling in cost structure, 130
    lessons learned, 126–128
    levels of costs, 126
    model checklist, 131–132
    Oberoi Hotels, 120–122

operating models (*continued*)
operating expenses, 126, 202
productivity gains, 127–128
real numbers, 129
Toyota Motor Company, 179–180
uniqueness, 127–128
value, 127
OpinionJournal.com, 144
opportunities, missing, 13
Ortega, Amancio, 200
outsourcing, 172
Overstock.com, 58
Overture analog, 72, 73

Page, Larry, 2, 69–74
PageRank algorithm, 69, 72
Pantaloon
analogs and antilogs, 22–23
category management, 23
founding, 21
India and, 15
International Retailer of the Year, 25
leap of faith, 24
lessons from, 25
Marks & Spencer and Zara, 23–24
Plan B, 24, 25
shopping experience, 24, 25
traditional Indian bazaar, 24–25
trial-and-error process, 15
Walmart, 22–23
Patagonia, 211
bankruptcy, 103
changing packaging, 104
contributing to society, 102
customers paying higher prices, 104
environmental values, 102, 104, 105–106
gross margin model, 93–94, 102–106
gross margins, 106
growth, 103, 104, 106
leaps of faith, 105
lessons from, 105–106
1% for the Planet, 105
Plan B, 103–105, 106
pricing decisions, 106
strong moral code, 102
values, 102–106
Patriot Act, 46
pay-as-you-go, 154
paying customers, 69–70
PayPal, 4
peer-exchanged data, 162
peer-to-peer (P2P) technology, 162–163
periodicals publishers, 140
Personify Inc., 53–54

Peters, Tom, 22
Phantom of the Opera, 83
Pieters, Marten, 196
Piette, Daniel, 181
Plan A
African Leadership Academy, 30
analogs, 27
business plans, 207
changes in, 33
Chouinard Equipment, 103
detailed description, 209
eBay, 97
Go airlines, 170
Google, 68–74
off target, 206
Price Club, 145
Project Hyacinth, 168
revenue models, 68, 82
Ryanair, 116–117
Shanda Interactive Entertainment, 79
Silverglide Surgical Technologies, 67
statistics, 1–2
street-testing, 5–9
Swaniker, Fred, 27
Toyota Motor Company, 100
what you don't know, 7
when it fails, 2
why it won't work, 3
ZoomSystems, 122–123
Plan B
African Leadership Academy, 30
Aggregate Knowledge, 57–60, 60
breaking industry rules, 10, 94, 181
building sponsor network, 48–49
as contingency plan, 212
Costco, 145–150
dashboarding to, 39–41
Development Space, 48–51
Dow Jones, 141, 143
evidence to support, 8
Go airlines, 170
Google, 70
industry, 33
legal, 162
not-fully-successful Plan A, 94
openness about journey to, 176
Pantaloon, 24–25
Patagonia, 103–105, 106
Ryanair, 117–119
Shanda Interactive Entertainment, 79–80
Silverglide Surgical Technologies, 77
Toyota Motor Company, 100–101
unique lessons about, 15–16
ZoomSystems, 123–124

Plan C
  Google, 70–72
  Shanda Interactive Entertainment,
    80–81
  Silverglide Surgical Technologies, 77
  Skype, 165
planning
  learning plan, 210–211
  merits and limitations, 205–206
  not delivering results, 206–208
  vagaries of operating costs, 129–130
Plan Z and Amazon.com, 181, 187
Polti, Georges, 14
positive cash flow, 180
poverty, 43
Powell, Michael, 165
predecessors, 14
Pressplay, 18
Price, Sol, 145
Price Club, 145, 148
prices
  customer purchases, 90
  gross margin models, 106
primary market data, 6
process and content, 10–11
Procter & Gamble, 26
production process, 182–183
productivity gains, 126, 127–128
products
  customer delight, 67
  margin mix, 90
  resolving pain, 67
  success and failure, 3
profitability, 135
profits, 130–131, 139
Project Hyacinth, 167–168
prototype dashboards, 40
The Publications Library, 142

qualitative issues, 43, 46
quantitative hypotheses, 62
quantitative measures, 43
questions, 7, 62
Quittner, Josh, 192

Raffles Junior College (RJC),
    27–28, 31
raising money, 160–161
RealEstate Journal.com, 144
real opportunities, missing, 13
Red Hat, 70
Re-Imagine!, 22
reinventing the wheel, 6

Renault, 28, 214
rethinking operating costs, 114–115
Reuters, 143
revenue, 65
  adequate gross margin, 89–90
  Amazon iterating, 189–191
  cost of goods sold, 90
  Costco, 150
  defining, 65, 91
  eBay, 97
  expected, 130
  Sam's Club, 150
  timing, 131
revenue models, 9
  adding dimension, 81
  Amazon, 191–192
  analogs or antilogs, 82, 84–85
  AuctionWeb, 95
  bug list, 83
  building and testing hypotheses, 84
  business model grid, 209
  Celtel International, 198
  checklist, 86–87
  cost of goods sold, 202
  customer delight, 67, 83
  customers to target, 84
  defining, 65–67
  evidence, 83–84
  evolution of models, 82
  expected revenue, 130
  generating revenue, 73
  Google, 67, 68–74
  how customers respond, 83
  key questions underlying, 66
  leaps of faith, 84
  lessons learned about, 82–84
  membership fee, 153
  move to free-to-play, 81
  paying customers, 67–68, 153
  Plan A, 82
  resolving customer pain, 67, 83
  Shanda Interactive Entertainment, 68,
    78–82
  Silverglide Surgical Technologies, 67–68,
    74–78
  timing issues, 153
  Toyota Motor Company, 179
  Zara, 183–185
RIAA (Recording Industry Association of
    America), 19
Rimer, Danny, 215
Rio, 18
Risk Management Association Annual
    Statement Studies and BizStats,
    129

risks
    focusing on, 42–43
    investors, 157
    needing to resolve, 15
Rivkin, Jan, 116
Roddick, Anita, 2
Rogers, 14
ROI (return on investment), 138
Romeo and Juliet, 14
Rothman, Simon, 97
Russian Federation economic
        development, 43
Ryan, Christy, 116
Ryan, Tony, 116
Ryanair, 10, 115, 169, 171
    aircraft, 117–118
    airline policies, 117
    analogs, 114–115, 169, 195
    Charleroi, Belgium, 118
    cutting costs, 127
    expanding service and low-price
        reputation, 117
    Internet savvy of customers, 118
    leaps of faith, 117–119
    lessons from, 120
    low-cost airline, 119
    operating costs, 115, 116
    operating model, 128
    passengers paying for extras, 119
    Plan A, 116–117
    Plan B, 117–119
    regional airports, 118
    saving commissions and
        operating costs, 118
    as "Wal-Mart of flying," 119

sales, 137
sales process, 182–183
Sam's Club, 145, 148, 150
Sandford C. Berstein & Co., 96
Schmidt, Eric, 71
Schwartz, Bruce, 124
scratch, not starting from, 14–16
Seal, 20
search engines, 52, 68–69
secondary data, 6–7
Second Life, 107
The Seven Samurai, 14
Shakespeare, 14
Shanda Interactive Entertainment, 179
    analogs, 79–80, 82
    average revenue per user, 81
    changing market, 80–81
    consumer delight, 78

Disney analog, 81
EZ Station, 81
gross margin, 151
Home Valley, 79, 85
initial public offering, 79
leaps of faith, 79, 80
lessons from, 82
licensing initial product, 85
massively multiplayer online role-playing
        games (MMORPGS), 79–80
pay-to-play cards, 79
Plan A, 79
Plan B, 79–80
Plan C, 80–81
revenue, 79–81
revenue models, 68, 78–82
Shanda Literature Limited, 81
subscription model, 79
user base, 81
Shanda Literature Limited, 81
Shearwood, Mike, 183
shopping experience, getting right, 24
Sierra Club, 106
Silverglide Surgical Technologies, 179
    developing forceps, 76–77
    Food and Drug Administration (FDA), 75
    leaps of faith, 75–77
    lessons from, 77–78
    licensing product, 85
    narrowly defined target market, 76,
        77–78, 84
    patented product, 75
    Plan A, 67, 75
    Plan B, 76–77
    Plan C, 77
    revenue models, 67–68, 74–78
    target market, 67–68, 75–76
    transitioning from Plan A to Plan B, 68
    venture capital, 74–75
Silverman, Josh, 166
Silverstein, Michael, 148
Sinegal, James, 146–148
Skype, 10, 212
    acquiring customers, 166–167
    beta version, 163
    comparing to Vonage, 165
    cut-rate calls, 164
    eBay and, 162, 165–166
    free calls, 163, 165
    gateways and hardware, 164
    initial investment, 163
    instant messaging, 165
    investment model, 161–167
    investors, 164–165
    journey from Plan A to Plan B, 160

leaps of faith, 163, 164
lessons from, 166–167
marketing, 161, 162
operating costs, 164
Plan C, 165
P2P technology, 160, 163
premium services, 165
registered users, 166
revenue, 165, 166
SkypeIn, 165
SkypeOut, 164, 165
starting, 162–163, 167
telecom industry and, 161–167
text messaging, 165
user base, 163
videoconferencing, 165
voice mail, 165
webcasts, 165
SkypeIn, 165
SkypeOut, 164, 165
Slim, Carlos, 144
Smith, Gower, 122–126
somebody else's cash, 136
Sony and ZoomSystems, 124
Sony Walkman, 17
sources of cash, 211–212
Southwest Airlines, 10, 116, 171
analogs, 117, 169, 195
disciplined growth, 117
good service, 168
unbroken profitability, 120
spot-on hypotheses, 61
Stabingas, Mark, 190
Stanford's Graduate School of Business, 26, 28
Starbucks, 2, 83
starting from scratch, 14–16
staying ahead of the pack, 73
street-testing Plan A
asking right questions, 7
being different, 6–7
framework to organize content, 9
guiding and tracking journey, 7–8
metrics, 7
not reinventing wheel, 6
process, 5–8
Stryker, 77
stuck in a rut, 13
style and leaps of faith, 183
sub-Saharan Africa, 193–194, 215
subscription-based model, 154
subscription-based periodical publishing industry, 140
Summer Academy, 29–30
suppliers and WIIFM, 154

Supply Change, 185
sustainable competitive advantage, 180–181
Suzuki, Ichiro, 100
Swaniker, Fred, 26–31, 214

Target, 200
Amazon, 190
Costco, 149
gross margins, 148
target market, 127–128
technology
Aggregate Knowledge, 55
productivity gains, 126
Tele2, 162
Tesco and negative working capital, 151
testing hypotheses, 208
theater, 14
Thorbeck, John, 185
Thorne, Jonathan, 74–78, 85
Toyoda, Akio, 102
Toyoda, Kiichiro, 98
Toyoda, Sakichi, 98
Toyoda, Shoichiro, 100
Toyota Motor Company, 107, 179, 213
basis for success, 98
boring image, 100
costs, 99, 110
efficiency objectives, 99
gross margin model, 93, 98–102, 102
gross margins, 99, 101, 179
growth, 99–100
high quality, 101
just-in-time supply chain processes, 154
kaizen, 100
lessons from, 101–102
Lexus, 100–101
low cost, 101
measurable results, 99–100
net loss, 102
operating model, 179–180
Plan A, 100
Plan B, 100–101
reliability, 99, 101
revenue model, 179
vigorously competitive, 102
worker productivity, 99
wreaking havoc on industries, 101
Toyota Production System (TPS), 99
Toys "R" Us, 190, 200
trade-offs involved in venture capital, 173–174
Tribe.net, 53
TripAdvisor, 73
Tutu, Desmond, 26

unearned subscriptions, 155
United Airlines, 116
United Kingdom incorporated
    companies, 129
United States economic development, 2
US Airways, 116
United World Colleges (UWC), 28, 31

value-based pricing, 107
variable operating costs, 129–130
vending machines antilogs, 123
venture capital, 173–174
venture capitalists, 174–176
virtual-goods entrepreneurs, 107–108
Visa, 51
Vise, David, 73
visionaries, 2
Vodafone, 196
VoIP (Voice over Internet Protocol)
    technology, 160
Vonage, 161, 165

Wabco UK, 151
Walkman, 17, 83
Wall Street Journal, 27, 139–143
Wall Street Journal Interactive Edition, 142
Walmart, 25
    category management, 22
    design and location, 24
    discount goods, 22
    modeling after, 23
    orderly stores, 24
    Pantaloon learning from, 22–23
    removing cost of middleman, 22
    shopping experience convenient, 24
    supercenters, 148
    supplier relationships and
        merchandising, 22
    thriving, 149
    unbroken profitability, 120
Walt Disney's entertainment analog, 80
Walton, Sam, 22
warehouse clubs, 145, 151
Washington Post, 142
Web analytics companies, 60
Webber, Andrew Lloyd, 14, 83
Web sites, 73
West Side Story, 14
Whirlpool and negative working capital, 151
Whittle, Dennis, 44–46, 49, 215
WIIFM (what's in it for me?), 154
Wilke, Jeff, 188
Wilke, Jim, 200

Winograd, Terry, 69
Wolfensohn, James, 44
working capital, 86, 134
    accounts payable, 137
    assets, 136
    business model elements, 152–154
    checklist, 155–156
    defining, 135–139
    inventory, 137
    liabilities, 136
    measuring in days, 137–139
    negative, 137–138, 211–212
    noncash portion, 136–137
    reducing, 137–138
    ROI (return on investment), 138
    sales, 137
    timing, 153, 201
working capital models, 9, 134
    Amazon, 189
    analogs, 155
    balance sheet, 154
    business model grid, 209
    Celtel International, 197, 198
    competitive advantage, 145
    Costco, 139, 149
    Dow Jones, 139
    favorable, 202
    lessons learned, 150–152
    paying before product or service is
        produced, 140–145
    revenue, gross margin, and operating
        models for, 201–202
    stretching too far, 154–155
    timing cash flows, 153, 201–202
    warehouse stores, 145
    Zara, 184, 186
The World Bank, 43, 44
The World of Legend, 80
World of Warcraft, 80
WSJ.com, 143
WSJ Online, 142, 144

Yahoo!, 69, 70

Zannino, Rich, 143
Zara, 10, 25
    affordability, 182
    assembly of goods, 183
    business model, 181
    cash in hand, 184
    clothing and accessories, 181
    cost of goods sold, 185–186
    customer delight, 199

customers, 23
design process, 182–183
distribution process, 182–183
fashionable clothing, 182
fashion preferences, 23
fast fashion, 23–24, 181–186
feeling of scarcity, 184
gross margin model, 185–186
gross margins, 182–183
international expansion, 182
inventory, 183, 184
inventory management, 23
leap of faith, 183
luring shoppers to return, 183–184
markdown merchandise, 182
new products for, 186
Pantaloon borrowing from, 23
pricing apparel, 182
production process, 182–183
retail marketplace, 182
revenue model, 183–184, 185
sales, 183
sales process, 182–183
slow fashion, 184–185, 199–200

strategy and business model,
    185–186
suppliers, 184
working capital model, 184, 186
Zennström, Niklas, 162, 174
ZoomSystems, 122
    competitive advantage, 127
    cost-saving replacement of labor, 115
    extending retail experience, 124
    labor productivity, 124
    leaps of faith, 123–124
    lessons from, 125–126
    location of stores, 123–124
    manufacturers, 124
    Motorola, 124
    operating costs, 124
    optical sensors, 123
    Plan A, 122–123
    Plan B, 123–124
    profit-sharing model, 125
    revenues per square foot, 125
    robotic store, 122–123
    scarce and expensive resources, 115
    Sony, 124

ABOUT THE AUTHORS

JOHN MULLINS—when he is not on a trip soaking up new knowledge about entrepreneurship in India, Africa, or some other emerging market—lives with his wife, Donna, mostly in London and occasionally in Colorado. He researches and teaches entrepreneurship and venture capital at the London Business School and in regular workshops on four continents. He is a veteran of three entrepreneurial companies, two of which he cofounded and one he took public. He is the author of the definitive work on assessing entrepreneurial opportunities, *The New Business Road Test: What Entrepreneurs and Executives Should Do Before Writing a Business Plan*. He has written numerous journal articles and cases on entrepreneurial companies, and speaks regularly to a variety of audiences on topics on entrepreneurship and venture capital.

RANDY KOMISAR lives in the beautiful hills of Portola Valley, California, with his wife, Debra Dunn, and his cunning canines, Lola and Rufus. As a partner at Kleiner Perkins Caufield & Byers, Randy helps fund and create some of tomorrow's most visionary companies. He has worked as an attorney in private practice, as the CEO of LucasArts Entertainment and Crystal Dynamics, as a cofounder of Claris Corporation, as CFO of GO Corporation, and as a janitor, baker, and music promoter. He is proud to have helped build such companies as WebTV, TiVo, GlobalGiving, and Cooliris, among others. He is the author of the bestselling book, *The Monk and the Riddle: The Art of Creating a Life While Making a Living*, as well as numerous articles on entrepreneurship and innovation. Randy has been a consulting professor at Stanford University, and he is a frequent speaker on entrepreneurship around the world.